T0331234

An Introduction to Energy Economics and Policy

Energy economics and policy are at the heart of current debates regarding climate change and the switch from fossil fuels to renewable forms of energy. They are also crucial in dealing with energy supply and security issues caused by global shocks such as the war in Ukraine. *An Introduction to Energy Economics and Policy* outlines pressing issues concerning current global energy systems, particularly energy production and use. It presents economic frameworks for evaluating policy goals and for understanding the major energy and climate challenges faced by industrialised and developing countries. Integrating insights from behavioural economics into the standard neoclassical approach, particularly the role of behavioural anomalies, this book offers a novel introduction to energy economics and policy and provides a fresh perspective on real-world issues in energy and climate. This title is also available as open access on Cambridge Core.

Massimo Filippini is Full Professor in Economics at *Eidgenössische Technische Hochschule Zürich* (ETH Zürich) and at Universitá della Svizzera italiana (USI). He is the director of the Centre for Energy Policy and Economics at ETH Zürich. He has been a visiting scholar at Massachusetts Institute of Technology and Harvard University and published over seventy scientific articles in energy and environmental economics.

Suchita Srinivasan is a senior scientist and lecturer at ETH Zurich. She studies environmental and energy-related issues in developing countries, as well as behavioural factors that hinder adoption of energy-efficient technologies. She has published papers in several field journals.

An Introduction to Energy Economics and Policy

MASSIMO FILIPPINI
ETH Zürich

SUCHITA SRINIVASAN
ETH Zürich

CAMBRIDGE
UNIVERSITY PRESS

CAMBRIDGE
UNIVERSITY PRESS

Shaftesbury Road, Cambridge CB2 8EA, United Kingdom

One Liberty Plaza, 20th Floor, New York, NY 10006, USA

477 Williamstown Road, Port Melbourne, VIC 3207, Australia

314–321, 3rd Floor, Plot 3, Splendor Forum, Jasola District Centre,
New Delhi – 110025, India

103 Penang Road, #05–06/07, Visioncrest Commercial, Singapore 238467

Cambridge University Press is part of Cambridge University Press & Assessment,
a department of the University of Cambridge.

We share the University's mission to contribute to society through the pursuit of
education, learning and research at the highest international levels of excellence.

www.cambridge.org
Information on this title: www.cambridge.org/9781009471817

DOI: 10.1017/9781009471831

First published 2024

A catalogue record for this publication is available from the British Library

Library of Congress Cataloging-in-Publication Data
Names: Filippini, Massimo, author. | Srinivasan, Suchita, 1988– author.
Title: An introduction to energy economics and policy / Massimo Filippini,
ETH Zürich, Suchita Srinivasan, ETH Zürich.
Description: Cambridge, United Kingdom ; New York, NY, USA : Cambridge
University Press, 2024. | Includes bibliographical references and index.
Identifiers: LCCN 2023050927 | ISBN 9781009471817 (hardback) | ISBN 9781009471831 (ebook)
Subjects: LCSH: Energy policy.
Classification: LCC HD9502.A2 F555 2024 | DDC 333.79–dc23/eng/20240221
LC record available at https://lccn.loc.gov/2023050927

ISBN 978-1-009-47181-7 Hardback
ISBN 978-1-009-47182-4 Paperback

Additional Resources for this publication at https://wp-prd.let.ethz.ch/exercisesfortextbookeep/

Contents

Additional Resources for this publication at https://wp-prd.let.ethz.ch/exercises
fortextbookeep/

Figures

Tables

Preface

In this introductory textbook on energy economics and policy, we present economic frameworks for understanding the major energy and climate challenges faced by industrialised and developing countries, and the energy and climate policy approaches that can be adopted to address these challenges. We give a similar weight to concepts in energy economics, as we do to policy design and implementation through an economic lens. In this book, we integrate insights from behavioural economics and thus provide a fresh perspective on issues that have traditionally been examined using a neoclassical economic approach. In the book, we also shortly address some issues in energy economics and policy in developing countries.

The book uses basic concepts of microeconomics concepts to flesh out the discussions and analyses. It presents insights that draw on both current energy and climate-related debates as well as the scientific literature and provides students the economic tools to analyse issues in the energy and climate sectors, as well as to critique policy. Although the book is centred on energy economics and policy, the fact that energy and climate policy share one goal, namely the switch to sustainable energy systems through the energy transition, it is important to include some aspects of climate policy into discussions on energy policy.

In the first part of this textbook, we consider the main problems with our energy systems and discuss the role that market failures (including behavioural anomalies) play in contributing to these problems. Then, we provide an analysis on energy demand and highlight how to use tools from investment analysis to make economic decisions in the energy sector. This leads to an analysis of the economic aspects of energy efficiency and on different market forms in the energy sector. In the second part of this book, we discuss the role of energy and climate policy instruments in addressing some of the problems that we highlight in the first part of the book. We conclude by illustrating criteria for policy choice, discussing different types of economic models in the energy sector, and elaborating on common policy evaluation methods.

In our textbook, we discuss the role of both traditional market-based instruments (such as taxes, subsidies, and permit trading systems) and non-market-based instruments (such as standards and direct control measures). We also present relatively newer policy instruments available at the disposal of governments (including nudges, once again drawing on the behavioural economics literature, energy labels, etc.). This perspective is relatively new to the field. All these measures can address the challenges that arise in energy sectors due to both traditional market failures and behavioural anomalies. We also provide some discussion on the role of climate policy, which is crucial given the current state of climate change and distinguish between the objectives of energy and climate policy.

Some potentially interesting aspects of this book are that (a) it includes a detailed discussion of both the traditional market failures and behavioural anomalies in the context of energy and climate policy, (b) a large section of the book involves a detailed discussion of energy and climate policy measures as well as their evaluation, and (c) the importance that is given to understanding the nature of problems in developing countries that are more likely to bear the brunt of global warming and climate change.

We provide some online exercises for each chapter to enable students to apply and verify their knowledge on each topic covered in the book. We also draw on several empirical studies from the literature, which are presented in boxes throughout the text, to enable students to better understand the real-world issues.

This textbook is suitable for undergraduate economics students, as well as students in other social sciences, engineering and environmental science. Moreover, this textbook could be used in introductory graduate courses in policy and business schools. A basic background in microeconomics is recommended; however, the material is broad enough for both economics students and non-economists.

Acknowledgements

We are grateful to the anonymous reviewers who helped us improve upon the book. We would also like to thank Sara Mohammadi, Shipra Mohan, and Lea Schlatter for excellent research assistance in preparing this book, as well as Davide Cerruti, Gustav Fredriksson, Fabio Haufler, Simon Pierre Le Ciezio, Adrian Obrist, Sebastian Rausch Bigyan Babu Regmi, Jonas Savelsberg, Samuel Schenk, and Tobias Wekhof for fruitful comments and discussions.

1 Energy Economics and Current Energy Systems

In this introductory chapter, we first present the discipline of energy economics, including a discussion on the analysis of policy instruments. We then describe the importance of energy for an economy, provide a synopsis of current energy systems using statistics on global energy consumption and greenhouse gas (GHG) emissions, and discuss some of the most pressing environmental and economic problems that are shaped by the prevailing fossil fuel-dominated energy systems.

1.1 What Is Energy Economics?

Economics is the study of how societies take decisions related to the production and consumption of goods and services to satisfy their needs in an efficient and sustainable manner, given scarce resources. These decisions are made within an economic system, with the goal of answering the following questions:

1. Which goods and services should be produced?,
2. How should we produce these goods and services?, and
3. For whom should these goods and services be produced?

The answers to these three questions are decided by different agents based on the type of economic system, that is, the markets in a market economy approach, the state in a planned economy approach, or both the market and state intervention in a mixed system. The last approach, that is, the mixed economic system is the one adopted by many societies around the world.

If we now consider the energy sector, we can also identify three fundamental questions that we should answer in this sector:

1. Which energy sources and energy services (such as heating, cooling, or lighting) should be produced?
2. Which technologies and energy sources should be used to produce goods and energy services?
3. For whom should the energy sources and services be produced?

Energy economics is the application of the principles of economics to the study of how energy sources can be managed and used in an efficient and sustainable way to produce goods and energy services. Moreover, energy economics helps to answer the three questions previously mentioned and helps to understand the role of the state in the management of energy sources that are scarce and partially non-renewable and polluting. Energy economics can also be used to study how the state can intervene in the energy sector through policies to promote more efficient and sustainable use of scarce resources and/or to promote more access to energy sources. As we will explain in Chapter 2, the functioning of energy markets is characterised by market failures, that is, situations wherein market forces such as demand and supply by themselves are not able to provide efficient and sustainable outcomes in terms of prices and quantities that maximise the welfare of society. In this context, state intervention is needed in the functioning of the energy markets to correct this failure. Therefore, an economic analysis of these policy instruments used by the state is essential. The discipline of energy economics includes an economic analysis of both the functioning of the energy markets and energy-related markets and of state intervention in these markets, that is, of policy instruments.

Economic analysis of energy systems can be based on using a microeconomic approach that studies the behaviour of individual agents such as consumers and firms, or on using a macroeconomic approach that provides an analysis of the economic issues at the aggregate level of an economic system. In this book, we provide an exposition based on a microeconomic approach that is integrated with some insights from econometric studies, that is, studies that use statistical and mathematical methods to evaluate issues in energy economics.

Although energy economics is largely oriented towards analysing issues from an economic efficiency perspective, it is also important to take into consideration equity-related issues such as access to energy, the impact of policy on income and wealth distributions, and the impact of pollution and climate change on the well-being of society. In this context, it is relevant to differentiate between positive and normative approaches in economics. Positive approaches provide insights into how economic systems function, that is, how households and firms make decisions, whether the allocation of resources is efficient, and how scarce resources are allocated among different economic agents. Normative approaches, on the other hand, shed light on the desirability of economic outcomes from society's point of view, for instance, whether the distribution of energy resources is equitable, or whether the impact of an energy policy instrument such as a carbon tax is equitable. Therefore, this approach involves making a value judgement.

In energy economics, we mainly use the scientific method, that is, models of energy markets as well as of the behaviour of different economic agents are developed. These models are tested using empirical analysis with real data. A model is a simplified representation of the real world and is based on a set of basic principles, as well as on some assumptions that allow the modeller to describe and analyse economic situations. The modeller emphasises empiricism, that is, evidence-based analysis. This type of analysis uses data and econometric methods to develop and test theories, and to evaluate the effectiveness of energy and climate policy, while being careful to distinguish between correlations and causality.

Moreover, these models are based on concepts of optimisation, in which economic agents are choosing, under some constraints, the best outcomes for themselves. Of course, in the real world, we can observe deviations from this optimal behaviour that we call 'behavioural anomalies', whereby economic agents may not always optimise their decisions. The models can be represented either using graphs or with some simple mathematical functions as well as more complex systems of equations. In this book, we will primarily use graphs with the goal of illustrating economic decision-making using intuition.

1.2 The Role of Energy in an Economic System

Energy is a pivotal driving force for any economic system, and its use is vital for enhancing the welfare of all agents within these systems.

The ultimate objective of any economic system is to enhance the well-being of both current and future generations of a society while taking into account the limits of natural resource availability as well as the Earth's constraints. Well-being is directly dependent on both material living conditions and on subjective perceptions of the quality of life. Energy is an essential determinant of both of these elements of well-being.

Energy plays a crucial role as a production factor in several sectors, such as the industrial, transportation, services, and residential sectors. Energy is used to run machines that transform materials into finished products, as well as to fuel vehicles, ships, trains, and aeroplanes to transport people and goods. Households use energy to produce energy services such as heating, lighting, cooking, and cooling which are crucial to satisfy their basic needs. Energy is also essential for the functioning of critical infrastructure such as telecommunications and health care, as well as important utilities such as power generation and water supply. More generally, access to affordable

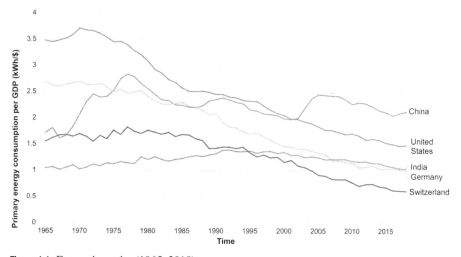

Figure 1.1 Energy intensity (1965–2018)
adapted from Our World in Data [1], sources of data include EIA [2] and the Energy Institute [3]

and sustainable energy sources is crucial to promote innovations, and productivity growth, which ultimately influences economic growth and enhances living standards.

While energy is an essential input in the production processes for goods and services, its role in contributing to production has generally declined over time, that is, reduced the total amount of energy consumed per unit of gross domestic product (GDP). For instance, in Figure 1.1 [4], we illustrate the values of energy intensity between 1965 and 2018 for a sample of Organisation for Economic Co-operation and Development (OECD) and non-OECD countries. We find that in general, energy intensity levels have declined over this period. This improvement does not imply, however, that the importance of energy has diminished; on the contrary, energy remains one of the main elements in promoting the well-being of all economic agents. This decline simply reflects technological gains over time, which have changed how societies use energy.

1.3   Energy Systems and CO_2 Emissions

1.3.1   Total Energy Consumption

In Figure 1.2, we present a graph that illustrates the trends in the total final energy consumption by source for the world. Upon looking at the graph, we observe a general reliance on the current energy systems on fossil fuels (coal, oil, and natural gas), which naturally leads to environmental and economic problems. Moreover, a large share of the global electricity supply is also generated using fossil fuels. Additionally, we observe that energy consumption is steadily increasing. This development is largely driven by an increase in energy demand in the growing developing countries, whereas in industrialised countries, it has mostly been stable.

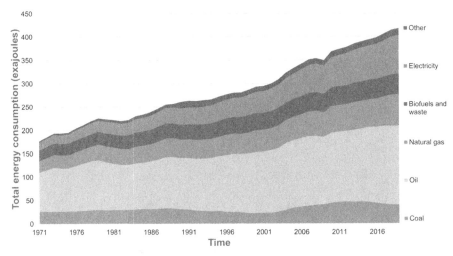

Figure 1.2 Total final energy consumption by source for the world [5]

One must note that the path being followed by the developing countries today, in terms of their growth in energy consumption, is one that has already been traversed by the current industrialised countries. Indeed, several industrialised countries experienced a significant increase in total energy consumption from the middle of the twentieth century, similar to the trend currently observed in China and India as well as in other developing countries. However, this increase was followed by a stabilisation, and in recent years a slight decrease in energy consumption. In the beginning, the growth in total energy consumption in industrialised countries was driven by the increase in population levels and in life expectancy that these countries witnessed, as well as by their economic growth. In the past decades, factors such as technological change, energy and climate policy measures, and low fertility rates have led to the stabilisation in levels of energy consumption. It is natural to expect this transformation in developing and emerging countries as well. However, as we will discuss later in this chapter, ensuring sustainable development in these countries would require that this increase in total energy consumption is largely met with renewable energy sources, and not by using fossil fuels.

Figure 1.3 presents a map that shows the total per capita energy consumption around the world, as of 2022. We see a clear divide between developing and developed countries with respect to per capita energy consumption. The value of this energy metric in several developed regions of the world, especially in the United States, Canada, Russia, Australia, Saudi Arabia, and the Nordic countries is much higher compared to that in the currently developing, or lower-income economies. We can observe that most countries in Africa, as well as several parts of South America, South Asia and

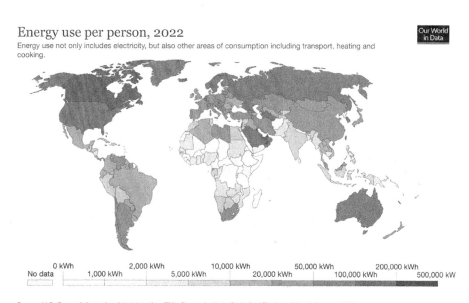

Energy use per person, 2022

Energy use not only includes electricity, but also other areas of consumption including transport, heating and cooking.

Source: U.S. Energy Information Administration (EIA); Energy Institute Statistical Review of World Energy (2023)
Note: Energy refers to primary energy – the energy input before the transformation to forms of energy for end-use (such as electricity or petrol for transport).
OurWorldInData.org/energy • CC BY

Figure 1.3 Total per capita primary energy consumption around the world (2022) [6]

Southeast Asia, have much lower levels of energy consumption compared to North America, Australia, and much of Europe.

1.3.2   Energy Consumption by Sector

For both industrialised and developing countries, it is important to evaluate the overall trends in aggregate energy consumption as well as in energy consumption by sector; this is helpful to identify the sources for the variations that we observe in aggregate consumption. Thus, in Figures 1.4 and 1.5, we will provide information regarding the structure of energy consumption by sector in a high-income country, Switzerland, and in a developing country, India, between 1990 and 2010. It is important to note that India has experienced an increase in total energy consumption over this period, compared to Switzerland, where levels of total energy consumption have stagnated.

Figure 1.4 shows the energy consumption in Switzerland split up by sector, including the residential sector, industry, services, and transport, for the years 1990 and 2020. We observe that the transport and residential sectors have contributed to a large share of the total consumption, while the shares of industry and commercial/public services are comparatively lower, and roughly of similar magnitudes to one another. Furthermore, this trend persists over time. In Switzerland, the buildings sector constitutes around 45 per cent of the total end-use energy demand [7]. This is tantamount to the case in several other industrialised countries, in which energy consumption in buildings for the provision of heating, cooling, lighting, and other energy services, constitutes a large chunk of energy demand.

Figure 1.5 illustrates the shares of energy consumption by sector for India, a large developing country, again in 1990 and 2020. These shares are different with respect to the shares that characterised an industrialised country such as Switzerland. In India,

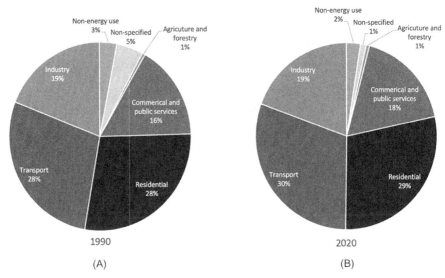

Figure 1.4 Total energy consumption by sector for Switzerland [5]

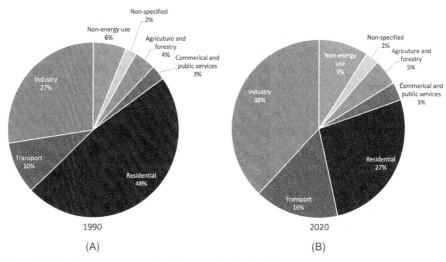

Figure 1.5 Total energy consumption by sector for India [5]

the shares of energy consumption across the industrial and transport sectors have grown rapidly, whereas, in Switzerland, we observe a general stagnation. As we can also observe that as of 2020, the industrial sector is responsible for the largest share of energy consumption, followed by the residential and transportation sectors. However, in the near future, India is likely to experience a significant increase in energy consumption in the buildings as well as the transportation sectors, due to both the installation of heating and cooling systems in buildings (primarily air-conditioning) and due to the increase in the number of private vehicles as levels of population and urbanisation skyrocket [8–10].

1.3.3 Energy Demand in the Future

The increase in energy demand in the future will be determined partly by increases in per capita income and urbanisation, and partly by increases in population. In the next decades, the world population is projected to increase to over 10 billion. This large increase in the world population, especially in developing countries, will naturally lead to an increase in demand for energy as well as energy services. For instance, in developing and emerging countries, energy demand in the transport sector can be expected to increase considerably in the next decades, especially as economic growth picks up. This increase will be amplified in emerging economies such as India and China in which population levels are still increasing (even if population growth rates have stagnated), while the number of vehicles owned per household is relatively low [9]. Currently, the population of countries that are classified as industrialised countries is estimated at around 1.2 billion. The combined population of China and India alone currently reaches a staggering 2.8 billion, with upward trends expected in both nations. Accordingly, the potential for an increase in vehicle ownership and energy demand in developing and emerging markets, mostly based in Asia and Africa, is enormous.

To satisfy this surge in demand, it will be crucial to promote sustainable private and public transportation modes such as electric cars, motorcycles, buses, and trucks, or vehicles with engines fuelled by renewable energy sources. It is also critical that the electrification of the transport system, to whichever extent it takes place, should be based on clean sources of electricity.

1.3.4 Greenhouse Gas Emissions

The main cause for the persistently high level of GHG emissions that we have observed over the past 20–30 years is that both the energy sector and the other sectors of modern economies are largely dominated by the use of fossil fuels. As of 2020, the composition of GHG was carbon dioxide (74.4 per cent), methane (17.3 per cent), nitrous oxide (6.2 per cent), and fluorinated gases (or F-gases) (2.1 per cent) [11].

1.3.4.1 Sources of Greenhouse Gas Emissions

It should be noted that the energy sector is the major contributor to GHG emissions, as shown in Figure 1.6 constituting almost 73 per cent of global GHG emissions. The agricultural sector is another important source of global emissions, being responsible for approximately 20 per cent of total emissions.

In this section, we will mainly present statistics on carbon dioxide (CO_2) emissions because of its dominant role in global warming. CO_2 is produced both from natural processes (such as during volcanic eruptions) and from anthropogenic sources (such as deforestation, land use changes, and the burning of fossil fuels). We must note that other pollutants are also significant contributors to climate change. For example, methane is a highly potent GHG, wherein one tonne of methane emission is equivalent to approximately 30 tonnes of CO_2 emissions [13]. This gas is released through natural sources and human activities, especially agricultural activities (such as rice cultivation and livestock breeding). With around 130 million tonnes of emissions from the energy sector on the global scale, methane also poses a serious threat to the climate [14].

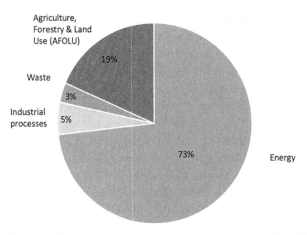

Figure 1.6 Global greenhouse gas emission by sector in 2016 [12]

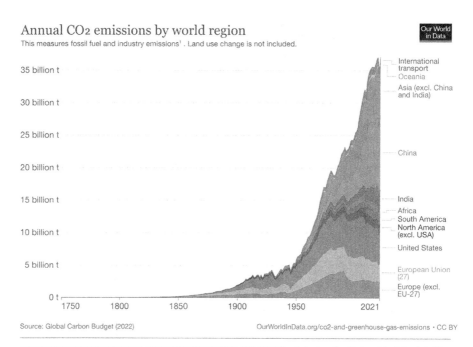

Figure 1.7 Annual fossil fuel carbon dioxide emissions (2023) [15]

Figure 1.7 illustrates world CO_2 emissions due to fossil fuel combustion from 1750 to 2020, by region. In the last 40–50 years, world CO_2 emissions grew steadily. However, if we look at the heterogeneity across regions, we can see that in the last decade, the amount of CO_2 emissions that arose in industrialised countries tended to decrease, whereas it has shown an uptick in the emerging-market and developing countries, as can be expected. It is also important to note that several industrialised countries, despite showing declines domestically, are still contributing to the global increase in CO_2 emissions through their imports, that is, CO_2 emissions generated in the production of goods that are imported from other countries.

Table 1.1 presents information regarding the per capita CO_2 emissions (measured in metric tonnes, as of 2020) for a sample of countries, as a result of burning fossil fuels for energy and cement production excludes land use change. This table presents information on emissions generated within the boundary of a country. However, as also previously discussed, these statistics fail to account for the emissions embedded in the import or export of goods and services, that is, the emissions being produced elsewhere, for example, due to goods that are imported. This is a significant omission in the accounting of emissions; for some industrialised countries, the inclusion of the embedded emissions in the total CO_2 emissions per capita is likely to lead to a large increase in their level of emissions. Per capita CO_2 emissions were relatively high in Australia, Canada, South Korea, Japan, and the United States, and to a lesser degree in countries such as China and Germany. Many of these countries use fossil

Table 1.1 CO_2 emissions (measured in metric tonnes per capita in 2020) [16]

Country	CO_2 emissions
Australia	14.77
Brazil	1.94
Canada	13.60
Switzerland	4.04
China	7.76
Germany	7.26
Spain	4.28
France	3.95
United Kingdom	4.60
Indonesia	2.07
India	1.58
Italy	4.73
Japan	8.03
South Korea	10.99
Mexico	3.04
Norway	6.73
Russia	11.23
United States	13.03
South Africa	6.69

fuels intensively. Naturally, population size also plays a crucial role in determining the quantity of emissions. As previously discussed, India emits relatively low levels of CO_2 compared to industrialised countries, on a per capita basis.

1.3.4.2 Which Countries Contribute Most to Global CO_2 Emissions?

The atmosphere can be considered, as discussed in more detail in Chapter 2, to be a global common resource, that is, a scarce resource that can potentially be exploited by everyone. More specifically, the atmosphere is a major sink for GHG emissions. As a sink, it has a limited capacity to 'absorb' emissions, and once that limit is surpassed, the ill effects of climate change become apparent, as we have already started to observe (through heatwaves, extreme weather events such as droughts and floods, a rise in global sea levels, and melting of glaciers).

Related to the use of the atmosphere as a sink, it is important to keep in mind that the industrialised countries, in which approximately 20 per cent of the current world population lives, have contributed to more than 50 per cent of the global cumulative emissions [12]. Therefore, the atmosphere has been exploited as a sink mostly by industrialised countries. In the discussion on climate policy strategies to address these ongoing (and expected) problems, it is also vital to know the actors that have contributed the most to the exploitation of this sink thus far.

1.3.5   The Relationship between Carbon Dioxide and Global Warming

As discussed and illustrated in the Intergovernmental Panel on Climate Change (IPCC) sixth assessment report [17], there has been a positive relationship between cumulative CO_2 emissions and the global surface temperature change since 1850. We should note that more than 90 per cent of scientists and researchers studying the Earth's climate support the notion of global temperatures increasing and acknowledge that the primary cause of this increase is anthropogenic emissions, that is, emissions produced as a result of activities of humans.

1.4   Main Problems Resulting from the Current State of Energy Systems

The current state of the world described in the previous section leads us to identify four major problems with present-day energy systems. We broadly classify these problems as: environmental and economic issues that can have both global and local effects, the non-renewable nature of resources, security of supply and geopolitical problems, and lastly, the inefficiency in the use of energy. In this section, we will discuss their importance and explain how they may pose a threat to the idea of sustainable development.

1.4.1   Environmental and Economic Problems

1.4.1.1   Environmental Problems and Global Effects

The current energy systems, dominated by fossil fuels, are creating global and local environmental problems. Globally, GHG emissions arising from fossil fuel combustion trigger climate change. Some changes have already started to materialise, such as extreme natural events, heat waves, the spread of infectious diseases, the occurrence of climate-related migration, and a reduction in production efficiency, and these changes are expected to intensify in the next few decades. Therefore, environmental problems at the global level pose serious threats to population health and give rise to potentially negative effects on production activities, on the levels of GDP, as well as on the well-being of all living beings. It is important to note that the effects of these environmental issues are likely not to be felt with an equal level of intensity by everyone around the world and that there exist strong disparities between different regions, with developing countries being affected relatively more by climate change.

Several studies in the scientific literature have analysed the long-term economic consequences of climate change. One of the first comprehensive studies on the economic impact of climate change on GDP was published in 2006 by Nicholas Stern. The report found that '... if we don't act, the overall costs and risks of climate change will be equivalent to losing at least 5 per cent of global GDP each year, now and forever. If a wider range of risks and impacts is taken into account, the estimates of damage could rise to 20 per cent of GDP or more' [18]. Two recent studies by Burke et al. (2015) [19] and by Kalkuhl and Wenz (2020) [20] analyse the regional impact of climate change on GDP. Both studies affirm that the negative impact on GDP is likely to be substantial, and could be more than 20–30 per cent for some developing countries by 2100. Additionally, both studies also clearly underline the stark heterogeneity of the impact of climate change on GDP, with emerging markets and developing countries likely to suffer more from climate change [19]. Of course, we have to keep in mind that these are long-run-oriented studies, and these results are derived on the basis of making certain modelling assumptions and do not factor in considerable uncertainty. Therefore, these results should be taken with a grain of salt. The main advantage of these studies is that they shed light on the possible effects of climate change and its heterogeneity, which is helpful for policymakers.

1.4.1.2   Environmental Problems and Local Effects

Apart from global problems, fossil fuel-dominated energy systems also have local impacts on human health and the environment. One of the most obvious negative effects is air pollution, which manifests through an excessive accumulation of Particulate Matter 10 (PM10), PM2.5, ozone, and other pollutants and is brought about by the burning of fossil fuels. Air pollution is also dubbed as the silent killer; with approximately 7 million deaths per year [21] being attributed to outdoor and indoor air contamination, it is one of the major environmental risks to human health. The level of air pollution varies considerably between regions of the world, and also between urban and rural areas within the same country. Its negative effects on health and well-being can also cause an indirect decrease in GDP. Being mindful of the heterogeneous effects once again, we should keep in mind that the most polluted urban areas in the world are located in developing and emerging countries, as can be observed from Figure 1.8, which plots average PM2.5 concentrations in some of the most polluted capital cities of the world in 2019 and 2020. According to guidelines from the World Health Organisation, annual average concentrations of PM2.5 should not exceed 5 $\mu g/m^3$ [22], and as we can see, these cities perform far worse in terms of air pollution.

1.4.2   Non-renewable Energy Sources

The second problem with current energy systems is their heavy reliance on the use of non-renewable energy sources, which is likely to lead to a scarcity of these resources. Furthermore, the projected increases in the use of these scarce resources (such as coal, oil, and natural gas) can lead to an increase in their prices, and thus potentially create social tensions and economic problems in society as well as across borders. Of course, to some extent, rises in prices can at least partially be stemmed by technological change in production and consumption activities. However, it is clear that our dependence on essentially unreplenishable sources of energy to fuel our lives not only has a severe environmental impact, but it can also have several economic and social implications.

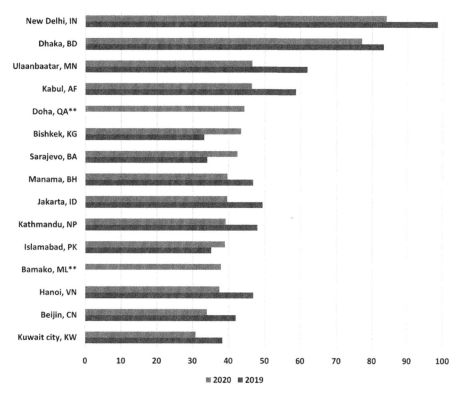

Figure 1.8 Average PM2.5 concentrations in the most polluted capital cities in the world in 2019 and 2020. ** Data for Doha and Bamako for 2019 was unavailable. [23–25]

1.4.3 Geopolitics and Security of Energy Supply

The third problem with current energy systems arises due to geopolitical circumstances. Oil reserves are primarily located in the Middle East (48 per cent) and in Central and South America (18 per cent), while gas reserves are concentrated in the Middle East (40 per cent) and in the Commonwealth of Independent States (Russia and eleven other republics that were formerly part of the Soviet Union (Commonwealth of Independent States (CIS))) (30 per cent). The consumption of oil and gas is predominantly concentrated in the OECD countries and in emerging economies such as China and India. Moreover, as previously discussed, a significant increase in energy demand can be foreseen in many developing countries. Such an increase in energy demand can lead to geopolitical tensions, which can negatively affect the security of energy supply for many industrialised and developing countries.

1.4.4 Inefficiency in the Use of Energy

The fourth and last problem is related to the efficiency of the use of energy. Current economic systems are wasteful in their use of energy, and this is a pivotal problem. Improving energy efficiency is the low-hanging fruit for ameliorating the extent of the other three problems discussed above, and for helping transform the current energy system. A study by the management consultancy firm McKinsey from 2009 calculated that in the United States, energy demand could be reduced by 23 per cent by improving energy efficiency, which amounts to savings of $1.2 trillion within a decade [26]. These findings are based on the adoption of a bottom-up approach (an engineering-based methodology that focuses on isolating the end-uses of energy, as well as detailing technological choices). On the other hand, using a top-down approach that analyses possible synergies between sectors and based on the estimation of econometric models, Alberini and Filippini (2018) [27] found that the potential for energy demand reductions through energy efficiency measures in the American residential sector was around 20 per cent of current demand, whereas Filippini and Hunt (2011) [28] estimated that across all the OECD countries, the potential energy demand reduction through energy efficiency measures was also around 20 per cent.

1.5   The Way Ahead: Energy Transition

The four problems that we discussed in the previous section clearly indicate that the current energy systems based on fossil fuels are not sustainable. Societies recognise that the solution to these compelling problems lies in the transformation of energy systems into those based on renewable energy sources and on the use of energy-efficient technologies. The ultimate goal is to develop a sustainable energy system, that is, an energy system that provides energy and energy services to the economic system while minimising the negative impact on the environment, considering the welfare of future generations. In this context, the term 'energy transition' is important to discuss.

1.5.1   Energy Transition

Energy transition refers to a structural change in the current energy system with respect to supply and demand. On the supply side, the energy transition implies a shift away from traditional fossil fuels such as coal, oil, and gas towards more sustainable and renewable energy sources, such as solar energy, wind energy, and hydropower. On the demand side, the energy transition involves the adoption of energy-efficient technologies, investments in digitalisation to optimise energy consumption, as well as making changes to consumption behaviour. Through the energy transition, governments want to achieve an energy system dominated by electricity produced from renewable energy sources within the next two to three decades. This implies, for instance, the electrification of some important sectors, such as land transport and heating. Other sectors, such as air transport, or some sub-sectors within the industrial sector are likely to substitute oil and gas and their derivative products with renewable energy sources such as biogas or hydrogen obtained using renewable sources ('green hydrogen').

Initially, the thrust on achieving an energy transition was mainly driven by concerns over climate change. During the last few years, governments and societies around the

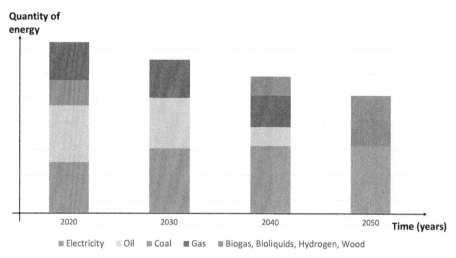

Figure 1.9 Energy transition and changes in the energy mix

world have realised that an energy system based on renewable energy can provide three other very important benefits, that is, an increase in the level of security of supply, an improvement in the level of air quality and, therefore, a reduction in the number of premature death and health costs due to air pollution, and the facilitation of energy access (particularly in developing countries) through decentralised systems.

Figure 1.9 is an illustration of a possible pathway of the transition of an energy system for a typical industrialised country from fossil fuels towards an energy system based on renewable energy sources and electricity produced using renewable energy. Starting from an energy system dominated by oil, gas, and coal, the transition results in an energy mix that is dominated by renewable energy sources such as biogas, hydrogen, biofuels, and wood and electricity produced from renewable energy sources.

An important point to note regarding the energy transition is the relevant decrease in total energy consumption due to the adoption of more energy-efficient technologies and the electrification of the transport and heating sectors. This is likely to be the case for industrialised countries. In developing countries, we expect a similar transformation towards renewable energy sources and an increase in overall energy efficiency, but we also expect an increase, and not a decline, in total energy consumption. This increase will be driven mostly by economic growth and population increases.

Regarding the transformation of the electricity sector in industrialised countries illustrated in Figure 1.10, we see that at the end of the transition process, the electricity production mix will be mainly based on hydropower, wind energy, solar energy, and geothermal energy. Of course, the electricity production mix is likely to be different across countries depending on their characteristics. We foresee this transformation taking place also in developing countries, although with a different path between 2030 and 2050.

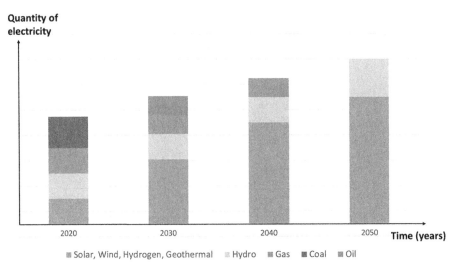

Figure 1.10 Electricity production mix for an industrialised country

Generally, it is expected that the electrification of sectors such as transport and heating will increase the electricity demand. Therefore, the energy transition implies that the suppliers will also increase electricity production, largely based on renewables. Note that in order to reach a well-functioning electricity system relying mainly on renewable energy sources such as solar energy and wind energy, which are characterised by intermittence in production due to meteorological factors, it is essential to:

- have a well-developed and interconnected electricity network that gives the possibility to move electricity from one region to another with flexibility, depending on the demand,
- have a well-developed electricity distribution network that enables the flexible and dynamic management of demand and supply using digitalisation (smart grids, smart meters, and smart appliances) as well as local storage facilities such as community-level batteries, and
- have a backup technology, such as gas-based power plants functioning with hydrogen, or technologies such as storage hydropower plants or large batteries that can be used during periods of supply shortages, which are mainly operated at the national level.

Some policymakers use the term 'energy transition' in combination with the term 'net zero'. This refers to a transition that is used to achieve an energy system characterised mainly by renewable energy sources, along with a small proportion of fossil fuel-based energy essential for sectors in which renewables cannot be employed. However, since the energy transition also implies achieving climate neutrality, that is, an energy system that produces zero CO_2 emissions, emissions from the sectors that still use fossil fuels must be captured and stored in dedicated repositories underground.

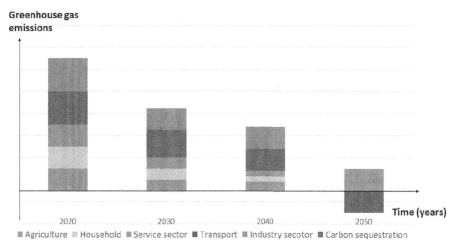

Figure 1.11 Energy transition and greenhouse gas emissions

In Figure 1.11, we illustrate the development of GHG emissions over time. Towards the end of the energy transition process, emissions are likely to be low, and, as discussed previously, they can be eliminated using carbon capture and sequestration technologies. For instance, emissions from industrial processes such as steel and cement production are likely to be captured from the production sites, and then transported and stored deep underground in geological formations.

The transformation of the current energy system into a system dominated by renewable energy sources and characterised by net zero GHG emissions generally implies additional costs in comparison to a system based on both renewable and non-renewable sources. However, it is important to keep in mind that this transformation is likely to also bring significant benefits to society. Of course, costs and benefits may vary a lot across different countries due to differences in their initial energy systems, their economic structures, and the socioeconomic characteristics of their populations. Generally, we distinguish between direct benefits and co-benefits of an energy transition. The direct benefits are obtained from the avoided negative climate change impacts, such as damages due to natural extreme events, agricultural yield losses, and adverse effects on labour productivity. Co-benefits result from the reduction of air pollution, greater biodiversity, enhanced water quality, and improved security of supply. It is, therefore, important to consider both costs and benefits (including these co-benefits) in all discussions about the energy transition, even though some benefits, such as the increase in air and water quality, as well as an increase in the security of supply, are not easy to estimate from an economic point of view.

The energy transition is an extremely essential but also challenging goal for societies to achieve. To reach this goal, we need to continue to invest in research and development activities to further enhance the exploitation of renewable energy sources, increase the level of energy efficiency, and digitalise the electricity sector. To ensure that they reach this ambitious goal, governments around the world are trying to design and implement effective energy and climate policies. In the second part of this textbook, we will discuss the most important policy measures that can be adopted by policymakers to address market failures and promote the energy transition. Of course, the ultimate goal is to choose a strategy to achieve the energy transition by maximising the difference between benefits and costs and by minimising possible negative distributional issues related to this transition.

Type of renewable energy sources for the energy transition

As we mentioned, to achieve the energy transition, we need to invest in renewable energy. In this box, we briefly describe different forms of renewable energy. Renewable energy is a form of energy that can be constantly replenished and is drawn from natural sources (such as water, biomass, sunlight, wind, steam or hot water within the Earth, or even waves). It can be used for electricity generation, space and water heating and cooling, cooking purposes (mostly in developing countries), and transport. Renewable energy sources should be distinguished from non-renewable energy sources, which are mostly drawn from fossil fuels (such as coal, gas, and oil) as well as from nuclear fuels that are exhaustible energy stocks, and thus only available in finite quantities.

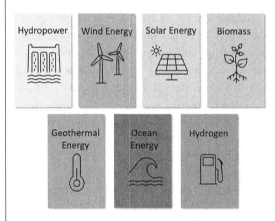

Figure 1.12 Types of renewable energy [29]

Figure 1.12 provides a snapshot of these main renewable energy sources. Hereon, we will briefly describe some of these forms of energy.

- **Solar energy:** In recent years, solar energy has become a very important form of renewable energy. Using the rays of the Sun as an energy source remains one of the most promising forms of clean energy. There are broadly three types of solar energy systems: photovoltaic (photovoltaic (PV))-based electricity systems, concentrated solar power-based electricity systems, and heating and cooling systems for water and spaces. PV-based systems use solar panels to directly convert sunlight to electricity. Smaller solar PV systems can power small appliances and individual homes, while many solar panels may be needed to produce electricity for several homes. Concentrated solar power systems are based on mirrors that reflect sunlight to a power tower, in order to focus it onto receivers that convert this to heat. This heat can either be used for electricity generation or stored. It is primarily used in very large power plants.

- **Wind energy:** Utilising the daily wind cycle to generate mechanical power or electricity is also one of the most common forms of renewable energy. Wind-based electricity is generated using wind turbines. They can be located on both land (onshore) and offshore. Wind turbines can either be individual structures or clumped together in what is called a wind farm. While individual turbines can generate enough electricity to power single homes, wind farms are needed for large-scale production.

- **Hydroelectric power:** Hydropower was one of the first renewable sources of energy used for electricity generation. Hydroelectric plants are located on or near a water source, and electricity is produced with the help of turbines. Run-of-the-river systems are those in which the water force of the current of a river causes a turbine to rotate, which then converts the mechanical energy to electrical energy. Storage systems, on the other hand, are built to accumulate water in reservoirs, from where it is released through turbines as and when needed to generate electricity.

- **Biomass energy:** Biomass is a renewable organic material, the source of which are plants and animals. Biomass energy is commonly used in many developing countries for the purposes of cooking and heating, but it is also used in many developed countries for transport (e.g., in the form of ethanol, which is a component of vehicle fuel in many countries) as well as electricity generation (by direct combustion, bacterial decomposition, or conversion to a gas or liquid fuel). Biomass sources can include wood, agricultural residue or crops, organic material in municipal solid waste, and animal manure.

- **Geothermal energy:** Geothermal energy is produced from the heat within the Earth. It can be used to heat buildings as well as to generate electricity.

- **Tidal/ocean energy:** Tidal energy is produced by the rise and fall of the ocean tides, as well as currents. Tidal electricity is generated with the help of tides turning turbines, similar to wind-based electricity. Tidal energy is at a relatively nascent stage of development compared to the other types, with very few commercial tidal power plants operating in the world.

- **Hydrogen:** Hydrogen is an energy carrier that is useful to store energy produced from other energy sources. It can be produced from a variety of renewable energy sources, and in this case, the it is a clean fuel, as well as non-renewable sources such as natural gas and nuclear power. Furthermore, it can be used for transportation as well as in electricity generation.

There are four main advantages of using renewable energy sources:

- Production of electricity is mostly devoid of polluting emissions.
- Resources used to produce these energy types are available at the local level (e.g., wind energy and solar energy), and they mostly use local technologies and know-how.
- The production costs are increasingly competitive.
- Countries can achieve a relatively high level of independence in generation with respect to other countries, and thus reduce the risk of international political crises arising due to energy shortages.

2 Market Failures and Behavioural Anomalies

In this chapter, we will discuss the economic factors that contribute to environmental and economic problems arising from the current energy systems, namely, the existence of market failures as well as behavioural anomalies. Then, we will briefly discuss how the government can intervene with energy and climate policies to correct these market failures and, finally, we will define the concept of sustainable development that can be considered as the ultimate goal of the government intervention in the economic system.

As we discussed in Chapter 1, the most important environmental problems arising from the current energy systems largely based on fossil fuels are climate change and air pollution. To facilitate the energy transition, several governments have introduced a policy mix including both energy and climate policy instruments. For these reasons, we believe that a discussion on energy policy should be supplemented with a discussion on climate policy. Moreover, as we will discuss in Chapters 7 to 9 of the book, several policy instruments overlap in terms of objective and their effects.

2.1 Introduction to Market Failures

In this section, we will provide a short overview of the five market failures that we think are most relevant and are often observed in production and consumption of energy and energy services. We will argue that the presence of behavioural anomalies can be considered to be a market failure.

As we know from introductory courses in economics, to function well and promote an efficient use of resources, a market (for any good or service) must be competitive and should satisfy the following conditions:

- There must be several producers and consumers.
- The product or service must be homogeneous.
- All economic actors (producers and consumers) must have all the information necessary to make informed and aware choices.
- No economic actor can influence the price, which in turn, must reflect all the costs determined by production and consumption.
- The economic actors must act rationally, that is, they must always consider the costs and benefits of making a choice, and therefore maximise their utility or profits.

When some economic actors deviate from behaviour which is considered rational from an economic point of view, a behavioural anomaly is said to occur, and this can lead to inefficient use of scarce resources in the market. Traditionally, while describing market failures in economics, textbooks often do not factor in behavioural anomalies and tend to treat them as economic problems that are distinct from market failures. However, in principle, behavioural anomalies can be thought of as manifestations of market failures; in this chapter, we will consider the existence of behavioural anomalies as a type of market failure, because they can alter the demand or supply in the market. As we will discuss in more detail, behavioural anomalies are important for understanding the glitches in the functioning of the markets for energy sources and in the markets for technologies used in producing and consuming energy services.

The presence of market failures impedes economic systems from reaching economic efficiency, that is, scarce resources are no longer efficiently utilised. The existence of the following economic phenomena gives rise to market failures:

1. Externalities
2. Public goods and common resources
3. Information problems (such as asymmetric and imperfect information) and principal–agent problems
4. Lack of competition
5. Behavioural anomalies

We must note that the 'traditional' market failures that we have mentioned above (1–4) are extensively studied and described in the field of neoclassical microeconomics, whereas behavioural anomalies (5) have only been introduced into economic discussions in the last decades, mostly by behavioural economists.

Neoclassical microeconomics assumes that while taking consumption or production decisions, consumers and producers are always rational, have willpower, and are looking to maximise gains for self-interest. For instance, according to the principles of neoclassical microeconomics, consumers and producers take decisions by weighing all the costs and benefits in order to maximise their utility functions, or their profit functions, respectively. In contrast, behavioural economics highlights the fact that the behaviour of economic agents can deviate from rational behaviour, that often they may have limited willpower, and that they may care about the well-being of others (and not just themselves) on some occasions. The difference between the two schools of economic thought (neoclassical and behavioural) is well described by Mullainathan and Thaler (2000): 'The standard economic model of human behaviour includes three unrealistic traits – unbounded rationality, unbounded willpower, and unbounded selfishness' [30].

As mentioned previously, the type of market failures that we have mentioned so far can lead to inefficiency in the use of resources. Note that there is another factor that makes government intervention important, even in the absence of market failures, namely the presence of a level of inequality that is unacceptable for society. A certain amount of inequality is a natural outcome of a well-functioning market because markets reward risk-taking and successful individuals, but often high levels of inequality are the outcome of poorly functioning markets, where individuals are unable to use their resources to their best advantage.

The functioning of energy markets and markets for energy services may also give rise to heterogeneity with respect to access to energy and energy sources that may be unacceptable for society. This situation can leave some households with insufficient or even no access to energy. The lack of energy infrastructure, as well as high prices for commodities such as electricity, gasoline, home appliances, or solar panels, can engender energy poverty. This situation is characterised by a lack of adequate, affordable, and reliable energy or basic energy services (for heating, cooling, lighting, mobility, and power) required to ensure a decent standard of living.

This problem is mostly observed in developing and emerging-market countries. However, industrialised countries can also experience the phenomenon of energy poverty (for example, due to an increase in commodity prices, such as oil and gas), although often with less severity. For instance, the introduction of subsidies to promote the installation of solar panels on the rooftops of low-income households can improve access to a sustainable form of electricity, and may even have positive spillover effects, such as fostering conditions to start a business (and increase household income), for example. The challenge for governments is to alleviate energy poverty and increase access to energy, by implementing policy instruments that promote the development of sustainable energy systems. This, in turn, can improve the levels of energy efficiency of the economy and help utilise clean and renewable energy sources effectively. For example, even though the introduction of fossil fuel subsidies for households that belong to the low-income classes could alleviate energy poverty, it will also likely lead to an increase in air pollution and contribute to climate change, and thus may not be the most sustainable policy that governments can implement (we discuss this issue further in Chapter 8).

From an economic point of view, the presence of market failures and problems related to ensuring universal energy access justify that most governments define and implement policies to improve economic efficiency, access to energy, and to reduce the levels of energy poverty.

2.2   Market Failures

2.2.1   Externalities

In economics, an externality is defined as a cost or a benefit that affects a third party during the production or consumption process of a good or a service, without any payment being made for it. Externalities can either be negative or positive, depending on whether a cost or a benefit is incurred by the third party. The presence of externalities is always a source of inefficiency in the use of resources. The term 'externality' means that an effect on the economic system is being determined outside the scope of the market, that is, the market is ignoring the cost or the benefit of an action, and thereby not ensuring that limited resources are used in an efficient manner.

Negative externalities occur when a decision creates costs to a third party, without any compensation for these costs taking place. For instance, a coal power plant may emit local air pollutants such as PM2.5 and global air pollutants such as CO_2. These emissions, as discussed in Chapter 1, create negative environmental and economic effects, and thus generate costs. If these costs are not included in the price of electricity produced by the coal power plant, a negative externality arises, and the polluter pays principle is not respected. As a result, electricity consumption in this setting is higher than what would be socially desirable, because the prevailing market price is lower than the price in the market where the environmental and social costs (also called external costs) from the generation of electricity from coal would have been taken into account.

Figure 2.1 describes the effect of a negative externality on the market equilibrium. The horizontal axis on the graph shows the quantity of an energy good (such as electricity produced by coal power plants), while the vertical axis depicts price levels. On the graph, two upward-sloping supply curves are present: one curve captures only the marginal private cost of the firms producing electricity using coal, whereas the other curve encapsulates both the private and external costs. In this setup, the equilibrium allocation is determined by the intersection of the upward-sloping supply curves with the downward-sloping demand curve. Generally, as depicted in Figure 2.1, the presence of a negative externality leads to the production (and consumption) of coal-based electricity at a higher level (Q) than the socially optimal level (Q^*). The optimal solution, from a societal point of view, is thus represented by the combination (P_2, Q^*), whereas without considering these environmental and social costs, the equilibrium on the market is characterised by the combination (P, Q). The triangle shaded in orange denotes the welfare loss when the firms ignore the external costs in their output decisions.

In the equilibrium that does not consider the social cost (i.e., the private equilibrium), an excess amount of electricity is produced and consumed (Q). As discussed

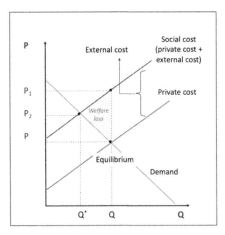

Figure 2.1 Negative externality

in more detail later, in order to reach the equilibrium situation (Q^*, P_2), the state could implement a policy, such as a pollution tax. The pollution tax is an example of a policy that would 'internalise' the negative externality in such a market, that is, the full costs associated with production and consumption would then be taken into account (or paid for), which would reduce the amount of coal used for electricity generation.

As mentioned before, externalities can also be positive. A positive externality is characterised by a decision that creates benefits to a third party, without a payment having taken place for it. In this case, the market produces a quantity of a good that is less than what is socially desirable. In the energy sector, this situation can arise with so-called learning-by-using spillovers, that is, the adoption of a new energy-efficient product, or a new renewable energy technology can create further knowledge about the product through its increasing use. This knowledge, which is based on the experience of using the new technology, will create a positive spillover for other potential adopters of this technology. Potential adopters will then receive information on the technology directly from the producers, as well as directly (or indirectly) from these early adopters. In the latter case, the potential adopters will receive useful information, generally without paying for it. Of course, the early adopters could also choose to only share the information with individuals who are willing to pay for acquiring it.

The installation of solar panels is a good example to illustrate the phenomenon of positive externalities. When a household installs a new and innovative technology such as a solar panel, the following positive externalities could materialise:

- The household that has installed solar panels can choose to share their experience after the installation and the first few months of operation of the technology. They can inform their friends, as well as other interested households, about the advantages and disadvantages of the investment, and the possible issues arising from its installation. To the extent that this knowledge sharing is not done formally or on a professional platform, and is thus not paid for, this is an example of a positive externality.
- The installation of solar panels in one household can also lead to an increase in the security of supply for the other households connected to the same grid. This is especially useful in areas with electricity shortages in the hours with solar power production exceeding its own consumption when the solar installation can feed excess electricity into the grid and contribute towards stabilisation of the system. This, once again, can serve as a positive externality for other households, as they can experience a more reliable electricity supply without paying for it.

Other types of positive externalities that can be observed in energy markets, particularly in the development of new products or technologies, are research and development (R&D) spillovers, where firms can acquire information generated by other firms, again without having to pay for it (this can, of course, also be controlled by using patent protection or with intellectual property rights).

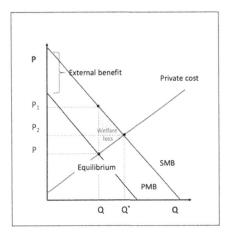

Figure 2.2 Positive externality

Figure 2.2 illustrates the effect of a positive externality on the market equilibrium. The horizontal axis shows the quantity of a certain energy good or service, while the vertical axis depicts price levels. On the graph, two downward-sloping demand curves are present: one curve that considers only the marginal private benefits (MPB) to the consumers, and another one that captures both the marginal private benefit and the external benefits incurred. This curve represents the marginal social benefits (SMB) from the consumption of the good or service. Therefore, the existence of a positive externality implies that the private benefits borne by the consumption of a good, which is graphically represented by the private demand function, are lower than the social benefits, represented by the social demand function. The equilibrium is determined by the intersection of these curves with the upward-sloping supply curve. Generally, the presence of a positive externality leads to production and consumption at a lower level (Q) than the socially optimal level (Q^*). The optimal solution for society is represented by the combination (P_2, Q^*), whereas without taking into account the positive externality, the equilibrium on the market is characterised by the combination (P,Q). The triangle shaded in orange indicates the welfare that is foregone when the consumers ignore these external benefits when making their consumption decisions. Also in this case, as we discuss in more detail later in the book, the state can intervene and address this positive externality using, for instance, a subsidy.

2.2.2   Public Goods and Common Resources

Another important market failure is the presence of public goods and common resources.

2.2.2.1   Public Goods

A public good is defined as a good that has two important characteristics: non-excludability and non-rivalry.

- **Non-excludability** is defined as the property that everyone can have access to the good and consume it, that is, it is not possible to exclude anybody from its consumption, and importantly, any person can consume the good without paying for it.
- **Non-rivalry** means that the consumption of the good by one person does not decrease the availability of this good to another person.

Examples of public goods related to the energy and climate sector are basic R&D activities on new energy technologies performed at research institutions and universities and awareness campaigns on climate change and energy saving. Another important example of a public good is investments made in infrastructure to protect entire regions, cities, or nations from the adverse effects of climate change. Consider coastal protection against rising sea levels, or riverbanks that protect against flooding. Such infrastructure can be considered a 'local' public good, that is, a public good that brings benefits to a localised population (and not the entire population of a country, for example).

The presence of a public good is a market failure because both the quantity produced and the price determined by the interaction of supply and demand in a free market do not correspond to the optimal combination of quantity and price that would maximise the welfare of society. Thus, the market mechanism underproduces the quantity of the good that would be optimal. The reason is very simple – the fact that people cannot be excluded from consuming a public good makes it impossible to charge a price for it. Therefore, the supply of the public good should be based on the voluntary financial contributions of people. If some or all individuals consume the public good without voluntarily paying for it, then we observe a free-rider problem. In this situation, economic agents undersupply the public good because they cannot recover all their costs. Therefore, to offer the optimal amount of public good for society, state intervention is necessary. This can be done by either imposing an obligation on everyone to pay a price for its use or by directly offering it to the public and financing it using general tax resources. An example in the energy sector is the financing of basic research in the field of energy efficiency or renewable energy generation at universities or the financing of public campaigns in favour of energy-saving behaviour.

2.2.2.2 Common Resources

A common resource has two characteristics: non-excludability and rivalry.

- **Rivalry** implies that the consumption or use of a resource or a service by one person reduces its availability to another person.

Common resources can be of two types – local and global. A common resource is considered to be local if the beneficiaries and users of the resource are located in regions close to the resource. Contrary to this, a common resource is considered to be global if its beneficiaries and users are effectively the entire world population. For instance, an alpine pond is a local common resource, while the atmosphere is a global common resource.

Unlike public goods, the functioning of market forces to decide the equilibrium quantity of a common resource and its price leads to the risk of an overexploitation of the resource, which can lead to its depletion. This phenomenon is also referred to as the tragedy of the commons. When a common resource is accessible to everyone without requiring a payment for using it, economic agents may try to maximise their utility in the short term, without thinking about the well-being of others, and even their own long-run utility.

For example, let us consider the exploitation of an alpine lake where a stock of fish is reared by some professional fishermen. To ensure that the number of fish does not decrease significantly over time, it is important that the conditions that allow the fish to reproduce are maintained. Thus, it is important to always keep a certain number of fish in the lake. On the other hand, we know that the income of every fisherman depends on the number of fish caught per day. In this situation, every fisherman may have an incentive to maximise his income in the short term, and thus maximise the number of fish caught per day.

If all fishermen end up adopting this strategy though, the stock of fish in the lake would drastically decrease. This would severely limit the reproductive cycle, and thus lead to a depletion in the number of fish in the long term. This would be an outcome detrimental to all fishermen.

One important common resource relevant to discussions on energy and climate policy issues is the atmosphere. The atmosphere is a layer of gases that protects the earth and allows people to live on it by ensuring stable temperatures on the planet. All living creatures receive benefits from this protection. As mentioned in the Chapter 1, in addition to protecting us, the atmosphere is used as a deposit or sink for the greenhouse gases (GHGs) emitted as a result of the production and consumption behaviour of modern society. It qualifies as a common resource because while everyone has access to it as a deposit, there is rivalry in its consumption due to the limits on its ability to store GHGs imposed by climate change.

Therefore, the problems related to climate change that we currently experience (and are likely to in the future as well) are due to the fact that societies around the world are overusing the atmosphere as a sink for GHGs, and therefore, are altering its protective ability. In this situation, if a country or a person decides to abate its GHG emissions, all other countries will also benefit from this reduction of GHGs. Therefore, a country that decides to abate its own emissions will create a positive externality for all other countries (and people). At present, countries are partially reluctant to unilaterally reduce emissions by implementing energy and climate policies. It is thus pivotal to define and implement international agreements to reduce GHGs and to manage this crucial common resource sustainably.

As illustrated in the Chapter 1, industrialised countries representing approximately 20 per cent of the world's population have already used about 50 per cent of the 'atmosphere' as a deposit of GHGs. This is an inequitable outcome for other countries that are on the path to growth and development, and it explains why many emerging market economies and developing countries ask for financial support and compensation/reparation, as well as more effort in reducing emissions from the industrialised countries during international climate negotiations.

Another example of a common resource is the land used for the production of electricity using renewable energy sources such as wind and solar. Suppose the most profitable land from the perspective of producing renewable energy is owned jointly by the members of a local community (and not by a private person or firm), without any corresponding land-use rights being assigned. In that case, there is a risk that the land may be exploited by all members of the community inefficiently. For instance, in the Alps, local communities often own favourable land to produce wind energy. Because this land is owned by all the members of the community, each of these owners could claim to have the right to install their own wind turbines. If this were to happen though, then the high density of the installed turbines will impede the efficient production of electricity.

To prevent the depletion of a common resource and to promote its sustainable use, there are three possible pathways we can follow:

1. The users and owners of a common resource should agree on some basic rules for limiting its use in order to avoid overexploitation problems. This is an interesting and practical solution in the case of local common resources such as the use of a lake for fishing, an alpine pasture to feed cows during the summer, or an alpine land to exploit wind energy. For example, the members of a local community could agree on the maximum number of wind turbines or solar panels that can be installed in an alpine and communal land by each member.
2. The state can intervene and impose rules, and possibly a price, for the use of a common resource.
3. A global institution can intervene to regulate the use of a global common resource. For instance, in the case of the atmosphere, global institutions such as the United Nations (UN) must intervene and encourage countries to sign international agreements to promote the sustainable management of resources. However, the current international discussions regarding climate change have revealed that it is difficult to define and implement effective agreements at the international level, as the UN has limited power to impose rules and sanctions on national governments.

2.2.3 Information and Principal–Agent Problems

2.2.3.1 Information Problems

Another important market failure is the lack of information for consumers regarding energy-saving technologies (also known as imperfect information) such as electrical appliances, cars, homes, and heating systems, or energy-producing technologies such as solar panels. As another example, in the market for adaptation measures against climate change, there exists a lack of information on technologies as well as on strategies that can improve resilience against climatic events (e.g., against flood risk, and excess heat). Furthermore, energy markets and markets for technologies used to produce energy services are characterised by asymmetric information between buyers and sellers. Asymmetric information arises when producers cannot convey or do not have incentives to provide the information that may be important for buyers. Therefore, one party in the market may have more information about a product or service than the other. These problems of asymmetric information and imperfect information can create inefficiencies in the energy market.

For instance, if heating system vendors primarily have knowledge of fossil fuel-based systems, they will tend to provide information to consumers on the advantages and disadvantages of fossil fuel-based heating systems in order to prioritise selling them over the systems that may be more efficient. The same goes for car dealerships prioritising the sale of internal combustion engine-based cars; employees of such dealerships may have stronger incentives to provide information that favours the sale of gasoline over electric cars. To overcome such information problems that could lead to market failures, the state could introduce energy labels, public energy consultancy services, and programmes and information campaigns in the energy industry.

Impact factors of household energy-saving behaviour: An empirical study of Shandong Province in China

In the empirical study of Shandong Province in China, Zhang et al. (2018) [31] explored the role of bounded rationality and the importance of information in addressing the cognitive limitations concerning energy-saving behaviour. Based on a survey conducted in the Shandong Province in China, the authors pointed out that several individual subjective factors and external factors can influence and shape the energy consumption of the residential sector ranging over several constructs, including behaviour, energy-saving intention, or sense of responsibility. They found that information about energy-related issues can help reduce boundedly rational behaviour in residential energy use and argued that it may be crucial in shaping the energy-saving behaviour of individuals. The study thus shows that policies that help in shaping energy-saving responsibilities, as well as information campaigns centred around enhancing energy knowledge, can guide users to adopt energy-saving behaviour and to make more conscious purchases.

2.2.3.2 Principal–Agent Problems

The principal–agent problem is characterised by the presence of an externality and asymmetric information. The most common case in the energy sector is when the owner of a building, the agent, has to make decisions regarding energy efficiency as well as the choice of heating system for the building. These decisions will have consequences on the tenants, that is, the principals. Externalities are said to arise in this case, because the decisions taken by the owner will have monetary consequences on the tenants. On the other hand, asymmetric information exists because tenants are not fully informed about the possible technological solutions that could be chosen by the owner of the building.

The result of this situation, also referred to as the split-incentive problem, is that the choices of the owners in terms of energy efficiency and choice of heating system might be optimal for them, but not necessarily for the tenants. Since the owners generally do not have to pay energy costs, they may not have incentives to invest in more modern, efficient, and sustainable heating systems (especially given their higher upfront costs) and in improving the energy efficiency of the building. Thus, minimal investments may be made in energy-efficient appliances or heating systems, even though they are characterised by lower operating costs (due to lower levels of energy consumption) which are borne by the users of the technology, in this case, the tenants.

In this situation, the losers are the tenants as well as society. The tenants lose out as they have to pay more for heating services, and society loses because it has to bear the brunt of pollution and energy inefficiency due to low energy-saving renovation rates and the presence of fossil fuel-based heating systems. It is clear that this situation tends to occur primarily in real-estate markets with excess demand. A similar principal–agent problem can also arise with respect to the adoption of adaptation measures in the building sector. The owner of a building may not have the incentive to install natural ventilation systems or greening and shading measures to deal with heat waves. To counter this problem, and the subsequent market failure, the state can introduce mandatory energy certification for buildings, or programmes and information campaigns about energy-saving and renewable energy technologies. Of course, conversely, it could also be the case that the tenant is the agent and the landlord is the principal. For instance, the landlord may pay for the utility costs of the tenant, in which case the tenant will have limited incentives to purchase energy-efficient appliances or to use energy judiciously.

Is There an energy efficiency gap in China? Evidence from an information experiment
Based on the results of an incentivised field experiment in the Chinese context, Beattie et al. (2022) [32] find that a lack of information may be an important driver of underinvestment in energy-efficient durables in the Chinese context. The results of the study revealed that Chinese consumers had imperfect information regarding the possible energy savings from using light-emitting diodes (LEDs) instead of incandescent lamps over a 10-year period. This discouraged them from making investments in energy efficiency, further exacerbated by the relative upfront costs of these technologies. They also found that providing information on these savings can augment the willingness to pay individuals for the more energy-efficient bulbs compared to the energy-inefficient bulbs. Thus, this study shows that imperfect information poses a barrier to investment in energy efficiency.

2.2.4 Lack of Competition – Monopoly and Collusive Oligopoly

The fourth market failure is a situation characterised by a lack of competition in the energy markets (such as for oil or electricity) and in the markets for energy technologies such as electrical appliances and heating systems.

2.2.4.1 Energy Markets

In Table 2.1, we present the types of market forms that can be observed in the markets for energy sources. It is important to distinguish the wholesale market (where the

Table 2.1 Energy resources and market forms

	Wholesale market	*Retail market*
Oil	Oligopolistic	Reasonably competitive (gasoline, heating oil...)
Gas	Oligopolistic	Natural monopoly
Electricity	In some countries reasonably competitive, monopolistic in others	Monopolistic for the transmission and distribution functions (natural monopoly). Retail is competitive in some countries, and still monopolistic in others
Coal	Reasonably competitive	Reasonably competitive

purchase or sale of energy to resellers takes place) from the retail market (where the purchase or sale of electricity is done with end consumers). It can be observed in Table 2.1 that several of the markets are not competitive, that is, the firms can exert market power to some extent and therefore influence the final price. For instance, the transmission and distribution of gas and electricity are characterised by relatively large initial investments to construct gas pipelines and electricity networks, and the presence of high economies of scale. The economies of scale imply a decline in average costs. If these average costs decrease up to the point where the resulting quantity supplied equals the market demand, then we observe a natural monopoly.

The term 'natural' is used to describe this form of monopoly, not because a key resource is controlled by a single firm or the government assigns to a single firm the exclusive right to use a natural resource, but because the inherent cost structure of these services implies that it is more efficient to have a single producer in the market, instead of several producers (namely, the existence of economies of scale). A natural monopolist can define the price of the product or service and the quantity to offer. If the monopolist is not regulated, then the monopolist will set a price and quantity to maximize profit and not society's welfare. Thus, the price and the quantity produced and consumed aren't optimal. Therefore, in the presence of a natural monopoly, it is important that policymakers create an authority to regulate the price and activities of the natural monopolist.

The oil and gas wholesale markets are generally characterised by an oligopolistic nature, that is, a market having a few firms. In this situation, firms can decide to compete, or to collude, in order to increase or influence the selling price. Therefore, collusive markets in the energy sector may also generate market outcomes that are not efficient from an economic point of view. If the firms operating in an oligopolistic market decide to collude by explicitly defining written (and binding) behavioural rules, then the firms form an official cartel with the goal to maximise profits. In this case, the price and quantity defined by the cartel are close to those of a natural monopoly. Organization of the Petroleum Exporting Countries (OPEC), which mediates negotiations for oil prices as well as oil production, is a well-known example of a cartel in the energy industry. Of course, in most countries, the creation of cartels is prohibited, and the states try to promote competition in these markets through the establishment and functioning of competition authorities that observe and regulate these markets.

Electricity markets, both wholesale and retail, can be very different across policy settings. For instance, some countries have introduced reforms in the electricity market (including some developing countries), whereas others are characterised by a monopoly. Generally, a reform of the electricity market includes the introduction of competition in the generation and retail activities, whereas the transmission and distribution of electricity tend to remain a natural monopoly.

As can be seen in Table 2.1, there are also markets that are reasonably competitive, such as the oil retail market. This means that they satisfy many of the typical characteristics of a competitive market.

In conclusion, the energy markets are mostly characterised by imperfect competition. Therefore, as we will discuss in more detail in Chapter 6, it is important to have strong competitive and regulatory authorities that monitor these markets in order to prevent either predatory or excessively high prices, low quantities, and little to no technological change as a result of limited R&D activities.

> **Emergence of a natural monopoly**
>
> In a study from 2014, Alaeifar, Farsi, and Filippini [33] documented the cost structure of the gas distribution sector in Switzerland. In their paper, they estimated the optimal size and economies of scale for a panel of Swiss firms for the years 1996–2000, leading to the finding that there were unexploited economies of scale [33]. Moreover, in the paper, the authors drew a figure based on the empirical results that shows three downward-sloping average operating cost functions, reflecting different levels of customer density (denoted by CUD), and therefore pointing out the existence of a natural monopoly.

2.2.4.2 Energy Technology Markets

The markets for technologies that produce energy services such as electrical appliances, heating systems, and cars are largely oligopolistic or monopolistically competitive markets. A monopolistic competition is a market structure characterised by differentiated products and freedom of entry and exit for firms. Therefore, the firms operating in a monopolistically competitive setup have both monopoly power (as monopolists) and freedom of entry and exit, as firms operating in competitive markets. The differentiation of the products is visibly present in the market for electrical appliances, and the market for heating systems. Given that in oligopolistic and monopolistically competitive markets, firms can exert some monopoly power, the price and quantity observed in such markets tend not to represent an efficient outcome from a societal point of view. In the case of oligopolistic markets, it is important to prevent a market failure due to collusion, which is achievable if the state establishes a competition authority. However, with monopolistic competition, significant state interventions are not always the optimal solution, first because the market power of each individual firm operating in this type of market is small, and second because monopolistic competition also provides benefits to society in terms of product diversity. Of course, in order to ensure that consumers can make informed and sound decisions in markets with differentiated products, the state could promote the introduction of labels, as well as websites that allow consumers to compare products. They can also implement regulations on the depth of information that must be provided by the producers to the consumers. Due to the complexity of the technologies used in the energy sector, the introduction of this type of measure is perhaps more important than in other sectors characterised by monopolistic competition. We will return to this discussion in Chapter 6.

2.2.5   Behavioural Anomalies

2.2.5.1   Behavioural Anomalies and Households

The most important behavioural anomalies that affect individual decision-making in the energy sector are ones related to bounded rationality, bounded willpower, and bounded selfishness/bounded self-interest. Jolls, Sunstein, and Thaler (1998) [34] describe bounded rationality as – '... an idea first introduced by Herbert Simon, refers to the obvious fact that human cognitive abilities are not infinite. We have limited computational skills and seriously flawed memories' (p. 1479) [34]. The theory maintains that individuals take decisions using just part of the information, and with cognitive constraints in analysing information and optimising decisions.

This means, in general, some individuals do not compare the costs and benefits before taking a decision, unlike the rational economic agent described in the neoclassical economic framework. These scholars also note that 'In addition to bounded rationality, people often display bounded willpower. This term refers to the fact that human beings often take actions that they know to be in conflict with their own long-term interests' (p. 1479) [34]. This concept of bounded willpower further questions neoclassical assumptions in the modelling of economic market transactions. Finally, the notion of complete selfishness in individual decision-making is also questioned by behavioural economic thought: '... the term bounded self-interest refers to an important fact about the utility function of most people: they care, or act as if they care, about others, even strangers, in some circumstances' (p. 1479) [34].

In Table 2.2, we have summarised and classified the most important behavioural anomalies that can influence decision-making in energy markets, and in the markets for energy technologies. These behavioural anomalies cause people to deviate from the rational and optimal behaviour that is assumed in standard economic theory. We have grouped these anomalies into three general categories – bounded rationality, bounded willpower, and bounded self-interest, to explain the three main deviations introduced by Jolls, Sunstein, and Thaler (1998) [34]. In the table, we also see how these anomalies may influence our decisions in situations related to energy and energy technology markets. For instance, consider bounded rationality and the specific behavioural anomaly of cognitive limitations. This is often an important factor that affects the investment decisions taken by people, that is, consumers may not make the effort or they may not have the skills to conduct evaluations or execute complex tasks, such as performing an investment analysis correctly (or doing a lifetime cost analysis before buying an electrical appliance). In addition to this, loss aversion, which arises due to *status quo* bias and the endowment effect, may induce people to keep using old

Table 2.2 Behavioural anomalies

Bounded rationality	
Behavioural anomalies	**Impact**

• Cognitive limitations in evaluating complex tasks
• Loss aversion: a pattern of preference for avoiding losses rather than acquiring equivalent gains
  • Status quo bias: a strong tendency to remain at the status quo
  • Endowment effect: humans assign greater value to specific goods that they own than to identical goods they do not own
• Framing effect: the choices of individuals can be influenced by the way the positive or negative aspects of the same decision are highlighted.
• Limited use of information
  • Limited attention paid to some information related to a decision
  • Limited salience of relevant information
  • Faulty priors/beliefs about which information is relevant
	• Difficulty to compute the lifetime cost of energy-consuming durables
	• Limited use of information that can be due to limited salience of the level of energy efficiency of a durable (cars, electrical appliances, etc.)
	• Heuristic decision-making (e.g., the use of a rule of thumb) instead of undertaking complex calculations
	• A tendency to keep old durables, to avoid changes in models and brands of durables

Bounded willpower	
Behavioural anomalies	**Impact**
• Attitude-behaviour gap: inconsistency observed between consumer attitudes and actions • Myopia in intertemporal choices: cognitive myopia/present bias, near future rewards, are valued higher than more distant rewards because of varying discount rates	• Individuals value the environment; however, they keep old appliances and do not behave accordingly • Due to myopia and present bias, consumers tend to give weight to the upfront cost of a durable or of an investment in energy efficiency and undervalue its future operating cost or benefits. • Individuals may underestimate current climate risks and tend to procrastinate on the adoption of adaptation strategies.

Bounded selfishness	
Behavioural anomalies	**Impact**
• Individuals give value to altruism (doing actions that benefit other people without receiving anything in return) • Individuals give value to fairness (treating people in a fair way, free from bias or injustice) • Individuals tend to care about social norms, that is, people try to exhibit attitudes and behaviours that are considered acceptable according to the prevailing societal norms.	• Social comparison of energy use among households may work to reduce energy consumption (e.g., through home energy reports) • Social comparison of energy-efficient investments among households

and energy-inefficient electrical appliances, or it may lead to a reluctance to switch models or brands (to more efficient ones), for instance.

Bounded rationality is also influenced by framing effects, which imply that the choice of individuals may be influenced by the manner in which the advantages and disadvantages of appliances, for instance, are presented. The choices of individuals may vary depending on how information about the energy efficiency of appliances is presented on energy labels. Related to this is the notion of limited use of information, whereby individuals may choose to pay more attention to some elements rather than to others, for instance, they may consider the upfront prices of an appliance to be more important than its operating costs.

Bounded willpower can be captured through the attitude-behaviour gap, as an example, that shows a wedge between beliefs and behaviour, as well as myopia. For instance, there may be a divergence between the attitudes of people towards investing in renewable energy sources, and their actual decision-making. Myopic preferences, on the other hand, imply that near-future rewards are valued more than distant rewards, because of varying discount rates. For instance, individuals may fail to recognise the operating cost savings from the use of energy-efficient technology and may weigh its purchase cost more heavily.

The third category of anomalies is bounded selfishness, which includes altruism, fairness, and social norms. From an energy perspective, social norms are more relevant, although altruism and fairness can also be important in some cases. For example, individuals who are altruistic in nature may choose to invest in sustainable technologies such as solar panels, even if they are not necessarily beneficial in their context from an economic point of view, as a way of contributing to the energy transition.

Social norms can play an important role in determining choices as well. From a neoclassical economics perspective, aligning choices with the prevailing choices of one's respective social group can be considered an anomaly. Think of the decision of a household to follow the crowd and buy gasoline-guzzling vehicles, simply because their neighbours or friends do so. Such behaviour is an example of a negative social norm. However, following social norms can also give rise to positive externalities, if the prevailing choice involves the adoption of more energy-efficient technologies or renewable energy sources. We will discuss the role played by some of these behavioural anomalies in hindering purchases of energy-efficient technologies in more detail in Chapter 5.

Adding fuel to fire? Social spillovers in the adoption of LPG in India

Households in many developing countries continue to use solid biomass (such as firewood) as a source of cooking fuel, even though it has negative ramifications on indoor air pollution, and thus on health. In this paper, Srinivasan and Carattini (2019)[35] investigated the role of social spillovers, or positive social norms, in the adoption of a relatively clean cooking fuel from this perspective, liquefied petroleum gas (LPG), in the Indian Context. The authors presented multiple pieces of evidence that together suggest that households were more likely to use LPG if the share of its adoption was higher in the same village or urban block, and that these effects were stronger for households belonging to social networks. The policy implications of this study relate to the use of social learning to facilitate the energy transition in developing countries.

As we mentioned in the introduction to this chapter, the behavioural anomalies mentioned in Table 2.2 are also a form of market failure, that is, the demand observed on the market due to the presence of these anomalies is not the same demand that we would have observed if consumers had acted rationally, and would not have deviated from the behaviour assumed in standard economics.

Figure 2.3 presents the effects of two categories of behavioural anomalies (bounded rationality and bounded willpower) on the market equilibrium. The horizontal axis shows the quantity of energy-efficient technology, while the vertical axis depicts price levels. On the graph, two downward-sloping demand curves are present: one curve accounts for the fact that consumers are rational and bias-free, whereas the other curve takes into account the presence of behavioural anomalies, and therefore possible bias in consumers. For instance, the presence of a *status quo* bias implies that the demand for new energy-efficient appliances is lower than one of the bias-free consumers. The equilibrium in this market is determined by the intersection of these curves with the upward-sloping supply curve. Generally, the presence of a behavioural bias leads to production and consumption at a lower level Q than the socially optimal level Q^*. The optimal solution from a societal point of view is represented by the combination (P_2, Q^*), whereas in the presence of a bias, the market equilibrium would be the combination (P, Q).

2.2.5.2 Behavioural Anomalies and Firms

So far, we have discussed how behavioural anomalies can affect the demand side of the market, that is, how they can characterise consumer decisions. However, Leibenstein (1966) [36] observed that it is also possible to individualise behavioural anomalies

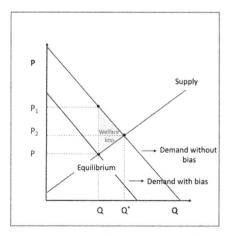

Figure 2.3 Impact of bias on market equilibrium

in the decisions of a firm. He suggested that the behavioural anomalies at the firm level can prevent them from minimising their costs of production. Leibenstein called this type of inefficiency in terms of using inputs X-inefficiency, although nowadays, the papers measuring the efficiency and productivity of the firms call it productive inefficiency.

Leibenstein, who can be considered one of the first behavioural economists, noted in particular that lack of motivation and lack of incentives (but not only these factors) could act as the reasons behind this production inefficiency, and used concepts from psychology to explain the inefficient behaviour of the managers of the firms [36]. He introduced the concept of selective rationality, where an individual is, at times, *homo economicus* and therefore rational, and at other times less than fully rational.

Selective rationality of a manager of a firm implies that he/she may not always be rational, that is, they may not always take optimal managerial decisions from the perspective of a firm. The magnitude of this selective rationality, which then may cause deviation from optimal behaviour as assumed in neoclassical economics, depends on the internal and external pressures on the firm. External pressures are determined by the type of market where the firm is active and by the shareholders. In a competitive market, from a production point of view, there is a significant level of external pressure to be efficient, while in a monopolistic market, these pressures are weaker, and shareholders are the main reason behind these external pressures.

Internal pressures, on the other hand, can be exerted either by the owner of the firm or even by the attitudes and personality of the manager. For instance, while managers may want to work as efficiently and well as possible, they may also be influenced by the instinct for impulsive behaviour. This may result in them minimising the effort exerted in work involving mental or physical strain and thus making decisions that are detrimental to the firm's welfare.

The presence of inefficiency in the production of goods and services usually manifests with higher costs of production, and therefore, the supply function of such a firm in the market is higher than the supply function of a firm with efficient production. Therefore, the optimal quantity and price combination will not be achieved. As previously discussed, some functions of energy markets, such as those for the distribution of electricity or gas to the end consumers, can be characterised as natural monopolies. In these markets, the possibility to observe inefficiency in production is still very high. In fact, several studies have shown that electricity and gas distribution firms are characterised by productive inefficiency [37, 38].

Persistent and transient cost efficiency – An application to the Swiss Hydropower sector
The goal of this study by Filippini et al. (2018) [39] was to measure the levels of cost efficiency of individual firms by applying the stochastic frontier approach and using an advanced econometric model specification, that is, the generalised true random effects (GTRE) model. The analysis was conducted on sixty-five Swiss hydropower firms for the period between 2000 and 2013. The results indicated

> a relatively high level of cost inefficiency in the Swiss hydropower sector of 21.8 per cent.

The behavioural anomalies described earlier have clear implications for the effectiveness of energy and climate policy instruments. In fact, most of the conventional market-based energy and climate policy measures, such as an energy or CO_2 tax, are based on the assumption that consumers and firms are rational. For instance, when policymakers introduce a CO_2 tax, they assume that consumers buying a new car, or installing a new heating system, will consider the increase in the cost of energy due to the tax while making their purchase decision. However, as we have discussed in this chapter, this assumption might be far-fetched, as some consumers may exhibit behavioural anomalies. For example, they may make decisions regarding which car or heating system to purchase without performing an investment analysis or calculating the lifetime cost of the durable. The consequence is that the CO_2 tax may not be as effective in reducing the consumption of fossil fuels as expected. Therefore, in order to define and implement energy and climate policy measures successfully, policymakers should consider that consumers and firms might not always act rationally.

2.3   Role of Energy and Climate Policies

From an economic point of view, the presence of a market failures justifies a state intervention in the energy and energy-related markets to promote an increase in economic efficiency. Moreover, the presence of a lack of access to energy sources and services may also justify a state intervention. The main goal of policies would be to correct these failures in order to promote economic efficiency and access to energy sources, increase the well-being of the population, and more generally, ensure the sustainable development of societies. In this section, we will briefly discuss the goals of energy and climate policies. A more detailed discourse is provided in Chapters 7 to 9.

We must remember that energy and climate policies are two different types of state interventions that seek to transform the current energy system (which is heavily dependent on fossil fuels) into a sustainable one. However, we must note that energy and climate policies are not necessarily synonymous, and as we will observe in the next section, energy policy often has more objectives to meet than climate policy. This is the reason for several countries defining goals and policy instruments for these two domains using separate laws or regulations. Despite this, given that both energy and climate policies promote the energy transition, it is important to discuss both in conjunction. Finally, we should also keep in mind that climate policy can comprise two different aspects; on the one hand, the most popular policies are mitigation measures, and, on the other hand, adaptation policies are also important.

2.3.1   Energy Policy and Climate Policy Goals

In Figure 2.4, we summarise the goals of energy and climate policy. Energy policy generally has three objectives: to guarantee an environmentally sustainable supply of

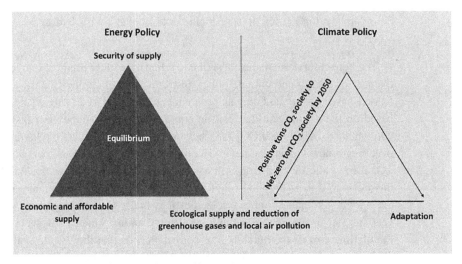

Figure 2.4 Energy policy and climate policy goals

energy, to guarantee the security of energy supply, and to guarantee an economically efficient and affordable supply of energy. In contrast to this, climate policy primarily has two goals, that is, to reduce the negative effects of climate change on society by reducing GHG emissions to zero and to improve society's resilience to climate change through adaptation policies. This second goal, even though not always highlighted, has emerged in importance as climate change worsens. The first of these climate policy goals is in line with the energy policy goal of having an environmentally sustainable energy system. We can therefore say that energy and climate policy share just one goal, that is, to guarantee an environmentally sustainable supply of energy.

It is important to keep in mind that the fact that these two policies do not have the exact same goals is very relevant in discussions related to climate and policy issues. For instance, in order to reach the energy policy goal of guaranteeing the security of supply, a government could decide to promote the construction of gas power plants that are used in case of exceptionally high demand, or if the import of electricity is problematic. Of course, the construction of these power plants will not contribute to reaching the goal of providing an environmentally sustainable supply of energy. This implies that in designing and implementing energy policy instruments, it is necessary to weigh the costs and benefits of each instrument against the three objectives, because of the presence of conflicts between these goals.

Another interesting example of state intervention is to promote the construction of solar Photovoltaic (PV) power plants, or solar panels. In this case, energy and climate policy do not necessarily share the same objectives. From an energy policy point of view, it is important to promote the installation of solar energy within the boundaries of a country, whereas from a climate policy perspective, even constructing solar PV plants abroad and importing electricity is a viable option. This is because climate policy is only concerned with the overall reduction of emissions by using sustainable energy sources; where this reduction of CO_2 emissions takes place does not really matter. This may not completely align with the goals of national energy policies, for example, which also aim to ensure the security of energy supply, a reduction of the carbon footprint within the country, as well as improvements in energy efficiency.

A more recent example is the provision of a subsidy for fossil fuels. In 2021, when the prices of fossil fuels increased, several European countries introduced fossil fuel subsidies for gasoline and diesel, which are well-known to be responsible for serious environmental problems. In this case, we clearly observe a situation where the objective of ensuring cheap and affordable energy clashed with the objective of promoting an environmentally sustainable energy system.

A last example is the case in which a country chooses to use coal power plants to produce electricity, and then either buys permits for the emissions or invests in projects that reduce CO_2 emissions in other countries. In this case, while the climate goals may be satisfied, local air quality still deteriorates. This may also not completely align with the goals of national energy policies, which would also aim to reduce the local negative impact of electricity production on air quality.

This misalignment arises because any policy implemented outside the country would not ensure domestic energy security, CO_2 emission reduction, air pollution, or energy efficiency improvements for the country itself. Through these examples, and largely due to the globalised nature of modern economies, we observe a clash in objectives, wherein the promotion of renewable energy production in one country that may have higher production costs than abroad need not be economically interesting but may imply domestic benefits such as security of supply and improved air quality. It is therefore important to keep such tensions across policy instruments in consideration while framing energy and climate policy.

2.3.2 Role of Governments in Adaptation Strategies

Adaptation to climate change can occur through adaptation goods that can either be public or private in nature. A public adaptation good is a good that provides protection not only to a firm or to a household but to several members of society. The construction of a riverbank that protects against flooding caused by climate change, the construction of coastal protection against rising sea levels, or the refurbishment of infrastructure such as highways or rail networks in order to be more resilient to hot weather are all examples of public adaptation goods. In these cases, the state should intervene and finance these goods. Another example of a public adaptation good is a public campaign that teaches society how to reduce its impact on the climate with behavioural changes; such goods should also be financed by either local or central governments, depending on whether the adaptation good is a local or national public good.

Examples of adaptation goods that are private are sandbags to protect a house from flood damage, a natural ventilation system in a building to reduce heat stress, construction that increases shaded areas inside or outside a building, and investments in green/blue spaces around the house. For these private adaptation goods, a government intervention cannot be justified by economic theory, because there is no clear market failure that can be identified.

2.3.3   Energy and Development

As discussed in Chapter 1, in the next few decades, the developing countries of the world will experience a significant increase in their energy consumption. For instance, in India, the expected increase in primary energy demand in the next few decades is expected to be about a thousand metric tonnes of oil equivalent. Therefore, in order to implement a globally sustainable energy system, it is vital that not only households and firms in industrialised countries but also those in developing and emerging-market countries immediately adopt energy-efficient technologies and use renewable energy sources.

The goal of reducing the negative effects of current energy systems can only be reached if both industrialised and developing and emerging-market countries implement ambitious energy and climate policies. Due to the differences in financial and technological resources in both types of countries to ensure mitigation as well as adaptation against climate change, and due to varying past contributions to climate change, it is worth to consider the possibility that industrialised countries help developing countries to abandon fossil fuel-based energy systems and to switch to more sustainable ones. In this context, industrialised countries could design and implement aid instruments that also promote the transformation of current energy systems into more sustainable ones in developing countries.

2.4   Sustainable Development

In the previous section, we discussed that one of the main objectives of energy and climate policy is the transformation of the global energy system into a sustainable one. This will promote sustainable development. This concept is, in a way, rather general and ambiguous. In the literature, we can find an institutional definition of sustainable development as well as some definitions based on different economic theories. In this section, we will first present the institutional definition and then the definitions included in the economic literature and based on economic theories.

2.4.1   Institutional Definition

The most important institutional definition of sustainable development has been introduced by the UN with the Brundtland Report in 1987: 'Sustainable development is a development that meets the needs of the present without compromising the ability of future generations to meet their own needs' [40].

This basic definition is rather general, although the importance of protecting ecosystems for future generations is indirectly stressed. The definition implies that demographic, social, and economic growth should take place at a level that is compatible with the constraints of our ecosystems. In 2002, policymakers at the UN World Summit on Sustainable Development (WSSD) in Johannesburg specified this definition. They underlined that to achieve sustainable development, it is important to find an equilibrium between three dimensions that are relevant to the well-being of

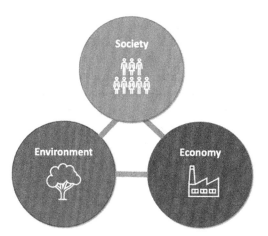

Figure 2.5 Dimensions of sustainable development

individuals and societies. Figure 2.5 presents these three elements – economic growth, social inclusion, and environmental protection.

- The environmental dimension captures the importance of preserving the functioning of the ecosystems over time.
- The economic dimension governs the generation of long-lasting growth of income and work.
- The societal dimension serves as a reminder to guarantee social inclusion and to ensure equally distributed wealth in the development process.

These dimensions are intentionally broad and capture many aspects of development, whereby valuable projects may involve multiple or even all dimensions. Related to these three dimensions, the UN has established seventeen specific Sustainable Development Goals (SDGs) that each country should try to reach by designing and implementing policy measures. Two of them, goals 7 and 13, are particularly relevant for energy and climate policy discussions. Goal 7 states that countries should aim to transform the current energy systems into affordable and clean energy systems, and goal 13 affirms that it is important to implement climate policy instruments to prevent the negative effects of climate change.

2.4.2   Definitions Based on Economic Theories: Weak and Strong Sustainability

The definition of sustainable development based on economic theory, and more specifically on economic growth theories, is similar to that proposed in the Brundland Report (1987) [40] but places more emphasis on the importance of transferring an amount of capital no less than the capital endowment of the current generation to the next generation. These theories state that in order to achieve sustainable development, the current generation must leave an amount of capital stock (including both physical capital and natural capital) equal to or greater than the amount of the current capital stock to the next generation.

In the scope of this definition, capital represents the ability to satisfy the needs of both current and future generations. Physical capital includes human-created tangible assets such as durable goods, infrastructure, and financial capital (i.e., money). Natural capital includes natural assets such as natural resource stocks, as well as land and ecosystems that provide environmental services. Note that in economic theory, and more specifically in growth theory, both physical capital and natural capital are considered as inputs which can be used to produce output along with another important input, that is, labour.

In economics, we can distinguish between two variants of this general definition of sustainable development that is based on the transfer of capital to the next generation. These two variants have weak and strong sustainability. Weak sustainability assumes that development is sustainable if the transfer of the stock of aggregate capital is not less than what exists in the present. Strong sustainability maintains that development is only sustainable if the transfer of the stock of aggregate capital is not less than what exists at present, and a critical level of natural capital is preserved.

The differences between the two definitions arise due to different assumptions about:

1. The degree of substitutability between physical and natural capital.
2. The critical level of natural capital to ensure a stable existence of ecosystem functions and supply of environmental services.
3. The amount of pollution and waste that the planet can absorb before ecosystems start to collapse.

To be more specific, we shortly present the assumptions behind weak and strong sustainability.

Weak sustainability assumes that:

1. The degree of substitutability between physical and natural capital is very high.
2. There is no critical level of natural capital needed to ensure a stable existence of ecosystem function.

On the other hand, strong sustainability assumes that:

1. The degree of substitutability between physical and natural capital is limited.
2. There is a critical natural capital level needed to ensure the existence of ecosystem functions.

Among economists that work on energy, natural resource, and environmental issues, some follow the neoclassical school of thought and tend to support the weak sustainability argument, while others belonging to the same school of thought tend to support strong sustainability. In addition, economists that belong to the ecological economics school of thought tend to also support strong sustainability. Weak sustainability implies that economic growth cannot be hindered by the limited availability of natural capital, because investments in R&D and technological change will always find a solution to overcome potential growth reductions that may be determined by the environment. Therefore, for economists who believe in weak sustainability, there is no tug of war between sustainability and continuous economic growth, under the condition that natural capital is replaced by the same amount of physical capital.

This school of thought indicates a high degree of technological optimism and a belief that energy and natural resource constraints can be overcome through technological advances. This optimism, however, is not shared by the second group of economists who support and believe in the concept of strong sustainability. These economists maintain that economic growth can be hindered by the limited availability of natural resources and that a certain level of natural capital is necessary to guarantee that the next generations are also able to satisfy their needs. Therefore, development is only sustainable if a critical (threshold) level of natural capital is preserved, in addition to the transfer of an amount of the stock of aggregate capital at least as large as the current one, to the future generations.

2.5 Issues in Developing Countries

In this chapter, we have explored the role of barriers, in the form of market failures including behavioural anomalies, in hindering the energy transition in developing countries. While most of these market failures pose challenges to the energy transition in both developing countries and in industrialised countries, we can expect some of them to be relatively more salient than others in developing countries. In the following subsections, we first discuss the traditional market failures that we think are more relevant in developing countries, namely the negative externality problem, credit constraints, as well as imperfect and asymmetric information. We also discuss energy access in light of the merit goods argument. These problems are likely to be grave in developing countries, given weak institutions, poor enforcement of regulations, and low average levels of education and income. These factors are also likely to play a role in determining the severity of some behavioural anomalies that we believe pose significant barriers towards energy-efficient investments, namely cognitive limitations, limited attention, and myopia/present bias.

2.5.1 Traditional Market Failures

The market failures discussed in the previous sections are ubiquitous in both developed and developing countries. In the following section, we discuss three of them that are particularly relevant for developing countries, namely externalities, merit goods, and information problems. One of the starkest exhibits of a negative externality problem, for example, is the level of air pollution in cities in developing countries that periodically witness levels of pollutant concentrations that are hazardous to human health. This is often the result of both the production of electricity using fossil fuel-based resources (such as coal) and a lack of basic air pollution controls (such as the use of filters or scrubbers), along with other factors such as the prevalence of rubbish dumps and landfill sites, which are common in informal settlements. Policymakers in developing countries often resort to using fossil fuel subsidies as a buffer for low-income households, however, economic intuition suggests that subsidies can lock in households as well as firms and can contribute to the negative externality problem. Once households start benefiting from subsidies, it is difficult to eradicate or reduce them without opposition.

Information problems are yet another type of market failure, whose effect on investments in energy efficiency can be amplified in developing country settings. Given low levels of education on average in low and middle-income countries (LMICs), as well as fewer government programmes to inform households about the need to switch to cleaner forms of energy (as well as its benefits), households are very likely to be imperfectly informed about energy-saving improvements. This can cause them to underinvest in energy-efficient technologies.

We can use the framework presented in Figure 2.3 to illustrate this and assume that we are considering the adoption of energy-efficient cars (either more fuel-efficient or electric). For this discussion, we assume that the demand without bias corresponds to the demand of informed consumers, whereas the demand with bias reflects the demand of uninformed consumers. If consumers are informed, the market equilibrium is represented by the quantity Q^*, which is socially optimal. On the other hand, in the more likely scenario of uninformed consumers (especially given the low levels of education in developing countries), the demand curve for energy-efficient cars is given by the leftward demand curve. The corresponding equilibrium would then be at quantity Q, which is inefficient from a welfare maximisation perspective. The quantity of energy-efficient cars that consumers buy in the private equilibrium, Q is lower than the socially optimal quantity of Q^*.

Another important market failure relevant in particular to developing countries is the presence of credit/liquidity constraints. Although not discussed as a major market failure in industrialised countries, it may be relevant for low-income households in these countries as well. Credit constraints may hamper the ability of households in poor countries to invest in more energy-efficient technologies that are relatively more expensive. Economic studies have shown that relaxing credit constraints for households in developing countries can result in households making higher investments in environmental protection. Addressing credit constraints among poor households may then imply introducing subsidies to ensure the affordability of energy-efficient durables, as well as expanding access to credit (which is more likely to work efficiently if credit-constrained households do not suffer from self-control problems).

Thus, policymakers can play an important role by enabling poor households to get credit more easily, either through microfinance lending or financial reforms. However, it is also imperative to keep in mind that the extension of credit to poor households may be difficult to implement from a practical point of view, due to the well-known problems of information asymmetry and adverse selection in credit markets, as well as the presence of informal channels of lending in low-income countries.

After having discussed these traditional market failures, in the context of developing countries, it is very important to mention the role of government intervention to promote energy access. In fact, in many industrialised and developing countries, electricity availability and supply are considered to be merit goods, that is, a good or service that society considers to be important enough to be offered to everyone, with the support of the state. In developing countries, because access to energy, in particular electricity, is not universal, the importance of merit goods is more pronounced. Therefore, policymakers continue to play a vital role in the development of electricity infrastructure, given the relatively large scale of investments needed for centralised electricity systems, despite significant steps also being taken towards the liberalisation of electricity markets. Many of these countries emphasised ensuring universal electricity access and achieving energy security, and public provision of electricity has promoted the affordability of this service as well as inclusiveness in some settings. Furthermore, assigning a merit for good character to electricity provision also ensured that governments were able to use centralised planning and system design to overcome coordination problems. It is, however, important to keep in mind that state involvement in electricity generation and distribution also created several inefficiencies in many developing country electricity markets, such as chronic electricity shortages, high system losses (such as due to theft), under-capitalisation, and inadequate extension of electricity services to poor households. For this reason, many developing countries have undertaken the process of electricity market reforms, which has also been supported by several international donor agencies and multilateral banks.

2.5.2 Role of Behavioural Anomalies

Like other market failures, behavioural anomalies are also a pertinent barrier towards energy-saving improvements in developing country settings. For example, low levels of education (and thus, low levels of cognitive skills) may hinder the ability of households to undertake lifetime cost calculations. In the absence of strict environmental regulations and enforcement, households may need to make repeated efforts to avoid exposure to air pollution, and for individuals with limited resources such as time and energy to make decisions, this can be exhausting. This may express itself in the form of a lower willingness to pay for improved air quality, for instance.

Furthermore, households may pay limited attention to the operating costs of durables and thus may end up prioritising their lower purchase costs (this effect may also be exacerbated by other market failures, such as credit or liquidity constraints). This, of course, will likely have implications on the efficiency of the durables that they end up purchasing.

Another relevant behavioural anomaly, namely myopia in intertemporal choices, may also give rise to suboptimal choices. It is commonly observed that economic agents exhibit myopic preferences that make them impulsively prefer smaller but faster rewards to larger but further away ones and that this impulsivity may decrease over time. For example, an individual might prefer to receive USD 100 today compared to receiving USD 110 tomorrow, but then if she had to make the same choice in the future, these preferences may reverse, that is, she may prefer to receive USD 110 in 31 days compared to the prospect of receiving USD 100 in 30 days.

Such preferences are one of the chief reasons for the low saving rates of low-income households in developing countries, who tend to prefer consumption today over consumption tomorrow, and they also explain why these households may be more likely to purchase durables that are less expensive but have relatively higher operating costs (compared to more energy-efficient durables). Importantly, this behaviour is compounded by credit or liquidity constraints, which is a reality for many households in developing countries: cash-strapped households who are either unable to borrow or face fluctuating cash flows might be even more likely to exhibit myopic preferences. As a result, they may not be able to invest in more energy-efficient (but also more expensive) assets.

2.5.3　Review Questions and Problems

The online question bank contains review questions and problems for this chapter, including solutions (see https://wp-prd.let.ethz.ch/exercisesfortextbookeep/).

3 Energy Demand–Theory and Empirical Analysis

In this chapter, we will introduce some theoretical as well as empirical elements of measuring energy demand. Understanding the factors that influence energy demand, and the demand for energy services, is very important, not only for firms but also for policymakers. For instance, information on the price and income elasticities of electricity demand can be used by electric utilities to design a new tariff structure, or by the government to estimate the impact of the introduction of a new energy tax. Furthermore, energy demand analysis is also useful to forecast future demand. Forecasting the energy demand is particularly important in developing countries where we expect a significant increase in the demand for energy services, and therefore, indirectly, also for energy because of increases in population and gross domestic product (GDP).

In this chapter, we propose a discussion based on microeconomic theory to highlight the role of the production process and of technology in determining energy demand. It is essential to understand that the energy demand depends on both consumption behaviour and on investment behaviour in technologies.

3.1 Introduction to Energy Demand Analysis

3.1.1 Energy Demand as a Derived Demand for Energy Services and Industrial Goods

In order to understand the demand for energy, it is important to keep in mind that it depends on the demand for both energy services and on the demand for goods.

Consumers and firms do not consume energy directly but instead use energy in combination with other inputs such as capital and labour to produce goods (e.g., cars, computers, and washing machines) and energy services (e.g., lighting, heating, and cooling, transport, cooking, and washing), that is, services produced by combining capital, labour, and energy, with energy playing an important role.

For instance, in order to wash clothes, a household must combine labour, capital (the washing machine), and electricity to produce washed clothes. As a result, the demand for electricity depends on the demand for washed clothes and on the level of energy efficiency of the washing machine. As another example, a firm that produces washing machines uses a combination of capital (equipment needed to manufacture a washing machine), labour, and energy to produce its product. Accordingly, its energy demand depends on the energy required to produce washing machines, the level of energy efficiency of the machines/capital used in the production process, and on the final demand for washing machines.

In this context, it is important to understand that the technology choice of households and firms (whether they purchase old and energy-inefficient, or new and energy-efficient technologies) can heavily influence energy demand for a long period. In fact, most of the machines, appliances, and general technologies used in the production of goods and energy services have a long lifetime. For instance, the typical lifetime of a washing machine is around 15 years, while that of a car is around 10 years, and the life of a heating system could be up to 20–30 years. This implies:

- The initial choice of technology has a long-term impact on energy consumption as well as on the type of energy used (renewable or non-renewable).
- The transformation of the current energy sector into a more sustainable one based on the use of energy-efficient technologies and renewable energy sources can take time.

3.2 Household Production Theory and Energy Demand

This next section will apply household production theory to the analysis of energy demand. This theory has been also used in several domains such as labour and health economics, and it can also help us to understand energy demand within the residential sector.

3.2.1 Key Functions of Household Production Theory

Household production theory is based on two key functions: the utility function and the production function. Following this theory, households purchase goods on the market, which are then used as inputs in the production process for energy services (ES), a component that appears as an argument in the utility function of the households, along with other goods. The production function, on the other hand, represents the production process for energy services. In the context of household production theory, a household wants to consume a reasonable quantity of energy services and other goods, given a predefined level of income, and wants to produce energy services using a production process that minimises the cost. As a simplification of this framework, a household is assumed to maximise the following utility function that includes two goods – energy services and other goods as described in Equation 3.1:

$$U = u(ES, OG) \tag{3.1}$$

U: Utility
ES: Energy services
OG: Other goods

The energy services (ES) are generally produced by the household using two inputs – energy and the capital stock (such as appliances and heating systems). The production function for the energy services can be described as follow:

$$ES = f(E, CS) \qquad (3.2)$$

ES: Energy services
E: Energy
CS: Capital stock

It must be noted that for the production of some energy services such as cooking, labour is also used as an input in the production process. In fact, to produce a meal, a household uses energy, an electric stove (i.e., capital), as well as time. In this case, another production factor (labour) would be added in Equation 3.2.

If we substitute the value of *ES* from Equation 3.1 into Equation 3.2, we obtain the following expression for the household utility function:

$$U = u(ES(E, CS), OG) \qquad (3.3)$$

U: Utility
ES: Energy services
E: Energy
CS: Capital stock
OG: Consumption of other goods

From standard microeconomic theory, we know that households try to maximise their utility function described in Equation 3.3 under an income restriction. Household production theory entails that households do this while minimising the cost of producing energy services. In the next subsection, we will describe this optimisation process that requires making:

1. A decision on the optimal combination of energy services and other goods that maximises utility subject to a given level of income.
2. A decision on the optimal combination of inputs that minimises the production cost in producing the optimal level of energy services.

From a mathematical point of view, these optimisation processes are simultaneous. We present this approach first graphically, and then using mathematical expressions.

3.2.2   Graphical Representation of Household Choices

Households face two optimisation decisions: the decision to optimise consumption (depicted in Figure 3.1) and the decision to minimise costs in the process of producing the energy services (illustrated in Figure 3.2).

On the one hand, households maximise their utility function, under a given budget constraint. In other words, they choose a combination of energy services and other goods that provide the highest level of utility to them, considering the constraints of their budget. Figure 3.1 shows this scenario with energy services (*ES*) on the horizontal axis and consumption of other goods (*OG*) on the vertical axis. The straight line gives the budget constraint and the convex curve represents the indifference curve. At point *A*, where the straight budget line and the convex indifference curve are tangential

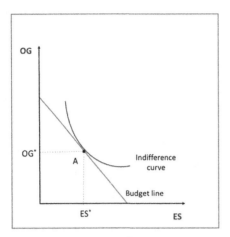

Figure 3.1 Optimisation of consumption

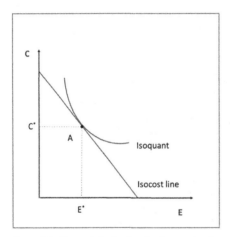

Figure 3.2 Cost minimisation in the production of energy services

to one another, the utility is said to be maximised. The optimal combination of other goods and energy services is thus represented by OG^* and ES^*.

On the other hand, households must also choose the inputs to minimise the cost of producing the chosen level of energy services. In Figure 3.2, capital (C) is shown on the vertical axis, while the level of energy production (E) is indicated on the horizontal axis. At point A, where the straight isocost line and the convex isoquant curve are tangential, the production costs for a predefined level of energy services

---

* A budget line represents all combinations of quantities of the two goods that can be consumed, given the prices of these goods and income; the indifference curve represents all combinations of the quantities of two goods that give the same level of utility to the consumer.

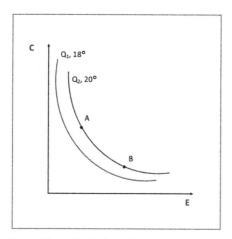

Figure 3.3 Optimisation of energy service production using isoquants

represented by the isoquant are minimised, where the optimal capital and energy production combination is given as $C^*, E^{*\dagger}$.

3.2.2.1   Example: Production of a Heating Service

Let us assume that a household is interested in producing an energy service, for example, the heating of an apartment. We can represent this production decision using isoquants. In Figure 3.3, two isoquant curves are shown, and we plot energy (E) on the horizontal axis and capital (C) on the vertical axis. The Marginal Rate of Technical Substitution (MRTS) is defined as the slope of the isoquant curves and can be computed as -MRTS = $\delta C/\delta E$. The isoquant closer to the origin in the graph (Q_1) represents all possible combinations of capital and energy that result in the heating of the apartment to 18°C, while the isoquant further away (Q_2) denotes all combinations that result in the heating up to 20°C. We must pay attention to the fact that the household can make a choice: it can decide to use a large amount of capital (e.g., to invest in insulation) and consume a low amount of energy in the process to obtain a particular heating level, or it can use a small amount of capital and thereby consume a large amount of energy to reach the same level of heating. Traditional buildings that tend to waste energy can be characterised by the combination of capital and energy represented by point B, whereas energy-saving buildings can be represented by the combination defined by point A. Nevertheless, both combinations of inputs lie on the same isoquant, and therefore give the households the possibility to produce the same level of heating.

In Figure 3.4, an isoquant and two different isocost lines are shown. On the vertical axis, we plot the quantity of capital (C) used in the production process, and on the horizontal axis, we have the amount of energy (E) required. The isoquant represents

---

[†] Isocost is a line providing all combination inputs that can be purchased with a given budget; Isoquant is a function illustrating all possible combinations of inputs that can be utilised to produce a given level of output.

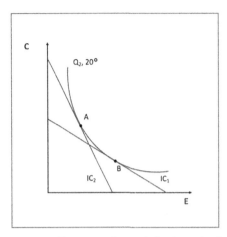

Figure 3.4 Energy service optimisation using isoquants and isocosts

the level of the energy service (Q_2) used in heating to 20°C. The isocost line 1 (IC_1) and the isocost line 2 (IC_2) have different slopes, that is, different values of the ratio of the two prices (that of energy and capital). IC_1 has a flatter slope than IC_2. In relative terms, IC_1 indicates that energy is cheaper than capital, in comparison to the situation represented by IC_2. Note that the different ratios of the energy price to that of capital can lead to varying optimal household decisions. The optimal combination of inputs is represented by the points where the relevant isocost curves are tangential to the isoquants. If the ratio of the two prices is represented by IC_1, a household would minimise the cost of producing the level of energy service (Q_2) with the combination of inputs represented by point B. In case the ratio of the two prices is represented by IC_2, the household would minimise the cost of producing the level of energy service (Q_2) with the combination of inputs represented by point A. This point A could represent either the construction of a new energy-saving building or the energy-saving renovation of an existing building. In moving from B to A, the households reduce energy expenditures.

When modelling energy demand, it is vital to distinguish between short-run and long-run scenarios. So far, we have looked at a scenario in which a household can freely choose and change inputs for the production of energy services. However, this flexibility is only available in the long run. Now, we will discuss a model of production in the short run, where the capital stock is fixed and cannot be changed. Once more, Figure 3.5 shows two isoquant curves with energy on the horizontal axis and capital on the vertical axis. In this scenario, the capital stock is fixed at C^*. In this case, a household can only decrease its energy consumption by decreasing the level of energy services produced. This could manifest in a reduction of room heating from 20°C to 18°C.

Of course, the question of which combination is the best for the household, that is, which combination minimises the cost to produce the energy service Q_2, arises from this optimisation exercise. Naturally, the optimal choice depends on the capital and

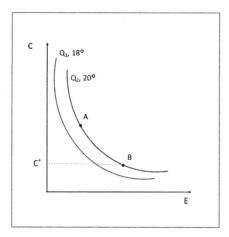

Figure 3.5 Optimisation of energy service production with fixed capital stock using isoquants

energy prices that determine the slope of the isocost lines at different points. If the isocost curve is tangential to the isoquant at point B, then the household is minimising the heating expenditures and the fixed capital stock is no longer a constraint. However, if the isocost curve is tangential to the isoquant at A, then the capital stock at C^* is binding, and the household has higher heating costs than it would in the long run at point A.

3.2.3   Analytical Representation of Household Choices

From a mathematical point of view, the optimisation problem of households involves the maximisation of the utility function subject to an income restriction, as well as the restriction related to the minimisation of production costs. The optimisation process in the long run (when all production factors and inputs are flexible or can be adjusted) can be represented as follows:

$$max\ U(ES(E,CS),OG)$$
$$s.t.\ C(P_E,P_{CS},ES) + P_{OG}OG \leq Y$$

(3.4)

U: Utility
ES: Energy services
E: Energy
CS: Capital stock
OG: Consumption of other goods
P_E: Price of energy
P_{CS}: Price of capital stock
P_{OG}: Price of other goods
Y: Household income

In the constraint in Equation 3.4, we substitute the expenditure for energy services (given by its price multiplied by its quantity) with a cost function to underline the fact that these services are produced by households. This optimisation exercise assumes that there are constant returns to scale so that the cost of producing energy services can be simplified as the price of energy services multiplied by the level of energy services produced given by the formula:

$$C(P_E, P_{CS}, ES) = P_{ES} \cdot ES \tag{3.5}$$

Upon the maximisation of the utility function under the constraints presented in Equation 3.4, four equations are obtained. These describe the demand for: energy services (ES), other goods (OG), energy (E), and capital stock (CS).

$$ES = f(P_{ES}, P_{OG}, Y) \tag{3.6}$$

$$OG = g(P_{ES}, P_{OG}, Y) \tag{3.7}$$

$$E = h(P_E, P_{CS}, ES, P_{OG}, Y) \tag{3.8}$$

$$CS = j(P_E, P_{CS}, ES, P_{OG}, Y) \tag{3.9}$$

In Equation 3.8, the household energy demand curve is in the long run. As can be deduced from the expression, the long-run energy demand depends on the price of energy (P_E), the price of the capital input (P_{CS}), the level of energy services produced (ES), the price of other goods (P_{OG}), and the household income (Y). The fourth expression represents the demand for capital stock, for instance, for appliances, heating systems, and so on, which is also very important for the analysis of energy demand.

In the short run, the capital stock is generally considered to be fixed, that is, it cannot be varied. For instance, in the short run, a household is not able to change an old and inefficient washing machine because of the increase in electricity prices. Often, households need time to substitute an old washing machine with a new energy-saving one. Therefore, it is normal to assume that the capital stock is fixed and therefore, the variation of the energy demand depends only on the variation in the demand for energy services. This implies that to reduce energy consumption, households can only engage in behavioural changes in energy consumption and not by investing in energy efficiency.

The optimisation problem faced by a household in the short run is almost identical to the long-run optimisation problem previously discussed. The only difference is that in the short run, the capital stock is fixed. The mathematical expression for the short-run problem is given by:

$$max \ U(ES(E, \overline{CS}), OG)$$
$$s.t. \ C(P_E, \overline{CS}, ES) + P_{OG} OG \leq Y \tag{3.10}$$

U: Utility
ES: Energy services
E: Energy
$\overline{CS}$: Capital stock
OG: Consumption of other goods
P_E: Price of energy
P_{OG}: Price of other goods

P_{ES}: Price of energy services
Y: Household income

From this optimisation problem, we obtain:

$$ES = f(P_{ES}, P_{OG}, Y) \tag{3.11}$$

$$OG = g(P_{ES}, P_{OG}, Y) \tag{3.12}$$

$$\underbrace{E = h(P_E, \overline{CS}, ES, P_{OG}, Y)}_{short\ run\ energy\ demand} \tag{3.13}$$

The third expression derived above ($E = h(P_E, \overline{CS}, ES, P_{OG}, Y)$) is the household energy demand curve in the short run. As can be deduced from the expression, the short-run energy demand depends on the price of energy (P_E), the fixed capital input ($\overline{CS}$), the level of energy services produced (ES), the price of other goods (P_{OG}), and the household income (Y).

This mathematical derivation of energy demand using household production theory is amenable for empirical researchers who want to perform an empirical analysis because it helps in specifying a model grounded in economic theory.

From the results of the optimisation process of the households in the short run as well as in the long run, we can learn three things:

1. In the long run, energy demand depends not only on the energy price but also on the price of the capital stock, that is, on the price of the technology that is used in the production process of the energy services.
2. In the short run, households are not able to change the capital stock. Therefore, the energy demand depends on the energy price, as well as on the level of capital stock. This implies that in the short run, the capital price is replaced with the capital stock.
3. The energy demand depends on the level of energy services consumed by a household, in both the short run and in the long run.

The models 3.8 and 3.13 are simplified representations of factors that influence energy demand. In empirical specifications, researchers generally augment these models with variables that represent geographical (cultural, climate-related, lifestyle-related, spatial organisation of the society, etc.) and technological factors (technical change and efficiency of the production process). Moreover, in case information on energy services is not available, researchers can use several socioeconomic variables (such as income, age, household size, dwelling size, etc.) to proxy the consumption of energy services.

3.3 Empirical Analysis of the Residential Energy Demand

As mentioned before, the main goals of these types of empirical analyses are:

- The estimation of the impact of price and income changes on energy demand.

- Analysis of the effect of socioeconomic and climate-based factors (e.g., age and climate) and of policy instruments (e.g., subsidies, standards, and carbon taxes) on the level of energy demand.
- Forecasting energy demand.

Empirical analysis of energy demand can make an important contribution to policy-making processes and is thus critical. Therefore, it is important to understand the methods for deriving the empirical results that are normally presented in scientific studies and reports. In this section, we provide a brief overview of this process.

3.3.1   Steps in the Empirical Estimation of an Energy Demand Model

Generally, researchers interested in the empirical estimation of an energy demand model follow five steps, as depicted in Figure 3.6. These steps are based on three components:

- Economic theory, for instance, household production theory.
- Data collection.
- Econometric methods (i.e., statistical and mathematical methods applied to the analysis of economic problems), such as regression analysis.

In the first step of the estimation of energy demand, researchers need to identify the main goals of their research. For instance, a study might set the aim to estimate price elasticity or the impact of a policy on energy demand.

In the second step, the empirical model needs to be specified while considering theoretical assumptions, such as the assumptions of household production theory.

The third step of the empirical analysis involves data collection and the construction of a data set. This step might be the most time-consuming step of the analysis.

Figure 3.6 Steps for estimating the energy demand and capital stock demand models

In step four, the econometric model is specified in more detail using an appropriate functional form (choice between linear, log-log, etc.) and the model is estimated using the appropriate econometric methods.

As a last step, the estimated coefficients have to be interpreted in the context of the research question asked.

It is important to note that there are several types of data that can be used in the estimation of an empirical energy demand model for the residential sector. On the basis of the level of aggregation, we can have either aggregated or disaggregated data sets. This data is either collected by a researcher, or by a data collector or a marketing company by doing a survey, or it could also be administrative data, that is, data collected on a regular basis by an institution such as a statistical office or a firm. While the former are called primary data, the latter are also referred to as secondary data.

A disaggregated data set includes information at the unit or individual level (for instance, on the levels of consumption, preferences, characteristics, etc., of households). An aggregated data set contains information aggregated to the local or regional (or even national) level. This kind of data is often collected periodically by statistical offices of governments. In the next subsection, we discuss in some detail elements of steps 2 and 4, which are relevant for empirical analysis and provide a simple example of the estimation of an electricity demand function.

3.3.2 Model Specification

Following household production theory, a simple empirical energy demand model as the one specified in Equation 3.14 should include the energy price (P_E), capital price (P_{CS}), level of energy services (ES), and the level of energy efficiency of the technology (EE), which is usually approximated by using a time trend (a continuous variable capturing the change in time), as explanatory variables.

$$E = h(P_E, P_{CS}, ES, EE) \tag{3.14}$$

From an empirical point of view, it is important to enrich model 3.14 using other explanatory variables that may influence energy demand, such as weather conditions, or institutional or cultural factors. This is important to account for other potentially observed factors that play a role in affecting energy demand.

An enriched energy demand model can look like the following expression:

$$E = h(P_E, P_C, P_{OG}, I, ES, G, T) \tag{3.15}$$

E: Energy demand
P_E: Price of energy
P_C: Price of capital
P_{OG}: Price of other goods
I: Income
ES: Level of energy services
G: Vector of geographical factors
T: Vector of technological factors including energy efficiency (EE)

Table 3.1 Energy resources and market forms

Model	Equation	Slope (dE/dP)	Price elasticity
Linear	$E = \beta_0 + \beta_{P_E} \cdot P_E$	β_{P_E}	$\beta_{P_E}(P_E/E)$
Log-log	$\ln E = \beta_0 + \beta_{P_E} \ln P_E$	$\beta_{P_E}(E/P_E)$	β_{P_E}

We should note that information on the level of energy services, for instance, on the frequency of cooking, or on the use of dishwashers and washing machines per week, is generally not available, or can be difficult to collect. To overcome this issue, empirical researchers have proposed to approximate the level of energy services with several socioeconomic variables, such as the number of rooms in the house, income, household size, age, gender, or number of children. Another difficulty for empirical researchers is to obtain information about the price of capital, that is, the cost of using appliances such as washing machines and heating systems and the capital stock. Researchers try to solve this problem by assuming that the capital price or capital stock is the same for all households or by applying a specific econometric method such as a fixed effects model, which takes into account any unobservable factors that are time-invariant and may explain energy demand.

3.3.3   The Typical Functional Forms for Demand Analysis

The two most used functional forms in the estimation of energy demand models for the residential sector are the linear and the log-log forms. Table 3.1 presents these two functional forms for a simple energy demand model with just one explanatory variable (P_E).

Using these functional forms, it is possible to compute price and income elasticities, which provide information on the impact of a price change (or income change) on the demand for a good. These can be categorised as short-run or long-run own-price elasticities (E_p), cross-price elasticities (E_{pc}), and income elasticities (E_Q).

The own-price elasticity of demand (E_p) measures the percentage change in quantity demanded of a good as a result of a percentage change in the price of the same good. The mathematical expression of the own-price elasticity is:

$$E_p = \frac{\Delta Q}{\Delta P} * \frac{P}{Q} \tag{3.16}$$

Where E_p is the own-price elasticity, Q is the quantity demanded, and P is the price of the product. A value of $E_p > 1$ indicates price-elastic demand, a value < 1 suggests price-inelastic demand.

The cross-price elasticity of demand (E_{pc}) measures the percentage change in the quantity of a product demanded by consumers as a result of a percentage change in the price of another product. The mathematical expression of the cross-price elasticity is:

$$E_{pc} = \frac{\Delta Q}{\Delta P_O} * \frac{P_O}{Q} \tag{3.17}$$

Where E_{pc} is the cross-price elasticity and Q is the quantity of the product demanded, and P_O is the price of the other product.

The income elasticity of demand I_Q measures the percentage change in consumption of a product as a result of a percentage change in the income of the consumers. The mathematical expression of income elasticity is:

$$I_Q = \frac{\Delta Q}{\Delta I} * \frac{I}{Q} \qquad (3.18)$$

Where I_Q is the income elasticity, I is the income of the consumers, and Q is the quantity demanded by the customers.

In the regression model using the linear functional form, the own-price elasticity is computed by multiplying the coefficient β_{P_E} with the price of energy P_E, and dividing by the level of energy consumption (E). Therefore, the value of the elasticity depends on the values taken by P_E and E. This implies that the elasticity varies with both the price level of energy and the level of energy consumption. In applied work, it is a common practice to measure elasticity at the mean or median point of the variables for P_E and E.

On using the log-log functional form, the defined own-price elasticity only depends on the coefficient β_{P_E}, that is, it is independent of the level of energy consumption. This is an interesting property of the log-log functional form, as it means that the elasticity may be directly inferred from the regression output.

3.3.4 Estimation of a Simple Electricity Demand Function: Example from a Developing Country

The following example, based on data on Indian households, serves to explain how an electricity demand function might be estimated in practice in an intuitive fashion, using a simplified model. The general model specification is denoted as:

$$E = h(P_E, Y) \qquad (3.19)$$

Using a log-log functional form, Equation 3.19 can be rewritten as:

$$\ln E = \beta_0 + \beta_{P_E} \cdot \ln P_E + \beta_Y \cdot \ln Y + \epsilon \qquad (3.20)$$

where:
E: Energy demand
P_E: Price of energy
Y: Household income
ϵ: Idiosyncratic error term

To estimate this model, we used household expenditure data collected by the National Sample Survey Organisation, Department of Statistics, Government of India. An enlarged version of this data set has been used for the estimation of more rich electricity demand models by Filippini and Pachauri (2004) [41]. Equation 3.20 is normally estimated using the popular regression-based econometric methodology – Ordinary

Table 3.2 STATA regression output of OLS estimation

Explanatory variables	Value of coefficient	Standard errors	t-values	$P > |t|$	95% confidence interval	
$\ln P_E$	−0.309	0.038	−8.12	0.0	−0.383	−0.234
$\ln Y$	0.762	0.023	33.18	0.0	0.717	0.807
Constant	−1.770	0.135	−13.16	0.0	−2.034	−1.506

Least Squares (OLS). Table 3.2 reports the STATA regression output of an OLS estimation of Equation 3.20 using information for a sample of 1999 Indian households. The value of the coefficient of determination (or R-squared) for this model is 0.35. This indicator provides information on the goodness-of-fit measure for linear regression models. A value of 0.35 indicates a good fit for a demand model estimated using cross-sectional data. The F-statistic for this model is 553, indicating that the model with these two explanatory variables provides a better fit than a model with no independent variables. The coefficient β_{P_E} is estimated to be −0.31, while the coefficient β_Y is estimated as 0.76. Given the functional form of a log-log regression, these estimates can be directly interpreted to be the price elasticity and income elasticity, respectively. The standard errors and t-values presented in the table can be used to ascertain the statistical significance of the estimation results. As a general rule, results are considered statistically significant if the t-value in absolute terms is equal to or larger than 1.96. At this value, the significance level of the estimation results is 95 per cent or higher, or the p-values (mentioned in the fourth column of the table) are lower than 5 per cent. As this condition is fulfilled for both of the coefficients, they can be said to be statistically different from 0. STATA is one example of statistical software that can be used for conducting econometric analysis of this nature. R, Python, and LIMDEP are some other software packages which are commonly used.

3.3.5   Estimation of a Capital Stock Demand Model

As shown in the theoretical discussion of household production theory, the demand for capital stock, that is, demand for electrical appliances, heating systems, and cars, plays an important role in determining the level of energy consumption. Therefore, the empirical estimation of this type of demand is also insightful. The demand for capital stock can be represented by the following model:

$$CS = j(P_E, P_{CS}, ES, P_{OG}, Y) \tag{3.21}$$

where:
CS: Capital stock or capital
P_E: Price of energy
P_{CS}: Price of capital
ES: Energy services
P_{OG}: Price of other goods
Y: Household income

The estimation of a capital stock demand model is similar to the one of an energy demand model with two small differences:

- First, the dependent variable measuring the capital stock can either be continuous (e.g., the installed capacity of electrical appliances in Watts, the capacity of a heating system, and the number of electrical appliances or cars) or dichotomous (ownership of an appliance, of a car, or of a heating system). A continuous dependent variable can take on any value in the range of the corresponding mathematical function, while a dichotomous dependent variable will only take on values of zero or one and can be used to estimate the probability with which a household is likely to own or buy an energy-efficient washing machine, for instance.
- Second, and relatedly, the econometric models used to estimate the demand for capital stock when the dependent variable is dichotomous are usually probit or logit regression models, that is, non-linear estimation models, and not the OLS method. Of course, some researchers in this case may also choose to use a linear probability model using the OLS method, and therefore reduce the non-linear specification to a linear one. However, this approach has some econometric limitations, as discussed by Greene (2018) [42]. In the case of the estimation of a capital stock demand model, researchers proceed in steps as with the estimation of energy demand models, and as previously illustrated in Figure 3.6.

3.3.6   Estimated Residential Energy Price Elasticities

Table 3.3 lists the values of the residential energy own-price elasticities obtained across several empirical studies. As these entries suggest, the majority of the values are less than 1. Moreover, studies that are able to estimate both short-run and long-run elasticities obtain, as expected, values for the short-run elasticities that are smaller than the long-run values. This is due to the fact that in the short run, as previously discussed, it is not possible to change the capital stock. Therefore, the only way to reduce energy demand in the short run is through a reduction in the use of energy. It is important to note that in Table 3.3, if we do not mention whether the computed elasticities are short-run or long-run in the first column, then the study does not distinguish between both time horizons in calculating elasticities.

Empirical Example of Using Energy Services in Electricity Demand Estimation
In a study on residential electricity demand estimation for Switzerland, Boogen et al. (2021) [43] estimated an empirical model derived by applying household production theory, and the study used disaggregated data on about 5,000 households collected using a longitudinal household survey. The electricity demand levels estimated in this study were said to depend on the level of energy services.

The authors described two different types of energy demand models, and both were estimated using a log-log functional form. One identification strategy was based on using household activities (such as cooking, washing, and entertainment) to infer the level of energy services, as electricity is consumed to provide these energy services; the other model specification used a number of household and socioeconomic characteristics to proxy for this variable [43].

In the first model specification, the demand for energy can be considered to be guided by the price of capital (P^K) (such as the prices of household appliances), the price of electricity (P^E), and the energy services (S) consumed by the household, as presented in Equation 3.22.

$$E^* = E(P^E, P^K, S^*) \qquad (3.22)$$

In the absence of data on energy services, however, we can also express the demand for electricity in a more simplistic form, by approximating the amount of energy services (S) using socioeconomic variables (denoted by (Z)) and household income (M):

$$E^* = E(P^E, P^K, M, Z) \qquad (3.23)$$

Of course, the use of socioeconomic variables to substitute for energy services can lead us to miss out on some important information and thus may result in omitted variable bias. The estimated price elasticity using both model specifications is around -0.7 in this study. This implies that the use of pricing policies can potentially help to reduce the consumption of electricity in Switzerland.

Table 3.3 Values of residential energy price elasticities

Elasticity	Energy Type	Region	Study
[−0.5, −0.4]	Electricity	India	Filippini and Pachauri, 2004 [41]
−0.2	Electricity	United Kingdom	Dimitropoulos et al., 2005 [44]
Long−run: [−0.7, −0.2]	Electricity	Japan	Hunt and Ninomiya, 2005 [45]
Short−run: [−0.1, −1.7] and Long−run: [−1.6, −1.5]	Electricity	G7 countries	Narayan, Smyth and Prasad, 2007 [46]
[−0.7, −0.6]	Electricity	OECD countries	Krishnamurthy and Kriström, 2015 [47]
−0.4	Electricity	Germany	Schulte and Heindl, 2017 [48]
[−0.5, −0.3]	Electricity	India	Chindarkar and Goyal, 2019 [49]
−0.06	Electricity	China	Li et al. 2020 [50]
Short to medium run: −0.7	Electricity	Switzerland	Boogen et al. (2021) [43]
[−0.36, −0.26]	Gasoline	India and China	Dahl, 2012 [51]
[−0.22, −0.13]	Diesel	India and China	Dahl, 2012 [51]
Short-run: −0.23 and Long-run: −0.51	Gasoline	Switzerland	Filippini and Heimsch (2016) [52]

Table 3.3 (cont.)

Elasticity	Energy Type	Region	Study
−0.73	Gas	Switzerland	Filippini and Kumar (2021) [53]
Long-run: −1.25	Gas	Forty-four countries	Burke and Yang (2016) [54]
Short-run: −0.08 and Long-run: [−0.08, −0.06]	Gasoline	USA	Coyle et al. (2012) [55]
Short-run: −0.16 and Long-run: −0.43	Gasoline	Fourteen OECD countries	Liddle (2012) [56]
Short-run: [−0.06, −0.15] and Long-run: [−0.06, −0.39]	Gasoline	Mexico	Crotte et al. (2010) [57]

3.4   The Empirical Analysis of the Industrial Energy Demand

Besides residential demand, another topic of natural interest is industrial energy demand. In this section, we will discuss how industrial energy demand can be empirically estimated.

According to production and cost theory, firms use inputs (in general – capital, labour, and energy) in a production process to produce goods, while trying to minimise their costs. We can represent the typical production function for the industrial sector as follows:

$$Q = Q(E,C,L) \tag{3.24}$$

where:
Q: Output
E: Energy
C: Capital
L: Labour

Generally, these inputs (energy, capital, and labour) can be substituted for one another in production. Given a predefined level of production, by substituting across inputs, firms can then attempt to minimise their costs.

The optimal choice of inputs to produce a predefined level of output by minimising costs can be represented either graphically or by using mathematical expressions. In the first illustration, in order to simplify the representation, just two inputs are considered: capital and energy. However, while using mathematical expressions, it is possible to consider all inputs in the empirical analysis.

As is apparent from Figure 3.7, with energy (E) on the horizontal axis and capital (C) on the vertical axis, the goal of the firm is to minimise its production costs (still captured by the isocost line IC_1) of achieving a predefined level of output (denoted by the isoquant Q_1). Such an optimal point is reached, as illustrated when the isocost line is tangential to the isoquant curve at point A.

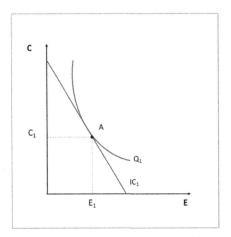

Figure 3.7 Finding the optimal choice of inputs

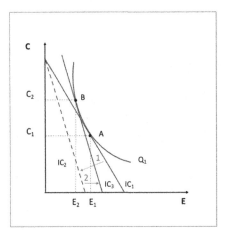

Figure 3.8 Impact of price increase on capital and energy demand of firms

It is useful to graphically represent the change in the energy demand of a firm when energy prices increase. This change is shown with the help of Figure 3.8 with capital (C) on the y-axis and energy demand (E) on the x-axis. If the price of energy increases, the isocost curve IC_1 changes its slope to reflect this change (as denoted by shift 1). In this case, the slope of the isocost line IC_2 is steeper (since energy prices have increased). When energy becomes more expensive, firms can buy less energy with the same amount of financial resources. However, with this rotation of the isocost line from IC_1 to IC_2, a firm can no longer maintain the same level of output (if it is constrained to the same cost). This is reflected in the graph by the distance between the rotated isocost curve IC_2 and the initial isoquant Q_1 denoting a specific level of output. In order to attain the original level of output denoted by Q_1, firms are forced to increase their cost, which would then lead to a shifting of the isocost curve from IC_2 to the IC_3 (denoted by shift 2). The final allocation of resources once again lies on the initial isoquant; however, the new combination shows an increase in capital and a decrease in energy inputs at point $B(E_2, C_2)$, compared to the initial capital and energy combination at point $A(E_1, C_1)$. The substitution of energy with capital can depend on many factors, such as the technology used for production, the sector or industry, the kind of goods that are produced, and so on. A measure of the ease with which a factor like energy can be substituted for another input is called the elasticity of substitution. This elasticity indicates the degree to which one input can be substituted with another input. From an empirical point of view, the elasticity of substitution is also an interesting parameter to estimate using empirical methods.

3.4.1 Energy Demand Function

In this section, we use mathematical approaches to derive input demand functions of firms, whereas in the previous section, we used the graphical approach. From a microeconomic point of view, it is possible to mathematically derive the firm-level energy demand model by solving a cost minimisation process. In this framework, a firm wants to produce an output using inputs; in general, labour, capital, and energy. The objective of the firm is to minimise its production costs, given its level of output. To derive an energy demand function in the long run, the minimisation problem is defined as:

$$\min (P_E \cdot E + P_C \cdot C + P_L \cdot L)$$
$$s.t. Q = Q(E, C, L) \tag{3.25}$$

Where:
P_E: Price of energy
E: Energy
P_C: Price of capital
C: Capital
P_L: Price of labour
L: labour
Q: Production output

Intuitively, this means that the firm tries to minimise the expenditures on production inputs, given the production function. From this optimisation exercise, we can derive the long-run demand functions for the three inputs – energy, capital, and labour, respectively:

$$E = h(P_E, P_C, P_L, Q) \tag{3.26}$$

$$C = c(P_E, P_C, P_L, Q) \tag{3.27}$$

$$L = l(P_E, P_C, P_L, Q) \tag{3.28}$$

As in the case of households, the short-run optimisation process for the firm is similar to the long-run optimisation, with the difference that capital is now a fixed input. Accordingly, the optimisation for the firm in the short run is given by:

$$\min (P_E \cdot E + P_C \cdot \overline{C} + P_L \cdot L)$$
$$s.t. \, Q = Q(E, \overline{C}, L) \qquad (3.29)$$

P_E: Price of energy

E: Energy

P_C: Price of capital

$\overline{C}$: Capital (fixed)

P_L: Price of labour

L: Labour

Q: Production output

From this, the demand functions for the two variable inputs in the short run are derived as follows:

$$E = h(P_E, \overline{C}, P_L, Q) \qquad (3.30)$$

$$L = l(P_E, \overline{C}, P_L, Q) \qquad (3.31)$$

From an empirical point of view, to obtain values of the elasticity of substitution, and own-price and cross-price elasticities of the inputs, the system of equations represented by Equations (3.26)–(3.28) or (3.30)–(3.31) is estimated. Another approach used in empirical studies is to add a cost function to this system of equations.

Researchers interested in the empirical estimation of elasticities of substitution can follow the same five steps discussed and depicted in Figure 3.6. The typical functional form used in this type of research is the trans-log functional form that is based on Taylor's approximation of a true function and thus includes squared and cross-terms of the explanatory variables.

3.4.2   Estimated Industrial Energy Price Elasticities

In Table 3.4, we exemplify the values of the price elasticities for firms and provide evidence from several empirical studies. These values are relatively low and indicate that the energy demand in the industrial sector tends to be rather inelastic. This means that it is not very easy to substitute away energy with capital. Some studies also estimate the elasticities of substitution, as depicted in Table 3.5. Based on a study for ten OECD countries, Kim and Heo (2019) [58] also provide a comprehensive review of the studies that estimate the elasticities of substitution and reach the conclusion that there is an asymmetry in terms of the elasticities of substitution of energy and capital, wherein they discuss that the substitution of energy for capital dominates (i.e., is easier) than the substitution of capital for energy.

Role of management practices in firm-level energy demand

A new stream of empirical economic literature has examined the role of management practices in determining the energy demand at the firm level, and several studies on industrialised countries have found that management practices are strongly correlated with reductions in energy intensity (energy demand per unit of output, measured in either physical units or in expenditure terms) (such as

Bloom et al. (2010) [59] and Martin et al. (2012) [60]). Grover and Karplus (2020) [61] investigated this question using cross-country data for a sample of countries, including some developing countries. The authors measured the effect of both general management practices (such as monitoring, incentives, targets, and operations practices) and energy-specific management practices (such as monitoring and target-setting related to energy efficiency) on energy intensity. They found that better general management practices were associated with declines in energy intensity (measured in expenditure terms), but not with declines in energy intensity measured in physical units. They attributed this difference, among other factors, to a focus of managers on saving costs, and not necessarily on mitigating environmental impact. Moreover, they found that energy-specific management practices didn't have any additional effects on improving energy intensity, over and above the general management practices. Thus, it is important to understand firms' incentives to reduce energy, as well as to what extent they may need to make adjustments such as capital investments in order to reduce energy demand. This study hints at the importance of future research to understand the role of management (as well as the behavioural traits of owners and managers) in determining energy demand at the firm level.

Table 3.4 Price elasticity in the industrial sector

Elasticity	Energy type	Region	Study
[−0.6, −0.4]	Electricity	United States	Kamerschen and Porter, 2004 [62]
Short-run: −0.2 Long-run: −0.2	Electricity (manufacturing)	United Kingdom	Dimitropoulos et al., 2005 [44]
Long-run: [−0.6, −0.5]	Electricity	OECD countries	Adeyemi and Hunt, 2007 [63]
Short-run: [−0.09, −0.3] Long-run: [−0.1, −0.6]	Electricity	Japan	Hosoe and Akiyama, 2009 [64]

Table 3.5 Elasticity of substitution in the industrial sector between energy and capital

Elasticity of substitution	Region and sector	Study
Energy with capital: 1.0295	Chinese machinery-based industry	Lin and Liu (2017) [65]
Capital with energy: 1.496	Irish manufacturing firms	Haller and Hyland (2014) [66]
Energy with capital: 1.543	Irish manufacturing firms	Haller and Hyland (2014) [66]
Energy with capital: 0.15–0.35	10 OECD countries	Kim and Heo (2013) [58]
Capital with energy: 1.11	Italian manufacturing firms	Bardazzi et al. (2015) [67]
Energy with capital: 0.602	Italian manufacturing firms	Bardazzi et al. (2015) [67]

3.5   Issues in Developing Countries

Developing countries face challenges in terms of ensuring universal access to affordable energy. Furthermore, given credit/liquidity constraints, many households (and firms) are unable to invest in energy-saving technologies. In this section, we will highlight two elements of household production theory that we believe are likely to be more relevant for developing countries. We first discuss how the household production theory may need to be modified to account for different sources of energy used in developing countries, and the opportunity cost of time in collecting these sources. We then discuss the role of income in determining investment decisions of households with respect to the purchase of durables such as appliances, given that these countries are likely to experience significant growth in the coming years.

3.5.1   Household Production Theory in Developing Countries

Energy demand in developing countries is usually met by using a variety of energy sources, and the 'energy-ladder' theory suggests that as household incomes increase, they are more likely to switch from dirtier to cleaner sources of energy. However, in reality, households often follow the 'energy-stacking' model, whereby they use multiple energy sources at the same time. In this context, the household production theory that we introduced earlier is an interesting theoretical framework to evaluate energy demand in developing countries. This theory should be augmented to account for (1) the differences in types of energy used and (2) time spent in acquiring energy (such as firewood, kerosene, charcoal, etc.) in developing countries. For the first point, the theory should consider that production functions change over time due to the use of different fuels or energy sources (as well as appliances). For the second point, the production function for energy services should incorporate labour/leisure as an input.

Many people in the developing world still live without access to electricity: the number of households without electricity increased between 2019 and 2021 in sub-Saharan Africa, for instance. The start of the pandemic in 2020 made it difficult for households to be able to pay for using grid-based electricity, which implies that many households began to rely on small systems that provided fewer energy services. As we will discuss in more detail in Chapter 4, while these systems are useful for increasing initial access to energy services, they may not be optimal for intensifying the use of energy. In a similar vein, the transition to clean cooking has also witnessed a slowdown in recent years. The fuel-stacking literature suggests that households often use dirtier fuels or energy sources in tandem with cleaner fuels, even when their income levels increase, and this has been observed to be the case for the use of cooking fuels in developing countries. Households may not easily switch to cleaner energy sources such as liquefied petroleum gas (LPG) or electricity in entirety, as long as it is possible to acquire firewood, charcoal, or kerosene at a relatively inexpensive cost. The pandemic also made it difficult for households to be able to pay for modern fuels, which implies that many households increased their use of traditional biomass and firewood, and spent more time at home with increased exposure to indoor air pollution. An application of household production theory to developing countries needs to take into account these facts.

Furthermore, as highlighted earlier, time spent collecting fuel can play a role in determining household welfare from using energy sources. Many households need to spend several hours collecting firewood for cooking or heating purposes, which has some opportunity costs (in terms of time spent for labour or leisure). This implies that labour/leisure should also be introduced as an input in household production theory, to make it amenable for developing countries. There is also an important gender dimension to this issue, as females in households are more likely to spend more time collecting fuel for cooking or heating purposes. Thus, different members of the same family can have different constraints, which is also important to consider when applying household production theory.

Given these considerations, financial support for poor households (such as through lower electricity tariffs or subsidised access to clean cooking fuels) may be necessary to hasten the switch to modern energy sources in these countries.

Economics of household technology adoption in developing countries: Evidence from solar technology adoption in rural India

Based on the case of solar-microgrid technology adoption, Aklin et al. (2018) [68] investigated the determinants of solar technology adoption by households in rural India. Potential differences across products were controlled for by offering identical solar technologies to all households in the study sample. The authors found that the main determinants of technology adoption decisions were high household savings and expenditures, along with an entrepreneurial attitude of the household members. On the other hand, community trust, acceptance of the risks related to the durability and quality of the product, and past fuel expenditures did not influence these decisions. Risk aversion was less important when compared to the entrepreneurial spirit of the people when adopting new technologies. However, the reliability of the technology played an important role in determining adoption. From this study, we learn that income and expenditure are important predictors of technology adoption, thus perverse policies such as providing generous subsidies for dirty fuels like kerosene have the potential to reduce the competitiveness (and appeal to consumers) of alternative renewable technologies such as solar power.

3.5.2 Energy-consuming Asset Ownership and the Role of Income

As we learnt from household production theory, capital stock is an important input in energy service production. Current levels of capital stock, such as appliances, are low on average in developing countries, but we can expect this to change, which will result in an increase in energy demand. Related to this point, a factor that is likely to contribute to the increase in energy demand in developing countries is a warming climate: for example, the demand for air conditioners is expected to increase significantly as many countries become warmer. Given that air conditioners consume significantly more energy than other cooling appliances, such as ventilators, this is also likely to catapult electricity demand.

While it is likely that only high-income households will start purchasing appliances such as air conditioners at the beginning, as incomes increase, this share is likely to increase as well. This has important implications for emissions, given that a large share of the electricity in developing countries continues to be generated using fossil fuels. On the other hand, energy efficiency levels have improved tremendously in the past few years, and at least some of these improvements are likely to continue in the coming decades. However, for sustained decarbonisation, other policies such as minimum energy efficiency standards, electricity pricing, as well as increased adoption of renewables, in particular solar, need to be implemented.

> The demand for energy-using assets among the world's rising middle classes
> Wolfram et al. (2012) [69] observed that there is an 'S-shaped pattern' between household consumption expenditure and energy-consuming asset ownership (such as refrigerators or cars); for instance, they showed that among the bottom 10 per cent of Mexican households in the year 2000 based on consumption expenditure, both fridge and car ownership were sparse. Middle-income households were more likely to become first-time owners of appliances and cars, whereas, at relatively higher levels of expenditure, adoption levels stabilised. At lower levels of income, due to the presence of credit constraints, for example, households may be unable to buy appliances or cars. Thus, ownership rates for durables such as appliances and vehicles are more likely to increase at middle-income levels (i.e., for households just emerging from poverty) than for upper-income households.

> A model of energy poverty and access: Estimating household electricity demand and appliance ownership
> Poblete-Cazenave and Pachauri (2021) [70] used a different approach based on a structural estimation approach to estimate energy demand. They relied on simulated data and incorporated different policy scenarios. The countries that they included in their analysis were Ghana, Guatemala, India, and South Africa. In the scenario analysis, the authors establish that higher levels of urbanisation and income growth were associated with higher electricity demand, even if population growth rates were reduced. An important result was that the share of electricity consumption for entertainment purposes (such as for televisions) was high in all countries and remained stable with income increases. On the other hand, the share of electricity consumption for food preparation and clothes maintenance only increased with increases in income. Thus, this study showed that there is significant heterogeneity in terms of the sources of increase in electricity consumption, and thus energy demand, among households in developing countries.

3.5.3   Review Questions and Problems

The online question bank contains review questions and problems for this chapter, including solutions (see https://wp-prd.let.ethz.ch/exercisesfortextbookeep/).

4 Economic Analysis of Energy Investments

In this chapter, we will focus on investments made by firms and governments in the energy sector, and on learning tools and methods that we can apply to evaluate investments in the energy and climate sectors, that is, that can help us to understand whether it is economically sound to make an investment, or not. Of course, these tools can also be applied to analyse investments undertaken by households. However, in this case, the benefits do not easily translate into 'revenues', because households usually do not produce and sell electricity or other services on a market. Nonetheless, a household can compute the lifetime cost of a project and compare it to the subjective economic value of the energy services produced by it. Furthermore, in situations in which a household has to decide between several technologies, for example, between heating systems that provide the same quantity and quality of heating services, the choice can be based on comparing their respective 'lifetime costs', an idea that will be discussed in more detail in Chapter 5.

The first part of this chapter will explain some important concepts for conducting a private investment analysis, that is, one in which economic agents do not factor in any potential social impact of their investment decisions at the time when they make the decision. This discussion will primarily focus on energy-sector investments performed by firms. We will then discuss the levelised cost of energy (LCoE), which is often used to evaluate returns from investments made in the energy sector. Next, we will briefly elaborate on the commonly observed notion of declining unit costs of production in the energy sector, applying the concept of learning curves that are useful in illustrating trends in investment costs. These can be used to define the amount of initial investments in the energy sector. Last, we will introduce social cost-benefit analysis, the notion of undertaking investment analysis from a broader perspective (factoring in the social costs and benefits of each decision). This approach can be applied to evaluate a hydropower project from a societal point of view, analyse the impact of the implementation of a policy measure to mitigate the long-term effects of climate change, and judge the economic effects of preventative adaptation investments.

4.1 Energy–Sector Investments and the Role of Discounting

An energy investment involves making a purchase of durable goods that are used in the energy sector. Different kinds of investments can be made by economic agents; for example, an individual may choose to purchase a new heating system or a new electrical appliance. Similarly, a firm may invest in a new power plant or in new production machinery. Governments may also invest in large-scale energy projects, such as electricity transmission lines or in adaptation projects, such as flood protection.

In doing an investment analysis, one compares the costs and benefits of a project over the lifetime of the investment. This comparison helps economic agents to decide whether to implement an energy project or not. For a firm, the benefits are mainly the revenues from selling a product or a service related to the realisation of a project. For a household, the benefits are the economic value of the energy services generated, for example, the heating services provided by a new heating system. From a government's perspective, on the other hand, the benefit from an energy project is the economic value of the services produced by the investment to society, for example, the protection services provided by a new flood wall that mitigates flooding risks.

Note that the discussion in this chapter will mainly focus on investments in the power sector; however, the same issues and methods of evaluating investments can be applied to other investments in the energy sector performed by firms such as in oil and gas, as well as in energy-intensive sectors such as the cement industry, or by households.

4.1.1   Characteristics of Energy–Sector Investments

Investments can be made by firms into any of the different functions in which energy is the final output. As Figure 4.1 illustrates, some investments may be made in the production of energy (such as in the extraction of oil or gas or in the production of renewable energy), others may be made in transport (such as in the processing of oil, gas, and electricity for the transport sector), and last, investments may also be made in the distribution of energy (for instance, in the setting up of a distribution network for gas or electricity). Note that while the transmission or transport of electricity entails the large-scale movement of electricity from a power plant to a substation, the distribution of electricity involves the transformation of high-voltage electricity at substations to lower-voltage electricity that can then be used by customers. These categories correspond to different types of functions or stages in the provision of energy.

Projects in the energy sector owned by firms and governments have some essential features that can make investments and their evaluation in this sector particularly challenging. These are:

- **Capital intensity:** Energy-sector projects are characterised by high initial investment costs.

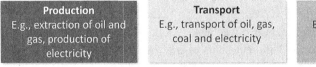

Production	**Transport**	**Distribution**
E.g., extraction of oil and gas, production of electricity	E.g., transport of oil, gas, coal and electricity	E.g., gas and electricity distribution

Figure 4.1 Investments in different energy functions

- **Capital specificity:** The physical capital in the energy sector tends to have a high degree of specificity, which means that it is difficult to find alternative uses for this type of capital.
- **Long lifespan of assets:** Most energy-sector investments have a long lifespan. For instance, a gas-fired plant can easily operate for 25–30 years, while a hydropower plant is able to produce electricity for up to 80–100 years. This implies that to perform a thorough investment analysis, one would need to collect information on both revenues and costs incurred over a relatively long duration.

Note that at least two of these features, that is, capital intensity and long lifespan, are also valid for investments performed by households. Asset specificity is more relevant for investments made by firms and the government. For instance, it is difficult to find alternative uses for drilling rigs used in oil extraction industries or for flood protection walls.

4.1.2 Investment and Net Cash Flow of a Typical Energy–Sector Project

A typical project in the energy sector realised by a firm (like most infrastructure-based projects) involves large outlays made at the outset when costs are incurred for setting up a power plant or a transmission line. During this period, revenues are most likely zero or negligible, as the plant is not yet operational. Figure 4.2 denotes the typical annual net cash flows, that is, the revenues minus operating costs, for a project from the date when the decision is made to set it up (denoted by time = 0 on the horizontal axis). The first three bars denote these initial (negative) cash flows due to the costs of setting up the project. In the following years, the project starts to yield revenues and the cash flows become positive, which is depicted by the remaining bars in the figure, and these may last over the lifetime of the project. Positive cash flows denote that the project

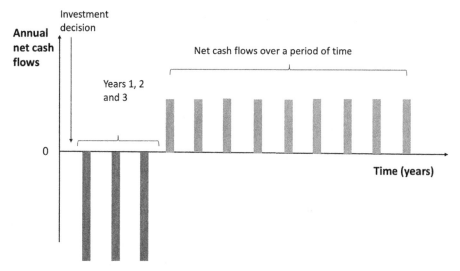

Figure 4.2 The life cycle net cash flows of an investment

yields revenues that are higher than the operating costs that are incurred. Of course, during the lifetime of a project, the cash flows can also be negative in some years.

Investment analysis first involves converting these cash flows made over different time periods to present-day values, that is, 'bringing' these cash flows to the present period (t − 0), when the investment decision is made. The conversion of future cash flows (negative or positive) to present-day monetary values is achieved by multiplying the value of the cash flow in time period t with the discount factor (w_t) for that time period, which is equivalent to weighting these cash flows. Closely associated with the discount factor is the notion of the discount rate (r). The discount factor used to discount cash flows of period t is defined as in Equation 4.1.

$$w_t = \frac{1}{(1+r)^t} \qquad (4.1)$$

The economic arguments for discounting future benefits and costs are twofold.

- **The time preference argument** reasons that individuals generally prefer to spend today rather than later, that is, they give more value to a dollar today than a dollar in 10 years. As consumers, we tend to be impatient; there is always a risk of falling ill, dying, or not being able to enjoy one's material wealth that nudges us to favour spending money today rather than tomorrow. This means that we should discount (i.e., downsize) any payment that we receive or make in the future when we convert it to present-day terms.
- **The capital productivity argument** put forth by economists suggests that since capital is inherently productive, one can invest his or her resources in one option today, at the cost of investing in an alternative option, to obtain some possible gains. The forgone financial gain when one invests in one alternative, but not in another one, is called the opportunity cost of the alternative. It is the value of the next best option, or of what is given up. These opportunity costs are another reason to discount future payments or revenues; by making an investment in the most profitable option today, investors forego the possible future gains from investing in other viable options.

In the case of firms, the capital productivity argument is usually more relevant, whereas for households, both arguments may be valid.

4.2   Investment Criteria: Net Present Value and Internal Rate of Return

4.2.1   Net Present Value and Internal Rate of Return

Let us look at Figure 4.2 again: when we are provided with information on the net cash flows of an investment over multiple periods, we should discount them to bring them to present value terms. Given the discounted net cash flows, we should then apply an investment criterion to evaluate each investment. The two most used criteria are the net present value (NPV) of a project and the internal rate of return (IRR) of a project.

The NPV is equal to the present value of the sum of the net cash flows (revenues minus costs) over all time periods during the life of the project, including those incurred in the present day (i.e., at t = 0). These cash flows are discounted by multiplying them with the respective discount factor for that time period. The following formula is used to compute the NPV:

$$NPV = \overbrace{\sum_{t=0}^{T} \frac{CF_t}{(1+r)^t}}^{\text{Sum of the net cash flows}} \tag{4.2}$$

where:

NPV: Net present value

CF_t: Net cash flow (revenue minus cost) in year t

r: Discount rate

T: Lifetime of the investment

We can interpret r as the firm's opportunity cost of capital, that is, the rate of return for the firm from investing in the best alternative project having similar risk. The NPV criterion for project evaluation suggests that any project that has a positive or zero NPV, that is, whose revenues are greater than or equal to the costs over the life of the project, is interesting from an economic point of view. If the NPV equals zero, there is no gain or loss from the project. If the NPV is negative, the project should not be considered for investment. In situations with similar projects, the project with the highest NPV should be chosen.

An alternative to the NPV as a criterion to take an investment decision is the IRR. The IRR is the value of the discount rate that sets the NPV of a specific project equal to zero. Mathematically, this can be written as:

$$0 = NPV = \sum_{t=0}^{T} \frac{CF_t}{(1+IRR)^t} \tag{4.3}$$

In order to obtain the IRR of a project, it is necessary to solve Equation 4.3. The IRR criterion for project evaluation is that any project that has an IRR larger than or equal to the cost of capital is worth investing in. In other words, if the rate of return on the project is higher than what one could get from investing money at the prevailing interest rate (or the cost of capital), then it is interesting to invest in the project from an economic point of view.

NPV and IRR are interrelated decision criteria because the IRR of an investment is defined as the discount rate required to make its NPV equal to zero. One of the advantages of the IRR is the possibility to compare investment projects having different lifetimes, based on their estimated rate of return. However, the IRR tends to be sensitive to the size of the project. In situations in which we are comparing two projects, one with a much lower initial capital outlay than the other, the IRR criterion tends to under evaluate the larger project. For instance, in the energy sector, we could imagine comparing an investment in a small hydropower plant with a large one, both of which have similar lifetimes. The smaller plant requires a lower initial capital outlay to be made in comparison to the larger plant. On applying the IRR criterion, it is likely that the larger project may not be realised. This is due to the fact that the IRR is derived by comparing the value of cash flows relative to the initial capital outlay of the project, and it tends to relatively 'undervalue' the higher potential cash flows of larger projects (in absolute terms) that are likely to also lead to higher profits.

Note that in performing an investment analysis using the NPV or the IRR criteria, one of the most challenging parts is to estimate the value of the cash flows, partially due to the long lifespan of these projects, and the difficulty in estimating future revenues and costs.

Finally, the NPV and IRR calculations should be done using either real values accounting for inflation in both cash flows as well as in the discount rates, or nominal values for both. This implies that if we use the nominal values of the cash flows, we should use the nominal value of the discount rate as well (i.e., the discount rate unadjusted for inflation), and *vice versa*.

As we will discuss later in the book, some energy and climate policy instruments can be designed to promote investments in renewable energy sources by increasing the NPV of such investments, for instance. One type of policy instrument that is often used is a subsidy to reduce the initial investment costs. These types of subsidies would increase the net cash flows from the project at the beginning (by reducing costs) and thus increase its NPV. In practice, these subsidies have been implemented in several countries, such as Switzerland, where the government subsidises investment costs for solar panels by up to 30 per cent.

4.2.2   Cost of Capital

In using the criteria discussed above, a certain cost of capital has been considered in the form of the discount rate. Here we provide a brief explanation of this important concept.

To realise energy-sector projects, firms need to collect financial resources that can be drawn from different sources. On the one hand, capital can be raised by using debt as an instrument, and on the other hand, the firm can also issue equity. Based on the use of these two sources, it is possible to calculate the discount rate using the so-called 'weighted average cost of capital (WACC)'.

The WACC is the weighted average of the cost of equity r_e weighted by the factor (E/V) and the cost of debt r_d weighted by the factor (D/V) (where the weights are the respective shares of financing through equity and debt). It can be represented as shown below:

$$r_{WACC} = WACC = \frac{E}{V}r_e + \frac{D}{V}r_d \tag{4.4}$$

Where:

r_{WACC}: Weighted average cost of capital (WACC)

r_e: Cost of equity (i.e., what shareholders expect as a return)

r_d: Cost of debt (i.e., the interest rate to be paid to the lenders)

V: Total market value of equity and debt

E/V: Proportion of equity financing

D/V: Proportion of debt financing

The cost of equity for a firm is influenced by factors such as the dividends paid per share issued by the firm, the current market value of the firm, as well as the dividend growth rate. The cost of debt is affected by prevailing interest rates as well as tax rates and tax regulations. Both of these factors are influenced by general market and economic conditions, risk of the investment, monetary and fiscal policy, corporate governance as well as financial stability.

An example of an energy and climate policy instrument to incentivise the adoption of renewable technologies by firms could be a reduction in their capital costs, for example, with a discount on the interest rate paid on debt. This would manifest as a reduction in the r_{WACC} and would increase the NPV of the investment.

Estimating the cost of capital for renewable energy projects

In a study, Steffen (2020) [71] empirically computed estimates of the cost of capital across forty-six countries over the period of 2009–2017. The author discussed the importance of the input data on the cost of capital and discount rates, and how it varied across different countries and technologies significantly, especially in the case of renewable technologies. The order of costs across different technologies was found to be consistent across countries, with offshore wind having the highest capital costs, followed by onshore wind and solar PV. Also, the cost of capital was significantly lower in industrialised countries, when compared to developing countries, and variations were also found within these two broad groups of countries, based on the level of economic development of the countries. This study seeks to highlight the large heterogeneity in the WACC across markets, which should be considered for cost-effective deployment of renewables and to mitigate financial barriers towards renewable energy investment.

4.2.3 Importance of Discount Rates in Investment Decisions

To illustrate the centrality of the discount rate in investment decisions, Table 4.1 includes values of the NPV of USD 100 calculated assuming different time periods and discount rates. For instance, USD 100 in 40 years would be worth USD 67.20 in today's money at a discount rate of 1 per cent, whereas it would be worth USD 0.10 in today's money at a discount rate of 20 per cent. This demonstrates the important role of discount rates in all investment analyses, including those in the energy sector. As investments in the energy sector are characterised by long life cycles, the discount rate chosen in any model, such as in a forecasting model, can decisively change the outcome of the prediction.

4.2.4 Example of Investment Analysis for a Power Plant

In Table 4.2, we present the information on revenue, cost, and net cash flows as well as the NPV of a hypothetical investment in a new power plant. The project spans a period

Table 4.1 NPV and the power of discounting

| | Time horizon in years | | | |
Discount rate	5 years	10 years	20 years	40 years
1%	95.1	90.5	82.0	67.2
2.5%	88.4	78.1	61.0	37.2
5%	78.4	61.4	37.7	14.2
10%	62.1	38.6	14.9	2.2
20%	40.2	16.2	2.6	0.1

Table 4.2 Investment analysis

Year	Cost (million USD)	Revenue (million USD)	Net cash flow (million USD)	Net discounted cash flow using discount rate of 5% (million USD)	Net discounted cash flow using discount rate of 1% (million USD)
0	700.00				
1	60.00	100.00	40.00	38.10	39.60
2	60.00	100.00	40.00	36.28	39.21
3	60.00	100.00	40.00	34.55	38.82
4	60.00	100.00	40.00	32.91	38.44
5	60.00	100.00	40.00	31.34	38.06
6	60.00	100.00	40.00	29.85	37.68
7	60.00	100.00	40.00	28.43	37.31
8	60.00	100.00	40.00	27.07	36.94
9	60.00	100.00	40.00	25.78	36.57
10	60.00	100.00	40.00	24.56	36.21
11	60.00	100.00	40.00	23.39	35.85
12	60.00	100.00	40.00	22.27	35.50
13	60.00	100.00	40.00	21.21	35.15
14	60.00	100.00	40.00	20.20	34.80
15	60.00	100.00	40.00	19.24	34.45
16	60.00	100.00	40.00	18.32	34.11
17	60.00	100.00	40.00	17.45	33.78
18	60.00	100.00	40.00	16.62	33.44
19	60.00	100.00	40.00	15.83	33.11
20	60.00	100.00	40.00	15.08	32.78
			NPV (million USD)	−201.51	21.82

of 20 years and has an initial outlay of USD 700 million. The total costs of the power plant include this initial investment cost, along with a yearly operating cost of USD 60 million over the entire life of the project. This cost generally includes expenditure for labour, maintenance, materials, and energy use (such as coal or gas). We have made the assumption that after the first year, the plant starts generating revenue of USD 100 million per year until the end of its lifetime. For the purpose of the investment analysis exercise, we calculate the NPV of the project assuming two different discount rates of 5 per cent and 1 per cent, respectively. We find that the NPV of the project is negative on using a discount rate of 5 per cent, that is, the project incurs a net loss of USD 201.51 million over the period of 20 years. Thus, the given investment is not worth making, economically speaking. On the other hand, we find that using a discount rate of 1 per cent generates a positive net cash flow for the project, and its NPV in this case equals USD 21.82 million. Using this discount rate, the project seems worth investing in. This example also shows us the importance of the choice of discount rates in NPV calculations.

4.2.5 Types of Risks Associated with Investments in the Energy Sector

Due to the high initial outlay, the long life cycle of a plant, and competition in the markets where the goods are sold (at least for some projects), realising an investment in the energy sector implies substantial risk and uncertainty.

From an economic point of view, we can use the term 'risk' when we can assign an objective probability to the likelihood of an event taking place. The use of the term 'uncertainty' is more prevalent in situations in which the probability itself is unknown. Therefore, in these situations, firms and individuals tend to use subjective probabilities or a qualitative assessment of the level of uncertainty of an outcome.

The four main types of uncertainties or risks that investments in the energy sector face are as follows:

1. **Construction risks:** for example, due to delays, technical problems, and cost overruns in the construction of a project.
2. **Cost risks:** for example, due to the introduction of new safety measures, changes in fuel prices, capital costs, or decommissioning costs.
3. **Market risks:** for example, risks arising due to competition from other technologies, or due to changes in consumer preferences or in demand.
4. **Policy risks:** for example, due to the change in regulations such as the introduction of subsidies for certain energy types.

In some cases, it may be possible for economists to form expectations based on past events or forecasts about the nature and severity of these uncertainties and, therefore, to assign a probability to an event. In other cases, it is more difficult to obtain information on the probability of an event occurring. Cost uncertainties, for one, are not always predictable when performing an investment analysis. After the Fukushima Daiichi nuclear disaster in Japan in 2011, for example, governments all over the world introduced more stringent safety measures on nuclear power plants, which increased production costs for nuclear energy. Developments such as this one cannot be foreseen at the point when an investment decision is made.

Generally, energy projects have different levels of risk across energy types. For instance, the construction of a nuclear power plant faces higher risks than the construction of a wind power plant, along the four dimensions discussed above.

4.2.6 Measures of Risk

In performing an investment analysis, the level of risk of an energy investment can be accounted for by using different approaches. In this chapter, we will briefly discuss two of them, that is, the risk-adjusted discount rate and the expected return/standard deviation approach.

A standard method is to use the risk-adjusted discount rate, that is, a discount rate which reflects or captures the risk associated with the cash flows of an investment. The risk-adjusted discount rate for a project is the sum of the risk-free rate of return (e.g., the rate of return on government bonds) and the risk premium associated with a project. The latter accounts for the risk of a project over and above what one may have received if they would have invested at the risk-free rate. The risk premium indicates the risk that characterises the investment and is generally calculated using the so-called Capital Asset Pricing Model (CAPM) developed in financial economics. Therefore, the risk-adjusted discount rate can be expressed as:

$$r = RFR + RP \tag{4.5}$$

where:
r: Risk-adjusted discount rate
RFR: Risk-free return
RP: Risk premium

The risk premium associated with a project compensates investors for 'systematic risks' that cannot be eliminated by risk diversification approaches, such as market risks and policy risks described above.

The second approach to take into account the level of risk of an investment is to measure risk using the expected value and the standard deviation over the NPVs of cash flows, which are computed using a risk-unadjusted discount rate. In this case, based on some information, a probability distribution is assumed for the different NPVs that can arise from a project. Using this distribution, it is then possible to calculate two measures that can be used for decision-making under the conditions of risk, that is, the expected value of these NPVs and the standard deviation.

The expression for the computation of the expected value of the NPVs is the following:

$$\bar{R} = \sum_{i=1}^{n} R_i p_i \tag{4.6}$$

where:
$\bar{R}$: Expected value of the NPVs
R_i: NPV in case i
p_i: Probability of case i
n: Number of possible outcomes

The standard deviation of the NPVs can be computed as follows:

$$\sigma = \sqrt{\sum_{i=1}^{n} (R_i - \bar{R})^2 p_i} \tag{4.7}$$

where:

σ: Standard deviation of the NPVs

$\bar{R}$: Expected value of the NPVs

R_i: NPV in case i

p_i: Probability of case i

n: Number of possible outcomes

The expected value of the NPVs and their standard deviations are measures that capture the various types of risks described above. For instance, construction, cost, market, and policy risks can influence the probability distribution of the NPVs, and thus have an impact on influencing both of these measures.

To show how to apply these concepts to investments in the energy sector, we provide the following example. Consider making a choice between investing in one of two projects: project A or project B. Due to the types of risks described above, the NPV of each project is determined with a certain probability distribution. These NPVs are given in column (1) for project A and column (7) for project B in Table 4.3. The corresponding probabilities are listed in columns (2) and (8), respectively. We present the products of each NPV with the corresponding probabilities in columns (3) and (9), respectively. On summing these values listed in columns (3) and (9), we find that the expected value of each project (denoted by $\bar{R}$) is equal to USD 4,100. In calculating this value, we have used Equation 4.6 mentioned earlier.

In columns (4) to (6), we present the values of the other elements that are needed to compute the standard deviation of project A (the corresponding values for project B are mentioned in columns (10)–(12)). For both projects, we use a value of $\bar{R}$ equal to USD 4,100. We can then compute the standard deviation of the projects using Equation 4.7 mentioned above, which is the square root of $\sum_{i=1}^{n}(R_i - \bar{R})^2 p_i$; this term equals 1,890,000 for project A and 29,306,000 for project B, thus yielding a standard deviation of USD 1374.44 for project A and USD 5413.50 for project B.

We can see that the expected values of the net cash flows are identical for the two projects. In this case, the choice between both projects can be made on the basis of the values of the standard deviations of these cash flows. The second investment has a standard deviation that is much higher than the first one (as can be seen from Table 4.3), therefore, it is riskier. For this reason, given that investors are generally averse to risk, the first investment will be preferable.

In case the expected values of the net cash flows are not identical, then the standard deviation can be a misleading measure of risk by itself, and we need to use another risk measure, that is, the coefficient of variation. This coefficient of variation is defined as the standard deviation of the NPVs divided by the expected value, such as:

$$CV = \sigma/\bar{R} \tag{4.8}$$

where:

σ: Standard Deviation of the NPVs

$\bar{R}$: Expected value of the NPVs

Let us assume now that Project B doesn't have an expected value of USD 4,100, but instead has a much higher expected value such as USD 20,000. The standard

Table 4.3 Calculating expected NPVs and standard deviations of projects A and B

Project	Project A						Project B					
Column	(1)	(2)	(3)	(4)	(5)	(6)	(7)	(8)	(9)	(10)	(11)	(12)
Parameter	R_i	p_i	$p_i * R_i$	$(R_i-\bar{R})$	$(R_i-\bar{R})^2$	$(R_i-\bar{R})^2\, p_i$	R_i	p_i	$p_i * R_i$	$(R_i-\bar{R})$	$(R_i-\bar{R})^2$	$(R_i-\bar{R})^2\, p_i$
	2,000	0.2	400	−2,100	4,410,000	882,000	1,000	0.4	400	−1,500	2,250,000	900,000
	4,000	0.3	1,200	−100	10,000	3,000	3,000	0.1	300	500	250,000	25,000
	3,000	0.1	300	−1,100	1,210,000	121,000	20,000	0.1	2,000	15,900	252,810,000	25,281,000
	5,000	0.2	1,000	900	810,000	162,000	2,000	0.3	600	−500	250,000	75,000
	6,000	0.2	1,200	1,900	3,610,000	722,000	8,000	0.1	800	5,500	30,250,000	3,025,000
Sum	$\bar{R}=\sum_{i=1}^{n}$ $R_i p_i =4,100$					$\sum_{i=1}^{n}(R_i-\bar{R})^2 p_i$ $=1,890,000$	$\bar{R}=\sum_{i=1}^{n}$ $R_i p_i =4,100$					$\sum_{i=1}^{n}(R_i-\bar{R})^2 p_i$ $=29,306,000$
Standard deviation						1374.44						5413.50

deviations of the two projects are the same as before, that is, USD 1374.44 for Project A and USD 5413.50 for Project B. In this case, if we compute the coefficients of variation (CV) for the two projects using Equation 4.8, we will get $CV_A = 0.34$ and $CV_B = 0.27$. Thus, Project B is more interesting than Project A from an investment perspective, given that it has a lower coefficient of variation, that is, a lower risk relative to its expected value.

Note that this second approach, based on the expected value of the net cash flows and on the standard deviation, can be refined by using simulation-based techniques that consider different probability distributions of all elements of the formula used in calculating the NPV of the cash flows, for example, the discount rate, revenues, and costs. Based on these different distributions, it is possible to obtain several hundreds or thousands of distributions of net cash flows, and thus calculate the expected NPV of the cash flows, the standard deviation, and the coefficient of variation. The decision-making process will still remain the same, as described above.

In case we don't have any information on the probability distributions of the cash flows, we are in a situation of uncertainty. Under these conditions, doing an investment analysis is more difficult, and one solution is to get an idea of the level of uncertainty of the investment, and thereby estimate a range of feasible benefits and costs, using sensitivity analysis. Given that uncertainty involves the decision-maker being unsure about the likelihood of different outcomes occurring, it may be possible only to make qualitative statements about the range of outcomes.

4.3 The Levelised Cost of Energy

The NPV approach is useful to evaluate different types of investment projects in the energy sector, such as in power plants, electricity transmission lines, or gas pipelines. For the evaluation of investments in new power plants, another approach that can be used is based on the calculation of the LCoE. The LCoE is a special case of the NPV calculation because it is the average price that yields a zero NPV. If the expected average price of electricity is greater than or equal to the LCoE, then it makes sense to invest in this technology.

The LCoE can also be defined as the price at which energy produced by a given technology should be sold, such that the revenues equal the costs over the entire lifetime of the technology.

The idea of the LCoE was conceptualised in the field of electricity economics to better compare the production costs of electricity using different technologies, even if these technologies may have different scales or lifespans. It is calculated by equating the present value of the sum of discounted revenues with the present value of the sum of discounted costs. It is important to note that the methodology of the LCoE was developed at a time when electricity markets were regulated, which meant that the price of electricity was assumed to be constant over time. With electricity market regulation, this was a justifiable assumption to make.

Consider the mathematical expression in Equation 4.9. On the left-hand side of this expression, we have the sum of the discounted revenues from the sale of energy/electricity (price per unit of energy P_{MWh} multiplied by the total amount produced in year i, MWh_i, summed over all time periods and discounted at the rate r) whereas, on the right-hand side, we present the sum of total discounted costs. These costs include the initial costs of investment I_i (which are most likely only incurred in the early time periods), the operating and maintenance costs O_i, fuel costs F_i as well as decommissioning and waste management costs D_i. We now set the total discounted sum of revenues equal to the total discounted sum of costs.

$$\sum_{i=0}^{T} \frac{P_{MWh} \cdot MWh_i}{(1+r)^i} = \sum_{i=0}^{T} \frac{I_i + O_i + F_i + D_i}{(1+r)^i} \tag{4.9}$$

P: Price
I_i: Investment costs in year i
O_i: Operating and maintenance costs in year i
F_i: Fuel costs in year i
D_i: Decommissioning and waste management costs in year i
r: WACC
T: Lifetime of the project

As previously defined, the LCoE is the price per unit of energy (P_{MWh}) that solves this expression. To be able to solve this expression for the LCoE, the implicit assumption is that price levels are constant, which is in line with the notion of regulated markets. Then, we can solve the expression as:

$$LCOE = P_{MWh} = \frac{\sum_{i=0}^{N} \frac{I_i+O_i+F_i+D_i}{(1+r)^i}}{\sum_{i=0}^{N} \frac{MWh_i}{(1+r)^i}} = \frac{Total\ life\ cycle\ cost}{Total\ lifetime\ energy\ production} \tag{4.10}$$

In Table 4.4, we present an example of computing the LCoE for new power plants using different technologies (for example, a residential-scale solar PV plant and a gas peaking plant), for an industrialised country. The rows of this table show the values used for the computation (and also the assumptions made), and the last two rows list the LCoE values with and without considering the external costs. Note that this is an illustrative example introduced for pedagogical reasons, and is based on some assumptions. A change in these assumptions, for instance, in the level of the investment per kW, in the degree of utilisation, or in the discount rate, can change the level of the LCoE significantly. In this simple example, we see that the production costs for the solar PV plant are lower than those of the gas-peaking plant.

Although the LCoE is interesting as an economic concept and quite useful, it has the following limitations:

- **Problem 1:** 1 kilowatt-hour of electricity produced during peak hours has more economic value than 1 kilowatt-hour produced during off-peak hours when electricity demand is low. In assuming a constant price, this variation is not captured by the LCoE.

Table 4.4 LCoE comparison across different power plants

	Photovoltaic	Gas
Initial investment [USD/kW]	1100	450
Installed capacity [MW]	0.50	1,000
Degree of utilisation	0.10	0.55
Discount rate	0.05	0.05
CO_2 price (USD/t CO_2)		30
External costs [USD/kWh]	0.0033	0.005
Lifetime [years]	30	30
LCoE without external cost [USD]	141.1	185.2
LCoE with external cost [USD]	144.4	190.2

- **Problem 2:** due to the inherent variability in renewable electricity generation, backup power and/or storage are often needed. This is an additional capital cost not accounted for in the LCoE calculation for renewable technologies such as solar or wind.
- **Problem 3:** comparing the LCoE of renewables to the LCoE of fossil fuel-based technologies is a meaningless comparison if negative externalities to the environment from the use of fossil fuels are not considered in the comparison. Generally, LCoE estimates do not include all the social costs of using individual technologies. For example, the LCoE of operating a coal-fired power plant includes the cost of CO_2 emissions (in terms of the cost of emissions based on charges, if any are imposed), but generally does not include the social costs that arise due to local pollution. To note that for some technologies, there is no general agreement in the scientific community regarding the exact value of these social costs. Some values of external costs for different technologies are presented in Figure 4.3. These values are important to keep in mind for a complete evaluation of investments in these technologies, since in the future, governments may introduce additional environmental taxes to systematically internalise the social costs of all technologies.
- **Problem 4:** the LCoE does not account for risks adequately (such as fuel supply risks, volatility of oil and gas pricing, and regulatory risks).

4.3.1 Example of LCoE Calculation for Different Technologies at an International Level

Every year, several studies and reports are published containing estimates of the LCoE for different countries. Some of these reports are published by national agencies, whereas others are published by international institutions such as the International Energy Agency. In this section, we present and discuss the values of LCoE estimated for the entire world, published by the International Energy Agency.

Figure 4.4 plots the LCoE for different technologies (renewable as well as non-renewable) based on information from twenty-four countries in 2020. These average values have been obtained by computing the NPV of each technology using a

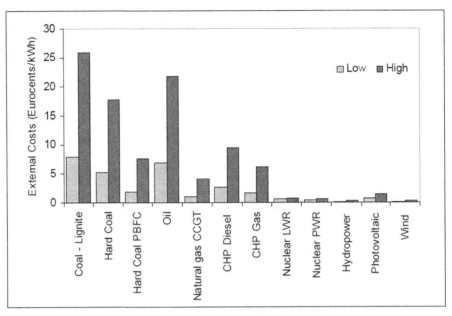

Figure 4.3 Estimated average external costs for different technologies in the EU [72]

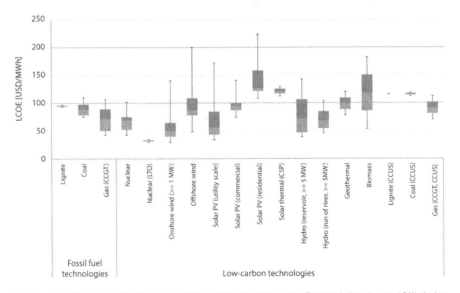

Note: Values at 7% discount rate. Box plots indicate maximum, median and minimum values. The boxes indicate the central 50% of values, i.e. the second and the third quartile.

Figure 4.4 Levelised cost of energy (LCoE) by technology aggregated over twenty-four countries [73]

discount rate of 7 per cent which is commonly assumed to be the case for industrialised countries and large developing countries (such as China). The information presented in this figure takes into account the specific investments needed to be made for each technology, within a range. The x-axis presents the different energy source types. We see, again, that there is significant heterogeneity in these values across technologies.

Solar PV (utility-scale) and onshore wind have reached LCoE levels comparable to fossil fuel-based technologies such as gas or coal. On the other hand, solar PV (residential), solar thermal, and geothermal technologies still remain relatively more expensive.

It is important to note that the calculation of the LCoE is based on making some assumptions such as on the level of the discount rate, the initial investment cost per kW, fuel prices, carbon price, and the lifetime of a plant. A change in the values assumed in the calculation can change the value of the LCoE significantly. Further, the values of the LCoE are also strongly influenced by national and local conditions. For instance, more or less favourable production sites for renewable energy generation, varying regulations and safety standards, heterogeneous fuel costs, and different levels of technical knowledge can lead to large regional and national differences in production costs.

In general, some renewable energy sources are competitive, while others remain relatively expensive as also shown in Figure 4.4. However, as we will discuss in further detail in the next section, generally the production costs of renewable technologies tend to decrease over time because of technical progress. On the other hand, the current competitiveness of coal power plants is relatively low compared to onshore wind and solar PV (utility scale). Furthermore, the introduction of new environmental taxes in the future, such as a pollution tax, will further affect the competitiveness of fossil fuel-based power plants.

By the same yardstick, some plants seem to have a low LCoE, such as nuclear power plants. However, we must keep in mind that these LCoE estimates are often theoretical, and based on making assumptions that may be unrealistic, and for which there is not always agreement in the scientific community. For example, sometimes the assumptions on construction time and on the average construction cost per kw (total overnight capital cost) tend to be optimistic.

4.4 The Learning Curve

We have seen in previous sections that the investment costs per kW are an important component of investment analysis. The value of this component can vary over time. Therefore, for investment analysis, it is important to have information on the evolution of these values over time. The learning curve can be a useful tool for this purpose.

The development of the production costs over time depends on two main factors, that is, technical progress and cost declines due to experience in the production of the technology. The learning curve provides policymakers and firms with important information on these kinds of developments over time and on the expectations of future costs of technologies.

4.4.1 The Learning Curve in the Energy Sector

The learning curve is a graphical representation of the trend in production costs as a function of the cumulative production volume of technology. It is thus a function

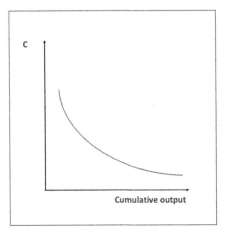

Figure 4.5 A typical learning curve

that describes the impact of learning and of experience acquired with an increase in the production volume on the costs. It can also be mathematically represented and estimated by empirical methods.

As an illustration, Figure 4.5 denotes the production costs (C) needed to produce one unit of output using a certain technology on the y-axis and the cumulative output of that technology on the x-axis. The illustrative curve shows the extent to which the production costs fall as the cumulative output increases. For instance, we could plot the cumulative number of solar panels produced by a firm against the average production cost per solar panel.

Theoretically, these cost reductions may be driven by two economic processes:

- **Learning-by-doing:** the learning effect operational at existing facilities and plants results in benefits from an increase in the efficiency and productivity of using equipment over time.
- **Learning-by-researching:** the benefits derived from investments in research and development may lead to the production of new knowledge as well as innovations.

Learning curves can be obtained empirically by plotting the cumulative output on the horizontal axis, and cost per output on the vertical axis or by using more sophisticated approaches based on econometric methods. Figure 4.6 provides stylised learning curves based on some data by International Renewable Energy Agency (IRENA) for different renewable energy technologies for the period 2010–2020, with the cumulative deployment plotted on the x-axis and the LCoE values plotted on the y-axis. The LCoE values are obtained by collecting information on global cost averages for electricity generated using solar PV as well as onshore wind energy. While costs have declined across both technologies, the decline has been steeper in the case of solar PV, which also had the highest levels of deployment. In fact, as can be seen from the figure, during the period from 2010 to 2020, the global weighted average LCoE of utility-scale solar PV projects declined by more than 80 per cent, whereas the decline was lower for onshore wind [74].

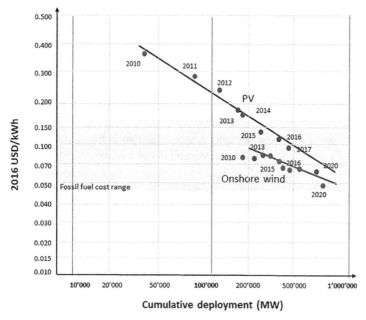

Figure 4.6 Learning curves for renewable energy technologies: adapted from IRENA [74]

From an econometric point of view, there are two types of learning curves that can be estimated, depending on whether we only consider learning-by-doing as a driving factor for cost reductions, or if we consider both learning-by-doing and learning-by-researching.

A one-factor learning curve illustrates the relationship between the unit cost of production of a technology and accumulated learning (normally captured by cumulative output/production). The underlying assumption behind this curve is the existence of only one kind of learning, namely learning by doing. The simplest and most common form of the one-factor learning curve can be written in mathematical form:

$$C_t = C_0 CP_t^a \tag{4.11}$$

C_t: Cost of unit production at time t
C_0: Average unit production cost at $t = 0$
CP_t: Cumulative output produced up to time period t
a: Elasticity of learning

The elasticity of learning a in the equation represents the percentage change in unit costs for a 1 per cent increase in the cumulative output produced up to the time period t, and is the parameter of interest derived from a learning curve. If one takes the logarithm of both sides of this equation, we obtain:

$$\ln C_t = \ln C_0 + a \ln CP_t + \epsilon \tag{4.12}$$

In this form, the equation can be easily estimated empirically, using identification strategies such as the OLS methodology. The term ϵ refers to the idiosyncratic error term, which captures unobservable variables not considered in the model. Such methods allow us to estimate the elasticity of learning. Once we have derived this estimate, we can also use it to calculate the learning-by-doing rate (LR), which is defined as:

$$LR_D = 1 - 2^a \tag{4.13}$$

The learning-by-doing rate is the fractional decrease in costs associated with a doubling of cumulative capacity or production.

Unlike the one-factor learning curve, the two-factor learning curve encapsulates both learning-by-doing and learning-by-researching. Learning-by-researching describes the association of per-unit production costs and the accumulated knowledge stock determined by research and development activities. A simple equation for the two-factor learning curve looks similar to the one-factor learning curve:

$$C_t = C_0 CP_t^a R_t^b \tag{4.14}$$

C_t: Cost of unit production at time t
C_0: Average unit production cost at $t = 0$
CP_t: Cumulative output produced up to time period t
a: Elasticity of learning
R_t: Knowledge stock up to time t
b: Elasticity of learning-by-researching

One can notice that the only difference in the mathematical expression of the two-factor learning curve from that of the one-factor learning curve is the inclusion of the term capturing accumulated knowledge stock and the elasticity of learning-by-researching. Taking the logarithm on both sides of this equation, we obtain:

$$\ln C_t = \ln C_0 + a \ln CP_t + b \ln R_t + \epsilon \tag{4.15}$$

As before, we can estimate this model empirically, using the OLS methodology, for instance. This will yield estimates for the elasticity terms a and b. As with the one-factor curve, we can then use these estimates to derive both the learning-by-doing rate, as well as the learning-by-researching rate, where the learning-by-doing rate is defined as previously, and the learning-by-researching rate is defined as:

$$LR_R = 1 - 2^b \tag{4.16}$$

As an example, in the economic literature, the average learning-by-doing rate computed for solar PV is about 20–25 per cent using a one-factor model. Using two-factor models, in general, the learning-by-doing rate tends to be high for solar PV among all energy types, and the learning-by-researching rate tends to be high for onshore wind [75].

4.5   Social Cost–Benefit Analysis

The construction of a power plant, such as a large run-of-river hydropower plant, yields revenues and costs for the firm that realises this project, but also generates benefits as well as costs for society. For instance, the construction of a large dam could reduce the risk of flooding along the river by regulating the flow of water and, therefore, creating benefits for the population living downstream from the dam. On the other hand, the construction of this dam may also create disamenities due to the reduced flow that may impede the ability of households living downstream to enjoy outdoor activities related to the use of the river. Therefore, if investment projects have the potential to generate significant costs and benefits for society, it is essential, from an economic point of view, to consider these effects when performing an investment analysis. These social aspects of investment projects are not considered in the typical private investment analysis approach that we presented earlier in the chapter. Therefore, to also incorporate the social effects of projects, we can perform a social cost–benefit analysis. This analysis is a form of investment analysis, usually performed by governments that considers both private costs and benefits of a project (which could be either direct or indirect), as well as its social costs and benefits (which include intangible costs and benefits) over the lifetime of a project. This is a useful tool that can be employed to evaluate the most important projects in the energy and climate sectors (such as building a new power plant or a gas pipeline or constructing embankments to prevent coastal flooding or flood protection walls near a river for a community). The main objective of using this methodology is to identify projects that can improve the overall welfare of a society. This method can be put to use either for evaluating the social value of a single project or to rank alternative projects to understand which one is most beneficial.

4.5.1 Steps of Doing a Social Cost–Benefit Analysis

There are typically three steps in doing a social cost–benefit analysis. The first step is to select the projects to evaluate or compare. The next step is to expound on the different types of costs and benefits that are needed to do a social cost–benefit analysis. Following the identification and monetary evaluation of these components, the sum of the benefits and costs for all projects can be compared. Collecting information on the indirect and external or intangible costs and benefits is the most challenging part of this analysis. Frequently, the information on the external costs and benefits is unavailable and, therefore, has to be estimated in separate studies.

The different steps in doing a social cost–benefit analysis are described in Figure 4.7.

After the first step of selecting the projects to be evaluated, as can be seen in Figure 4.7, the second step includes the evaluation of different types of costs and benefits, namely primary, secondary, and intangible, that we explain below. The third step is to compute the sum of the discounted benefits and costs for all projects and compare them by choosing an appropriate discount rate. We will discuss this in more detail in the next subsection.

Primary Benefits and Costs

- **Primary benefits:** these equal the value of the goods and services produced if the project is implemented (such as the electricity produced by a power plant). Primary benefits can be measured by summing up the total revenue and the consumer

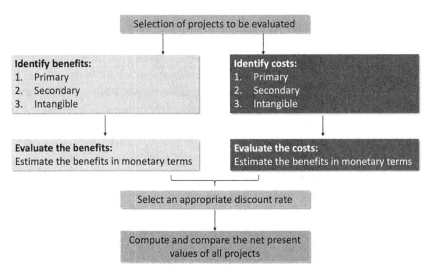

Figure 4.7 Steps in doing a social cost–benefit analysis

surplus. In case the value of the consumer surplus is unknown, the value of primary benefits from a project can be approximated by the total revenue generated. However, this simplified approach underestimates the benefits and therefore may introduce imprecision in the analysis.

- **Primary costs:** primary costs comprise input costs of the project, such as capital, labour, and energy, as well as operational and maintenance costs. These should be evaluated using the notion of opportunity costs, that is, if there is no alternative use of input, then its opportunity cost is said to be zero. For example, the opportunity cost of unemployed people is zero, whereas for employed people, it is the highest wage they could get in the next best job that they could find in a labour market.

Secondary Benefits and Costs

- **Secondary benefits:** it is important to account for indirect benefits that may manifest during the project, such as reduced flooding damages due to the construction of a dam. These types of benefits are called secondary benefits.
- **Secondary costs:** like secondary benefits, secondary costs might also arise in the form of indirect costs of a project. For example, building a dam along a river may decrease the flow of water downstream, and this could increase the production costs of a commercial fishing farm.

Intangible Benefits and Costs

- **Intangibles:** one of the most difficult aspects of conducting a social cost–benefit analysis is the evaluation of intangibles. Intangibles are goods and services whose economic value is not revealed in prices because they lack a market; thus, assigning a price to them is impossible. These are also called non-market goods. This also means that it is not possible to observe the revealed demand for these goods or their quality. For instance, it is quite difficult to evaluate the social cost of air pollution due to the construction and operation of a coal-fired power plant or the loss of biodiversity due to the construction of a hydropower plant. Furthermore, it is difficult to assign an economic value to the protection offered to villages from reduced flood risk due to the construction of a dam along a river that regulates the flow of water.

Another example of adaptation projects is flood protection on the sea shore. This type of investment aims to protect the local community from the increased risk of damage caused by flooding. These are large-scale public investments that entail the construction of dams, embankments, dikes, and so on. These are fairly common in the Netherlands; for instance, the storm surge barrier at the Hollandse IJssel, an economically important region below sea level near Rotterdam, protects the area from floods. For these types of investments, the government performed a social cost–benefit analysis that considered, apart from the large initial construction costs, benefits such as increased safety and reduced damage to infrastructure and buildings, and the mitigated negative impact on agricultural yields. Intangible costs and benefits are extremely difficult to measure, making a social cost–benefit analysis relatively non–trivial compared to a private cost–benefit analysis.

In economic literature, several methods have been developed to evaluate the value of non-market goods. We can distinguish between methods based on stated choice and revealed choice. One of the most commonly used stated choice methodologies is contingent valuation, which normally involves doing a survey to infer the willingness to pay for a non-market good or an improvement in its quality in a hypothetical situation. For instance, we can use this method to elicit the willingness to pay for the possible improvement in air quality in urban areas that is likely from a hypothetical project. Another method based on the stated choices of individuals is the choice experiment, which differs from contingent valuation methods in that individuals are not directly required to express their willingness to pay, but end up doing so indirectly, by making choices between different hypothetical goods having different attributes (such as its environmental impact). Using information on these choices, and differences in the attributes across the goods, it is possible to estimate the value of an environmental attribute to individuals.

An example of a revealed preference method is the hedonic pricing method. This method is based on the theory that the price or value of a good depends on different characteristics, including its environmental attributes. The effect of changes in these attributes on the price can be assessed using regression-based methodologies. Another method usually used for revealed preference analysis is the travel cost method. In this case, the demand for a non-market good, for instance for preserving an alpine valley that is likely to be submerged due to the construction of a hydropower plant, is inferred by observing the visit frequencies to this valley and calculating the cost incurred by the visitors to get there. This cost includes not only the transport costs but also the opportunity cost of time. With information on travel costs and frequency, it is possible to estimate a demand function for non-market goods using econometric methods, and thus it is possible to have an estimate of the willingness to pay to protect this environment.

Incremental benefits of air quality improvements

Several cities around the world are affected by severe local air pollution. One possible solution to decrease the level of air pollution, at least partially, is to substitute old inefficient diesel buses with new electric buses using electricity produced from renewable energy sources. Figure 4.8 presents the marginal social benefit (MSB) function for improved air quality that can be used to identify the incremental benefits of introducing electric buses. This project is said to improve air quality because of the reduction in the number of fossil fuels burned, which will also reduce the number of local pollutants such as PM_{10} emitted. On the x-axis, we plot the quantity of PM_{10} abated, whereas on the vertical axis, we plot the MSBs from reducing the emissions of PM_{10}.

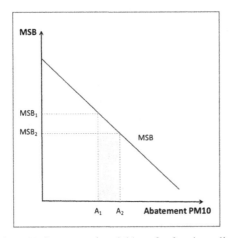

Figure 4.8 Incremental social benefits for air quality

The marginal social benefits function represents society's willingness to pay for the benefits obtained from a reduction of PM_{10} emissions, in terms of the improvement in air quality. The shaded area represents the incremental benefits from a decrease in PM_{10} emissions from A_1 to A_2. Of course, in Figure 4.8, we are assuming that we can observe the demand for pollution abatement. However, we know that there are no explicit markets for several environmental goods, and, therefore, it is not easy to estimate the incremental benefits. In these cases, as discussed previously, economists have suggested several approaches to derive the benefits from improvements in environmental quality, or more generally, the benefits of using goods and services not traded on a market.

The local socioeconomic impacts of large hydropower plant development in a developing country

In a study on Brazil, de Faria et al. (2017) [76] evaluated the local socioeconomic effects of sixty-six hydropower plants built from 1991 to 2010 across various counties in Brazil. They used econometric methods to evaluate their impact while considering counties in which hydropower projects were planned, but not yet built as the control group. The authors found that while the establishment of hydropower projects led to an economic boom in the short term (within 15 years of construction), these effects did not persist beyond that time. Also, they did not find a significant effect of hydropower projects on average incomes, life expectancy, as well as on other socioeconomic indicators. The findings of this paper lend support for taking a deeper look at costs and benefits over varying time horizons before constructing energy–sector projects, especially in developing countries, where capital costs may tend to be high.

4.5.2   Net Present Value Criterion

The concept of the NPV also applies as a decision criterion for doing a social cost–benefit analysis. From a mathematical perspective, this is done by rewriting the cash flows in the formula of NPV as the difference between societal benefits and costs, substituting the discount rate with a social discount rate, and subtracting the initial investment, as shown:

$$NPV = \sum_{t=0}^{T} \frac{B_t - C_t}{(1 + r_s)^t} - I \tag{4.17}$$

where:
NPV: Net Present Value
I: Initial investment cost
B_t: Societal benefits in period t
C_t: Societal costs in period t
r_s: Social discount rate

Note that values of I, C, B, and r should either all be measured in real terms, with an adjustment for the inflation rate, or all be measured in nominal terms.

The NPV criterion for social project evaluation suggests that any project that has a positive NPV, that is, benefits that exceed costs over the life of the project, is interesting from both economic and social perspectives. This criterion is based on the Kaldor–Hicks Criterion which states that if a project makes some individuals better off, and others worse off, then the project will increase social welfare if the winners, at least hypothetically, can compensate the losers while maintaining higher welfare. Moreover, this criterion implies that between similar projects, the project with the highest NPV should be chosen.

We must note that in general, evaluating the income and wealth-based distributional effects of a project is quite important, however, it is generally not considered when doing a social cost–benefit analysis.

Nevertheless, one could think of assigning weights to the benefits as well as costs, depending on the number of economic agents that experience these due to a project. For example, in a developing country, the construction of a hydropower plant will benefit households belonging to the middle and upper classes who consume electricity more than households that do not own appliances and perhaps have to leave their homes so that the plant can be built. In this case, one could consider giving less weight to the benefits and more weight to the costs of displacing poor households, especially in an economic equity-oriented society.

4.5.3   The Social Discount Rate

In Section 4.1, we discussed the rationale for discounting when doing an investment analysis. The social discount rate reflects the rate of substitution of society between present and future consumption. Two arguments were put forth: the time preference argument and the capital productivity argument. These arguments are equally valid in the case of discounting while doing a social cost–benefit analysis. An additional rationale for discounting also arises in this case, namely economic growth and decreasing marginal utility of income – today's investments and technical change are likely to give rise to economic growth, which implies that future generations are likely to be richer than present generations. Thus, their marginal utility from each unit of income will be lower, that is, each unit of currency will be worth less in the future when everyone enjoys higher incomes than it is today. Therefore, discounting is an important way to consider this decline in the marginal utility of income.

The definition of the social discount rate is critical and always creates much discussion since the value of NPV is strongly influenced by this rate. A high social discount rate corresponds to a high social value of consumption today relative to consumption in the future, or a high social value of the costs today relative to costs in the future. In other words, it implies that the consumption and costs of future generations are valued less than current consumption and costs. The extent of the impact of the discount factor on estimations is best explained using an example. Consider a social discount rate $r_s = 4$ per cent. If the discounted period is 50 years, such a discount rate would result in a discount factor (w) of 0.14. This implies that a gain or loss in 50 years would be valued at only 14 per cent of its initial value now $(w_{50} = 1/(1.04)^{50} = 0.14)$. This is an extremely low value, which illustrates the potential sensitivity of the NPV calculation to the choice of the social discount rate. It is important to keep in mind that in the energy and climate sectors, we typically have projects with long lifespans. For instance, a hydropower plant can have a lifetime of up to 80–100 years. The benefits of adaptation projects can also last up to 100–150 years.

In all these cases, the choice of discount rate profoundly influences the evaluations. A high discount rate will dramatically reduce the value of the future benefits of reducing the damages of climate change, that is, the benefits for future generations. Likewise, a high discount rate implies that the long-term costs associated with the treatment and storage of nuclear waste are meagre. However, future generations will need to pay these costs, giving more weight to the costs than the one assumed in doing the cost–benefit analysis. Therefore, by choosing a high discount rate, current generations are not fully taking into account the benefits and costs of these investments for future generations.

4.6   Issues in Developing Countries

As we learnt in this chapter, investment analysis in the energy sector can have important repercussions on the energy transition towards renewables. We will now discuss three issues that we think are relevant for investment analysis in developing countries, namely the growth of decentralised energy systems and the role of renewable energy technologies in developing countries and the importance of social discount rates.

In many developing countries, given the abundance of resources such as sunlight, water, and wind, and the decline in renewable energy production costs, the transformation to cleaner sources of energy is inevitable, even though fossil fuels may still remain dominant in some settings. One apparent (and already underway) outcome of this transition is the growth of decentralised energy systems: we will first discuss these systems in this section, which have paved the way for affordable and clean energy access for millions in the developing world. We will then discuss the role of policy in facilitating the transition to renewables in developing countries. Last, given that investments in public projects entail knowledge of the social discount rates, we will discuss relatively high social discount rates in developing countries, underlining the method of computation and how it can have an impact on the values of this parameter.

4.6.1   Application of Investment Analysis: Growth of Decentralised Energy Systems

There are vast differences in terms of access to electricity across the world; however, many parts of the developing world, particularly in Africa, are far from achieving universal access to electricity. Furthermore, the quality of electricity supply is poor in many countries, and this implies frequent blackouts and load-shedding events, which can have serious consequences on the benefits of electrification.

While designing policy instruments to promote electrification in developing regions, policymakers face several challenges. Some of these are high electricity connection charges (especially to extend grid electricity to remote rural areas), high operating costs, low population density in rural areas, difficult terrain, unreliability in supply, as well as a lack of finance for adequate investment in infrastructure.

Moreover, extending electricity access is not the panacea for all problems related to electricity. Ensuring the reliability of electricity supply and power quality (with minimal interruptions, blackouts, and voltage fluctuations) remains an enormous technical and financial challenge in many developing countries.

Decentralised systems such as solar home systems as well as micro/mini-grids offer households living in rural, remote areas the possibility to easily connect to electricity by 'leap-frogging' centralised systems. The benefits of these decentralised systems that rely almost exclusively on renewable technologies are that they provide an affordable means to acquire reliable access to electricity (even though the cost per kWh of some of these options may be higher than that of grid connections) and are relatively cheaper and cleaner than using diesel generators. One of the disadvantages is that the smaller systems make it impossible to use multiple or high-power appliances.

Thus, from the policymaker's perspective, performing a cost–benefit analysis is important to understand whether it is worth extending the electricity grid to the rural areas, possibly at a high cost, or whether to emphasise subsidising or promoting the use of decentralised systems, which can serve to extend access to energy to these households. Given that these are relatively small-scale systems, policymakers may choose to ramp up investments in building or extending grid infrastructure over time, prioritising the adoption of these systems in the short run.

An investment analysis from a private point of view is also interesting in this regard. Consider a situation where households living in remote areas are looking to acquire access to electricity and have two possibilities: either connecting to the grid (if it is available nearby) or investing in an off-grid system (such as a solar home system). In the first case, the initial investment costs for a grid connection may, in many cases (especially in low-income countries), be very high, and the theoretical benefits may also be relatively large (compared to the off-grid system). On the other hand, several challenges related to supply, such as poor reliability and quality of electricity and transmission and distribution losses, may make these benefits less likely to materialise. In the case of the off-grid system, while households may pay less upfront, the magnitude of benefits realised also generally tends to be smaller (given the smaller scale of these systems). However, with low or no transmission losses and a relatively stable electricity supply, households are better assured of receiving these benefits. The choice between the two forms of electricity will depend on how high the grid connection costs are and the magnitude of discounted benefits. Households can then undertake an investment analysis and compare the two options (in terms of their NPV) to decide which one they prefer.

4.6.2   Levelised Cost of Energy in Developing Countries

The primary challenge for the larger deployment of renewable energy, not just in developing countries, but also in developed countries, is their somewhat higher cost of installation, and in the case of solar and wind, their short-term variable character.

The opportunities offered by renewable energy technologies in developing countries are paramount: for instance, most parts of the developing world are well endowed with sunlight and wind. The LCoE for renewable energy technologies has declined in many developing countries in recent times due to a combination of factors: technological progress, a decline in operating costs (due to declining labour costs with technical progress, as well as economies of scale), and a decline in investment costs (which is a result of both technological improvements and policy). These trends are also likely to continue, which suggests that economic policy must be supportive of renewable deployment in developing countries, and policymakers could prioritise this as a short-term energy policy goal to facilitate decarbonisation.

The inherent intermittence and variability of renewable power production implies that developing countries must invest in backup systems as well as storage, and improve forecasting to benefit from their use. Greater research and development (R&D) efforts are needed to advance technical knowledge, increase efficiency, and reduce the costs of storage and backup technologies. Even though installation costs have fallen over time for these technologies even in developing countries, it remains important to increase capital investments in reducing variability, which should be supported by innovation-based policies. Furthermore, investments also need to be made in the grid infrastructure, such as in extending the network and in digitalisation. These investments are important for extending the grid to remote areas and ensuring that clean electricity is used by households and businesses.

Role of policy for promoting investments in solar energy in developing countries

Ondraczek et al. (2015) [77] discussed the importance of financing costs in determining the LCoE for solar PV. They argued that in developing countries, the WACC was generally higher than in developed countries (due to higher costs of capital) and that this difference between both sets of countries contributed more to variations in LCoE across countries than differences in solar potential. They highlighted that policymakers in developing countries should emphasise de-risking renewable sector investments and promoting access to cheap finance, to reduce the cost of borrowing, as has also been argued in other studies cited in this chapter.

4.6.3 Social Discount Rates

As we saw in Section 4.5, the choice of social discount rate is an important determinant of the evaluation of the social costs and benefits of a public project. In many developing countries, the market interest rate (or rate of return on private sector investments) is used as the social discount rate in cost–benefit analysis, and this typically tends to be high (in the range of 10–12 per cent). The use of such high discount rates may discourage projects having relatively high upfront costs, with benefits spanning several time periods (such as investments in renewable power projects).

An alternative to calculate social discount rates, in such settings, may be to use the real interest rate at which these countries can borrow. Some economists argue that this measure correlates better with the cost of borrowing for governments, who are most likely to be funding these projects. This would imply a real discount rate of about 5 per cent, which is lower than the current social discount rate used in many countries. This is also the approach used in many industrialised countries. Of course, if sovereign debt yields were to increase due to changes in macroeconomic conditions in the country, the real interest rates may increase, and then the social discount rate should reflect these changes.

4.6.4 Review Questions and Problems

The online question bank contains review questions and problems for this chapter, including solutions (see https://wp-prd.let.ethz.ch/exercisesfortextbookeep/).

5 Economics of Energy Efficiency

As discussed in Chapter 1, it is important to promote the adoption of renewable energy sources, modify our lifestyles, and increase energy efficiency to reach the energy transition. Currently, the economic systems of industrialised and developing countries are still characterised by significant levels of inefficiency in the use of energy, that is, by production and consumption processes that waste energy. Therefore, improving energy efficiency is one of the cheapest and most environmentally friendly strategies to transform the energy sector. For this reason, since the oil crises of the seventies of the last century, several countries worldwide have implemented important energy policy instruments to promote energy efficiency and reduce the wastage of energy.

In this chapter, we will introduce the definition of energy efficiency, discuss the approaches that can be used to measure it, and elucidate some of the common barriers towards achieving a high level of energy efficiency.

5.1 Energy Efficiency

5.1.1 Definition

While the definitions of energy efficiency vary between engineering and energy economics, in this book we provide a definition based on the microeconomic theory of production. In this theoretical framework, as depicted in Figure 5.1, and discussed in Chapter 3, alongside capital (such as insulation in a building and ventilation systems) and labour, energy is considered to be an essential input used in the production of goods such as machines, cars, and in the production of energy services such as heating and cooling.

This implies that the demand for such inputs depends on the demand for energy goods and services.

The relationship between the use of energy inputs and outputs is used to measure the level of energy efficiency. A production process is said to be energy efficient if it is not possible to produce the same level of energy services or goods with less energy. Similar efficiency measures can be defined for the other production inputs as well (e.g., labour efficiency or capital efficiency). More generally, the overall level of productive efficiency is based on the relationship between inputs and the output, that is, the final good or service produced.

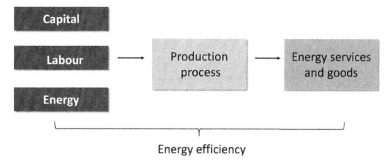

Figure 5.1 Energy efficiency and productive efficiency

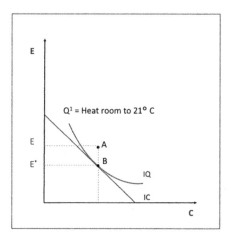

Figure 5.2 Inefficient use of technology

5.1.2   Reasons for Inefficiencies

Inefficiencies in the use of energy can arise in at least three situations: inefficient use of technology, inefficient combination of inputs to produce output, or employment of obsolete technologies.

In Figures 5.2 to 5.4, we illustrate these three situations that can give rise to energy inefficiency using isoquant and isocost lines. All graphs depict a simple production model with capital (C) on the x-axis and energy use (E) on the y-axis, as well as an isocost line (IC) and an isoquant curve (IQ). All points on the isocost line depict combinations of inputs with the same total cost, while all points on the isoquant curve are combinations of inputs that yield the same output. In the following examples, the energy service produced is the heating of a room to 21°C.

Consider a situation in which the inefficient use of technology leads to a loss in energy efficiency. In our example related to the production of a heating service, this could mean that a household does not use an optimal amount of energy to heat the room. This is shown in Figure 5.2 by the combination of capital and energy represented by point A (which is a point at the same output temperature of 21°C). At this point, if the capital input is held constant and the energy consumption is reduced from E to E^*,

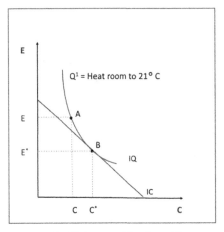

Figure 5.3 Inefficient combination of inputs

the desired level of output (i.e., the desired heating temperature) can be achieved using less energy at point B. In the context of heating, for example, situation A could arise when, during the winter, windows are kept open longer than necessary, which leads to a loss of heat. It may also arise if the use of a heating system is not optimised, such as when heat pumps are operational even if they are not required, or the parameters of the heating systems are not optimised.

Energy inefficiency resulting from a suboptimal combination of inputs is best explained through Figure 5.3. Here, the combination of inputs used to produce a room temperature of 21°C is represented by point A. At this point, the level of capital C is lower than the optimal one C^* and the household is using too much energy E. For instance, a building could still have been equipped with old single-glazed windows instead of new double-glazed windows. In this situation, if capital is increased to the optimal level C^*, for instance, with the substitution of the old with the new more insulated windows, it is possible to reduce the energy consumption to E^*, that is, the optimal combination of inputs represented by point B can be reached.

We should note that the use of energy-saving double-glazed windows can still be considered a standard technology. In fact, one classical approach currently used in the building renovation sector to improve heat retention is to use double-glazed windows instead of single-glazed windows.

Dependence on obsolete technologies is the third situation that characterises an inefficient use of energy. This could manifest when the household does not adopt newer technologies that can produce the same energy services or goods using a lower energy input. In the graph in Figure 5.4, old and new technologies are each represented by an isoquant. Note that both the isoquants denote the same level of output (heating a room to 21°C). Old technologies in the building sector are characterised by structures having poor insulation, no double-glazing of windows, and inefficient heating systems. New technologies in buildings imply better insulation and an air ventilation system equipped with heat exchangers that reduce energy consumption.

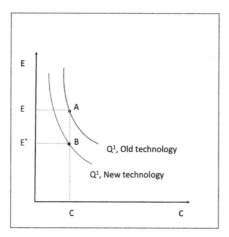

Figure 5.4 Use of obsolete technology

Generally, these technologies provide more comfort in terms of lower noise levels, uniform temperatures, and better air quality, in addition to energy savings.

Figure 5.4 represents a situation in which consumers can choose between buildings with old technologies, or buildings with more modern technologies. Let's assume now that a household chooses to live in the building with the old technology, and that it chooses the inputs in the combination characterised by the point A (with inputs E and C). The alternative for the household would have been to choose to live in a new building, and for instance, choose the input combination represented by point B. In this case, point B is characterised by the use of the same level of capital as at point A, and would have implied a reduction of energy consumption from E to E^* without changing the achieved output. Thus, the use of obsolete technology in this case leads to higher levels of energy consumption than is possible with newer technologies.

5.2 Measurement of Energy Efficiency

There are three main approaches for measuring energy efficiency empirically: partial indicators, econometric approaches, and bottom-up engineering approaches. Two of these approaches – partial indicators and econometric approaches – are discussed in this chapter, because they better capture the concept of energy efficiency based on microeconomic theory, as discussed in Section 5.1. Additionally, the analysis of energy efficiency can either be done at a relatively disaggregated level, for example, using data from firms or households, or at an aggregated level with data from countries, regions, or cities.

5.2.1 Partial Indicators

When a partial indicator approach is used to measure energy efficiency, the simple ratio of the total output to energy consumption is computed, whereby both outputs and inputs can be measured in either quantity-based or monetary units.

Two central partial indicators in the literature are energy productivity, which is the ratio of the total output of a good or service to the total energy consumption, and energy intensity, which is the opposite, that is, the ratio of energy consumption to output. For instance, in the context of the efficiency of buildings, energy productivity could be measured as the ratio between the size of a house, measured in square meters, and the amount of energy consumed, measured in kilowatt-hours (kWh) or in British thermal units (BTUs), whereas energy intensity would be measured as the ratio between the amount of energy consumed and the size of a house. Another important example of the use of a partial indicator is the measurement of the level of energy intensity of an economic system. In this case, the level of energy intensity can be measured as the ratio between energy consumption at the country level (measured in BTUs) and GDP.

One of the advantages of the use of partial indicators to measure energy efficiency is the simplicity of the calculation. However, while these indicators provide a system to rank households, firms, countries, and regions on the basis of energy efficiency, they suffer from important limitations. For example, the differences in the levels of energy efficiency of households and firms obtained with partial indicators can arise due to several factors, such as climatic conditions, building age, differences in the technologies adopted, household size, type of firm, and behavioural components. Similarly, differences in the level of energy efficiency of economic systems across countries or regions may arise due to differences in their economic structures, the presence of energy-intensive sectors in some regions/countries, climatic conditions, or the level and type of urbanisation.

As a result of the uni-dimensional information that partial indicators provide, this approach cannot be used to easily benchmark or compare performances across different units, such as houses or countries. The risk in using the partial indicator approach would be to perform an unfair comparison of economic agents and countries. For instance, one country could be characterised by a low level of energy productivity or a high level of energy intensity because of cold weather conditions that require a high level of consumption of heating services, and not necessarily because of being a society that is wasteful in energy use.

Table 5.1 mentions the level of energy productivity and energy intensity for a sample of countries. We observe a great variation in the values of energy productivity measured across countries. For instance, some countries such as France and Italy exhibit relatively high levels of energy productivity, while Canada and India fare relatively worse. A part of this difference may be explained by an inefficient use of energy; however, it may also be due to other factors such as the climate, or the presence of heavy industries that can contribute significantly to energy consumption.

An interesting example of an indicator of energy intensity at the household level is the ratio of the energy consumption of a heating system to the size of the house. Figure 5.5 shows a histogram of frequencies (represented on the y-axis) across different energy intensity (EI) levels (x-axis), plotted using information from a sample of Swiss households. In this case, energy intensity is measured in units of KWh per square meter. Importantly, the figure illustrates that there is vast heterogeneity

Table 5.1 Cross-country energy consumption comparisons [78] [79]

Country	Primary energy consumption (TWh)	GDP (billions of 2020 USD)	Energy productivity (GDP/Energy)	Energy Intensity (Energy/GDP)
Australia	1,780.44	1,400	0.79	1.27
Brazil	3,445.40	1,840	0.53	1.87
Canada	3,948.35	1,740	0.44	2.27
China	39,360.93	14,300	0.36	2.75
France	2,688.65	2,720	1.01	0.99
Germany	3,649.98	3,860	1.06	0.95
India	9,460.98	2,870	0.30	3.30
Indonesia	2,475.35	1,120	0.45	2.21
Italy	1,770.42	2,000	1.13	0.89
Japan	5,187.15	5,080	0.98	1.02
Mexico	2,144.65	1,270	0.59	1.69
Norway	490.78	403	0.82	1.22
Russia	8,279.18	1,700	0.21	4.87
Saudi Arabia	3,065.43	793	0.26	3.87
Singapore	986.02	372	0.38	2.65
South Africa	1,500.24	351	0.23	4.27
South Korea	3436.34	1,650	0.48	2.08
Switzerland	313.93	703	2.2	0.45
The United Kingdom	2,177.83	2,830	1.3	0.77
The United States	26,291.36	21,400	0.81	1.23

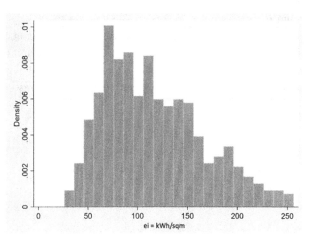

Figure 5.5 Energy intensity at the household level
Source: Data collected at CEPE (Centre for Energy Policy and Economics at ETH Zürich)

in energy intensity levels; some Swiss households in the sample merely consume 25 kWh/m^2, while others consume up to ten times as much. As mentioned, partial indicators only provide limited information, as the values of energy intensity do not convey the reasons for the observed differences. In fact, some of the households included in this sample live in mountainous areas where the heating requirements are higher than for households in the valleys.

5.2.2   Econometric Approaches

The second approach for measuring energy efficiency is based on using econometric methods and estimating different types of models, some of which are discussed in this chapter. One important econometric approach is the stochastic frontier model of energy demand, which has been introduced by Filippini and Hunt (2011, 2016) [28] [80]. This approach is based on the use of a special econometric method that enables estimating a frontier function based on data at the household, firm, or country level.

Generally, a frontier function indicates the maximum or minimum level of an outcome variable that an economic agent can attain in production or consumption activities. In the context of energy demand, a frontier function shows the minimum quantity of energy needed to produce any given level of goods and/or energy services.

In Figure 5.6, we present the situation of a household that is producing and consuming an energy service. The horizontal axis shows the level of energy services produced (ES), the vertical axis indicates the level of energy consumed (E), and the curved line represents the energy demand frontier function. This simple frontier function shows the minimum level of energy needed by an economic agent, in this case, a household, to produce any level of energy services. At an energy service production level of ES_1, energy inefficiency exists if instead of E_{pro}, the observed energy consumption is at the level E_{obs}. The level of inefficiency can be read as the vertical difference or ratio between points A and B.

Empirically speaking, this inefficiency is estimated using an econometric model, that is, the stochastic frontier model. In Figure 5.7, energy consumption (E) is again plotted on the vertical axis and energy services (ES) on the horizontal axis. The black and dark grey data points in the figure represent combinations of energy consumption

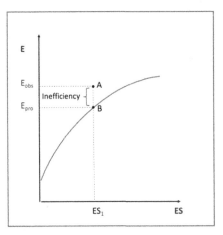

Figure 5.6 Frontier demand curve and inefficiency

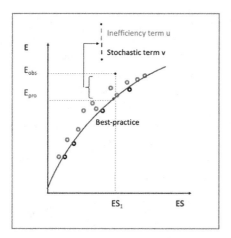

Figure 5.7 Stochastic frontier demand curve and inefficiency

and services observed for a household, a firm, or a country. The vertical distance between the dark grey points and the stochastic frontier is made up of both an inefficiency term (μ), which indicates the level of energy inefficiency, and a stochastic term (v), which is the typical residual term of a regression model, and captures unobserved variables and accounts for a lack of perfect goodness of fit.

In order to estimate the level of energy inefficiency of an economic agent, the researcher should first specify an energy demand function. For instance, for households, the energy demand frontier function could be specified as:

$$E = f(PE, HS, AS, HDD, ES, EINEFF) \tag{5.1}$$

Where:
E: Energy demand
PE: Energy price
HS: Household size
AS: Area or size of dwelling
HDD: Heating-degree days
ES: Level of energy services
$EINEFF$: Level of inefficiency in energy use

After having specified it, the researcher should collect data on all the variables included in such a model as that in Equation 5.1, and estimate it using an econometric methodology that derives the coefficients of the variables as well as the two components of the general error term, that is, μ and v. For instance, the econometric specification of model 5.1 using a log-log functional form can be expressed as follows:

$$
\ln(E) = \alpha_0 + \alpha_p \ln(PE) + \alpha_{HS} \ln(HS) + \alpha_{AS} \ln(AS)
$$
$$
+ \alpha_{HDD} \ln(HDD) + \alpha_{ES} \ln(ES) + v + \mu \tag{5.2}
$$

In this example, the natural logarithm of a household's energy demand is for instance explained through the natural log of the energy price (PE), of the household size

(HS), of the area or size of the house (AS), of the heating-degree days (HDD) (a measure of how many days the temperature was less than a threshold temperature, and by how much, indicating cold weather severity), of the level of produced energy services (ES), the stochastic term (v), and the level of energy inefficiency (μ). The researcher will first estimate the model by applying a maximum likelihood-based estimator, and then using a formula to split the general error term into the two components. Afterwards, the level of energy inefficiency can be calculated using the values of μ. We should note that the level of inefficiency measured by μ may be due to inefficient use of technologies in generating energy services as well as due to inefficient investment decisions, that is, the choice of energy-inefficient technologies.

The main advantage of using this econometric approach (over the partial indicator approach) is that it provides a fairer comparison of the levels of energy efficiency of households; the econometric specification includes explanatory variables that can potentially explain differences in consumption across households, which may also be factors beyond the household's control, such as the number of heating degree days or household size. To note, that the level of inefficiency may be due inefficiency behaviours in consumption or investment.

Stochastic frontier energy demand function

A study on the level of energy efficiency of US households conducted by Alberini and Filippini (2018) [27] computed a level of energy inefficiency of approximately 25 per cent among US households. This implies that US households could potentially have saved up to 25 per cent of their energy, without reducing the number or level of energy services consumed. In another study on the level of residential electricity demand in Switzerland, Blasch et al. (2017) [81] found that the aggregate level of inefficiency in the use of electricity was around 30 per cent among Swiss households. These studies suggest relatively high levels of energy inefficiency at the aggregate level in these countries, with the potential for improving energy efficiency.

5.3   Investment in Energy Efficiency

As discussed in Chapter 4, investment decisions in the energy sector can heavily influence the level of energy demand and energy efficiency of a household, firm, or country, and over long periods. This is because technologies used in the production of energy services have a very long lifespan. For example, a heating system may have a lifespan of around 30 years, and windows have a lifespan of around 20–30 years. This implies that a suboptimal investment choice from an energy point of view can have negative repercussions on energy consumption for a very long time. These investment decisions are rather complex, as they depend on a multitude of factors, such as the initial prices of technologies, their operating costs, expected prices, discount rates, behavioural factors, policy measures, and the long lives of these technologies. In this subsection, we will focus on investments made by households.

A quantitative and qualitative analysis of the super-efficient equipment programme subsidy in India

Troja (2016) [82] discussed the growing need for energy efficiency in the Indian energy sector, which is facing unprecedented pressures due to high population growth and urbanisation rates. The main focus of this study was to analyse the impact of a policy, the Super Efficient Equipment Program (SEEP) in the housing sector. The aim of this scheme was to reduce energy consumption in the residential sector in India, by incentivising producers, that is, by providing subsidies for the production of more energy-efficient fans. The author accounted for economies of scale and the market power of producers. Additionally, he used an econometric model to factor in the preferences and behaviour of consumers. He found that the SEEP was able to achieve its goal of reducing energy consumption, but only to some extent. The weaker-than-expected results arose because even despite the subsidies, the more efficient fans tended to cost about INR 300 (about $5) more than regular fans. Also, the demand for fans was rather price inelastic. These two factors contributed to the low switching rates between the less efficient and more efficient technologies. The author suggested various government interventions that could help promote energy efficiency in India, such as:

1. To impose bans on the consumption and production of technologies that are inefficient.
2. To undertake information and awareness campaigns to highlight the resulting costs and energy-saving benefits.
3. To evaluate programmes such as SEEP using econometric models, to fully understand their impact.

5.3.1   Investment Decisions

Investment decisions influence the stream of benefits and costs over a long period of time. This implies that appropriate investment levels in energy efficiency can be identified through intertemporal optimisation, as is done in microeconomics. To take such a decision, individuals need to collect information and make assumptions regarding the future, especially regarding their usage and future energy prices. They then need to perform an investment analysis (as discussed in Chapter 4) or calculate lifetime costs. If it turns out that the benefits that manifest from investing are the same across all technologies and the lifetimes are similar, then the use of lifetime cost, that is, the sum of the upfront cost or initial price and the operating costs incurred during the lifetime of the technology, is a viable means for decision-making. However, if the said benefits vary with the type of technology, then the use of an investment analysis that fully considers all the costs and benefits over the lifespan of a technology would be more appropriate to conclude. In this chapter, we focus on the discussion of using lifetime costs as a criterion for making investment decisions. For example, if a household wants to buy a heating system, then this household should compare the lifetime costs of the potential heating systems with similar lifespans that could be installed in their house.

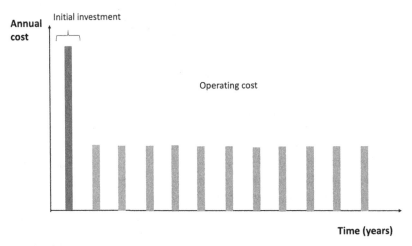

Figure 5.8 Lifetime costs

5.3.2   Lifetime Cost Calculations

Lifetime costs are obtained by summing the initial purchase price (initial investment) of the technology with the operating costs of the technology over its lifetime. In Figure 5.8, the first vertical bar (the red bar) represents the initial fixed costs paid for the purchase of the new durable or technology, and the subsequent bars (blue bars) indicate the operating costs that are incurred over its lifetime.

Sometimes, we can observe situations where the initial price of a durable good, for instance, a washing machine, is lower than the price of an alternative model that is relatively more energy-efficient and that consumes less electricity. However, if one were to consider the lifetime costs of these two washing machines, we may well observe that the washing machine having a higher initial price would actually have lower lifetime costs, because of its relatively lower operating costs (compared to the cheaper washing machine).

The formula for the computation of the lifetime cost of a technology used to produce energy services is:

$$LTC = P^I + \sum_{t=1}^{T} \frac{P_t^E \cdot C_t}{(1+r)^t} \qquad (5.3)$$

Where:

LTC: Lifetime cost (present discounted value (PDV) of a stream of costs over time)

P^I: Price of the durable

P_t^E: Energy price at period t

C_t: Energy consumption at period t

r: Discount rate

t: Time

T: Total lifespan of the durable

In this expression, the first term P^I refers to the initial cost and the composite term $\sum_{t=1}^{T} \frac{P_t^E \cdot C_t}{(1+r)^t}$ indicates the total operating costs, which depend on the price of energy (P_t^E), the level of energy consumption (C_t), the discount rate used to calculate the present value of future cash flows (r), as well as the lifetime of the durable (T).

We should note that in cases where the choice set includes durable goods such as cars, appliances, or heating systems that are somewhat dissimilar, information on the lifetime costs is still important in the decision-making process but is likely to not be the only determinant of the final choice made by individuals. In this case, individuals will consider the lifetime costs as well as other characteristics of the durable good when making their choice.

5.3.3   Examples: Comparing Lifetime Costs of Cars and Refrigerators

As an example to compare the lifetime costs of two cars, Table 5.2 provides real data on two similar car models that could have been bought in Switzerland in the year 2020. As can be seen from the table, one car is more energy-efficient; however, it is also characterised by a higher purchase price. Further, the different efficiency ratings have an impact not only on the operating costs but also on the level of the annual registration tax. For the diesel model, there is an annual registration bonus of CHF 214, that is, the amount of registration tax paid by owners of this model is CHF 214 less than that paid by owners of the gasoline car. Due to the better fuel economy of this car, its lifetime cost is lower than the lifetime cost of the gasoline-powered car. This calculation has been done assuming a lifespan of 10 years, usage of 10,000 km/year and a common discount rate of 3 per cent. If a consumer were to only compare the purchase prices of these cars, then the consumer may have chosen the gasoline car. However, by considering total lifetime costs, the choice should be expected to reverse.

Another example of the computation of the lifetime costs is summarised in Table 5.3, which shows details of two refrigerators with similar characteristics. Fridge

Table 5.2 Lifetime costs of cars

	Ford focus SW 1.5 SCTi 150	Ford focus SW 1.5 TDCi 120
Fuel type	Gasoline	Diesel
Fuel price	CHF 1.43	CHF 1.75
Efficiency rating	F	A
Fuel consumption (L/100 km)	5.6	3.8
Initial price	CHF 26,200	CHF 27,800
Registration tax (ZH bonus)	CHF 268	CHF 54 (CHF 214 bonus)
Fuel + tax + price	CHF 36,880	CHF 34,990
Fuel + tax + price + CO_2 tax	CHF 37,430	CHF 35,485

Source: Data collected at CEPE

Table 5.3 Lifetime costs of refrigerators

Appliance	Discount factor	Electricity price ($/kWh)	Consumption per year (kWh)	Expenditure per year ($)	Initial price ($)	Lifetime cost for 10 years ($)
Fridge A	0.03	0.25	100	25	3,000	3,213
Fridge B	0.03	0.25	200	50	2,900	3,327

Source: Data collected at CEPE

A is more expensive at purchase; however, due to its lower energy consumption compared to Fridge B, the lifetime cost of Fridge A is lower than that of Fridge B. If a consumer only compares the purchase prices of the two appliances, then he or she will probably choose Fridge B. However, if a consumer considers the total lifetime costs, then the consumer should choose Fridge A. Again, as with the previous example, we should keep in mind that we are discussing the choice between two very similar refrigerators. The calculation has been done assuming a lifespan of 10 years, an electricity price of 0.25 dollars per kWh, and a discount rate of 3 per cent. We should keep in mind that with sufficiently high discount rates, the less efficient fridge may look more attractive from a lifetime cost perspective, because the operating costs will be more heavily discounted. For instance, individuals with high subjective discount rates may then prefer to buy Fridge B compared to Fridge A.

5.4   Energy Efficiency Gap

5.4.1   Private and Social Perspectives

In some situations, consumers or firms do not adopt durable goods that minimise their lifetime costs when facing a choice between very similar goods. This describes the inefficient behaviour of consumers or firms, that is, there exists a gap between the optimal choice and the actual choice they make.

There are two definitions of the energy efficiency gap: one definition is focused on a private perspective, while the other definition is based on a social perspective. From a private perspective, an energy efficiency gap arises when economic agents do not opt for the most energy-efficient technology, even though this technology may minimise their private lifetime costs and is therefore cost-effective. In this situation, we have the following inequality:

$$P_e^D + \sum_{t=1}^{T} \frac{P_t^E \cdot C_{et}}{(1+r)^t} < P_I^D + \sum_{t=1}^{T} \frac{P_t^E \cdot C_{it}}{(1+r)^t} \tag{5.4}$$

Where:
P_e^D: Price of the efficient durable
P_I^D: Price of the inefficient durable
P_t^E: Energy price at period t

C_{et}: Energy consumption at period t for an energy-efficient durable

C_{it}: Energy consumption at period t for an energy-inefficient durable

r: Discount rate

t: Time

T: Total lifespan of the durable

Both sets of lifetime costs (the one for the efficient technology on the left-hand side of the expression above and the one for the inefficient technology on the right-hand side) are based on an energy-efficient usage of the durable or technology, but one technology (the efficient one) is associated with lower operating costs due to lower energy consumption.

   An energy efficiency gap, from a social point of view, is said to occur when consumers or firms do not opt for the most energy-efficient technology, even if it minimises social lifetime costs and is therefore cost-effective. Mathematically, this can be expressed as the following inequality:

$$P_e^D + \sum_{t=1}^{T} \frac{P_t^E \cdot C_{et}}{(1+r)^t} < P_I^D + \sum_{t=1}^{T} \frac{P_t^E \cdot C_{it} + EC_t}{(1+r)^t} \tag{5.5}$$

Where:

P_e^D: Price of the efficient durable

P_I^D: Price of the inefficient durable

P_t^E: Energy price at period t

C_{et}: Energy consumption at period t for an energy-efficient durable

C_{it}: Energy consumption at period t for an energy-inefficient durable

r: Discount rate

t: Time

T: Total lifespan of the durable

EC_t: External costs at period t for the energy-inefficient durable

On the right-hand side of this inequality, the social cost of using the inefficient technology (EC_t) is included in the operating costs. Note that even though we do not mention external costs on the left-hand side of this expression, we cannot always rule out that efficient technologies do not have external costs. An example to illustrate these different lifetime costs could be the choice of a heating system using renewable energy on the left-hand side of the inequality, in comparison to a heating system relying on oil on the right-hand side. The environmental impact of the oil-based heating system is represented by the social cost EC. It is important to note that the absence of an energy efficiency gap from a private perspective does not imply that there is no social energy efficiency gap. In fact, we can observe situations where the least efficient and most environmentally damaging technology has lower lifetime costs than the most efficient and sustainable technologies, if we do not consider the external costs. In such cases, the decision of consumers who choose the technology that damages the environment is an optimal decision from a private point of view, but it is not optimal for society.

Table 5.4 Factors contributing to energy efficiency gap

Traditional market failures	Behavioural anomalies	Non-market failures

• Negative externalities
• Imperfect information
• Asymmetric information
• Split-incentive/ principal–agent issue
• Positive externalities
• Capital market imperfection
	• Bounded rationality
	  • Cognitive limitations to performing an investment analysis
	• Loss aversion
	  ○ Status quo bias
	  ○ Endowment effect
	• Limited attention
	• Present bias
	• Bounded willpower
	  • Cognitive dissonance
		• Hidden costs
		• Uncertainty

5.4.2   Barriers to Energy Efficiency

Several factors contribute to the energy efficiency gap, each of which can be categorised as either traditional market failures, behavioural anomalies that can also be considered to be market failures as discussed in Chapter 2, or non-market failures. Table 5.4 presents the barriers to energy efficiency investments.

The most important market failures that serve as barriers to investments in energy efficiency, which we also discussed in Chapter 2, are recapped here. As already mentioned, the presence of negative externalities implies that the operating cost of using energy-inefficient and polluting technologies does not capture the true social cost and, therefore, these technologies may appear to be less costly for buyers. Asymmetric and imperfect information imply a situation wherein buyers of energy technologies may be partially ignorant of the existence of new and energy-efficient technologies, while sellers, having more knowledge, could try to exploit this information to their advantage, potentially hurting the welfare of buyers. Split incentives arise when the person or institution ultimately responsible for making investments in energy efficiency (the agent) is not the one responsible for the payment of bills for energy consumption. Positive externalities give rise to situations in which the early adopters of a new energy-efficient technology share their experiences of using it with potential (new) adopters without being paid for this service. Imperfections in the capital market can also serve as a barrier to energy-efficient investments.

The presence of behavioural anomalies, as also explained in Chapter 2, may further create barriers towards achieving energy efficiency. For instance, the presence of cognitive limitations may lead to difficulties in computing the lifetime costs of different energy technologies. This situation could induce the buyer of an energy technology to choose a technology based on the purchase price, and not on its lifetime costs. Likewise, buyers may give limited attention to the future operating costs of an energy technology, because they are not as salient as the purchase price at the moment the consumer makes the purchase decision. In this case as well, the lifetime costs are not being factored in. Furthermore, the presence of status-quo bias and/or the endowment effect, that is, a tendency to give more value to technologies that are owned and better known, also reduces the probability of opting for new energy-efficient technologies. Finally, the presence of the so-called cognitive dissonance gap and myopia in intertemporal choices can create additional barriers to investment in energy efficiency. We observe a cognitive dissonance gap when there is a mismatch between our beliefs and actions. For instance, we may believe that buying a less powerful car is essential for the environment, yet fail to do it. Myopia is mainly due to present bias, that is, the tendency of people to give more weight to rewards in the near future rather than in the distant future, because of varying discount rates. For instance, buyers may give more weight to the upfront cost of a heating system and tend to undervalue future operating costs.

Finally, non-market failures may also serve as barriers towards energy efficiency investments; examples include the hidden costs of installing and operating a new energy technology or uncertainty about the advantages and disadvantages of using this new technology. For instance, a wood pellet-based heating system has some hidden costs, such as the time it takes to load the stove with wood or to clean the stove. The uncertainty about the true advantages of owning a new energy-efficient technology can also be large, because of its long life cycle, as previously mentioned, and the irreversibility of typical energy investments.

For instance, the real advantages of using a heating system based on new technology can only be assessed after 15–20 years. Moreover, in this case, delaying the decision to adopt a new heating system in order to acquire more information about its functioning from other adopters creates an option value. Such situations imply that the implicit discount rate used by the buyers to value these technologies is likely to be much higher than the one defined by the market, and therefore, the importance of future operating costs in the investment analysis diminishes.

From an energy policy perspective, it is important to underline that only the presence of barriers in the form of market failures and behavioural anomalies (and not non-market failures) justify state intervention.

Finally, it can be interesting to see how some of the barriers discussed and illustrated in Table 5.4 affect elements of the expression used to compute the lifetime costs. For instance, as can be seen in Equation 5.6, limited attention suggests that individuals do not completely consider the operating costs ($P_t^E \cdot C_t$) in their choice. Present bias influences the choice of the discount factor; consumers characterised by present bias tend to give more weight to the initial price than to operating costs. Bounded rationality, which can be characterised by the endowment effect, *status quo* bias, or cognitive limitations, influences the exactitude with which individuals undertake calculations of lifetime costs.

Given that investment decisions are very relevant for the energy transition and behavioural anomalies can be important barriers, in Section 5.5, we propose an in-depth discussion on the role of bounded rationality, cognitive skills, and knowledge in decision-making strategies related to households' investments in the energy sector.

$$P_E^D + \sum_{t=1}^{T} \frac{\overbrace{P_t^E \cdot C_{e_t}}^{\text{Energy cost: limited attention}}}{\underbrace{(1+r)^t}_{\text{Discount factor: present bias}}} < P_I^D + \sum_{t=1}^{T} \frac{(P_t^E \cdot C_{i_t}) + \overbrace{EC_t}^{\text{Externality}}}{(1+r)^t} \tag{5.6}$$

5.5   Bounded Rationality and Energy-related Financial Literacy

As we discussed in Section 5.4 of this chapter, in order to make informed decisions on the purchase of durables, individuals and firms need to have information as well as the skills to perform an investment analysis or to compute the lifetime costs. In this section, we explore the role of bounded rationality, and in particular the lack of financial or investment knowledge and skills in the selection of the decision-making strategy related to the choice of energy technologies in more detail. We are, therefore, interested, to discuss more in details the specific anomaly of cognitive and knowledge limitations related to investment decisions.

5.5.1   Decision-making Strategies

A household or a firm may adopt two kinds of strategies in the choice of a new energy technology (such as an electrical appliance or a heating system), as described in Figure 5.9. An economic agent who adopts a rational decision-making approach will make the effort to actually calculate the lifetime cost of various possible technologies, and then choose the technology that minimises these costs based on the upfront price, energy price, intensity of use, the discount rate, and the lifetime of the technology.

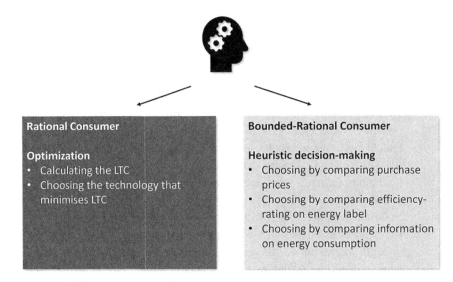

Figure 5.9 Different decision-making strategies

A less rational economic agent would adopt a heuristic decision-making strategy, which in this context could involve making the decision based on a simple comparison of purchasing prices, efficiency ratings, energy consumption levels, as well as technology choices.

Generally, the choice of the decision-making strategy depends also on the level of financial knowledge for making investment decisions in energy technologies. This type of knowledge can be measured using the energy-related financial literacy concept, which is defined as 'the combination of energy-related knowledge and cognitive abilities that is needed in order to take decisions with respect to investments for the production of energy services and their consumption' (Blasch et al., 2021) [83]. In general, consumers who have higher levels of energy-related financial literacy tend to follow a more rational decision-making process than consumers or firms characterised by low levels of energy-related financial literacy.

To measure the level of energy-related financial literacy, researchers organise surveys with households, asking questions related to:

- Their knowledge of energy consumption, energy prices, as well as on levels of energy efficiency of energy technologies.
- Their ability to calculate the lifetime costs in simple situations.
- Their capacity to know and use interest rates in simple calculations.

For instance, Blasch et al. (2021) [83] use the following question to measure the ability to compute the lifetime cost: 'Suppose you own your home, and that your fridge breaks down and you need to replace it. As a replacement, you can choose between two alternatives that are identical in terms of design, capacity, and the quality of the cooling system. Fridge A sells for CHF 400 and consumes 300 kWh of electricity per year. Fridge B has a retail price of CHF 500 and consumes 280 kWh of electricity per year. Assume that the average cost of energy is CHF 0.20 per kWh, that the two models both have a lifespan of 15 years and that you would get a return of 0 per cent from any alternative investment of your money. Which purchase choice would minimise the total costs of owning the fridge over its lifespan?'

- Fridge A
- Fridge B
- Fridges A and B are equivalent in terms of total costs
- Don't know

In this case, the correct answer is Fridge A, that is, the less efficient fridge actually has a lower lifetime cost.

Empirical studies suggest that in general, both in industrialised and developing countries, the level of energy-related financial literacy is weak [83, 84]. One implication of a low level of energy-related financial literacy is that individuals will tend to ignore the lifetime costs during the decision-making process. Indeed, some studies indicate that people with low levels of energy-related financial literacy tend to adopt less energy-efficient technologies [83].

Empower the consumer! Energy-related financial literacy and its implications for economic decision-making

Blasch et al. (2021) [83] measured the levels of energy-related financial literacy by conducting a relatively large-scale European household survey, and explored the socioeconomic factors that influenced its levels. The empirical results showed that energy-related financial literacy was low, with female respondents faring worse than males. This gender gap existed in various countries: females were found to have lower levels of literacy compared to males in Italy, Switzerland as well as in the Netherlands. The total score used to assess energy-related financial literacy was based on the number of correct responses in eight questions, with the score for each correct answer being 1, and there was no penalty for wrong answers. The empirical results also suggest that survey participants did not perform equally well in all aspects of energy-related financial literacy. Knowledge of energy prices was relatively low, and only 45 per cent of the participants answered questions about calculating the lifetime cost of appliances correctly. Most importantly, the authors empirically show the association between limited energy knowledge and skills in performing investment analysis on the adoption of energy-efficient light bulbs. The results reported in this study suggest that introducing programmes that increase the energy-specific financial knowledge could increase the adoption of energy-efficient durables.

Energy-related financial literacy and bounded rationality in appliance replacement attitudes: evidence from Nepal

Filippini et al. (2019) [84] studied the level and determinants of energy-related financial literacy using a sample of 2000 Nepalese households from Biratnagar, Nepal, the second largest city in the country. The empirical results indicated that the level of income, education, and gender played an important role in determining their energy-related financial literacy. Furthermore, the econometric analysis provides suggestive evidence that higher levels of energy-related financial literacy were associated with more rational decision-making. The paper showed that energy-related financial literacy could contribute towards ensuring sustainable development over the coming decades, as increased knowledge about lifetime costs and improved computational abilities may facilitate investment in energy-efficient technologies in developing countries.

5.6   Rebound Effect

Adopting a more energy-efficient technology generally reduces energy consumption per unit of energy services produced. This reduction in energy consumption leads to a reduction in the cost of producing energy services, at least a reduction in the variable costs (namely, energy costs). In turn, the decrease in the production cost per unit produced of energy services may increase the demand for the same. This may reduce the impact on energy consumption of the new, more efficient technology. This phenomenon is called the rebound effect.

For example, an increase in the energy efficiency of a car results in lower levels of gasoline consumption per kilometre, and thus at the margin, a lower cost per kilometre driven. This reduction in cost per kilometre may lead consumers to drive more kilometres, and thus chip off some of the energy savings due to the increase in fuel efficiency. As an extension of this example, some of the money saved in road transportation due to lower gasoline consumption could be used by the consumer in other energy-using activities, such as flying in aeroplanes for travel more frequently. This, again, would lead to a smaller overall reduction in energy use than initially projected. The first effect, that is, the change in energy consumption from the utilisation of the new technology, is called the direct rebound effect, whereas the second change, that is, the change in energy consumption in other activities unrelated to the use of the new technology, is called the indirect rebound effect.

The rebound effect can be illustrated graphically. For pedagogical reasons, in Figures 5.10 and 5.11, we assume that adopting a new energy-efficient technology leads to a decrease in the total costs of producing the same amount of energy services (represented by the parallel shift of the isocost line).

In Figure 5.10, we illustrate the effect of the introduction of an energy-saving technology on the optimal use of two inputs, energy and capital, and on the cost of producing the energy service. The vertical axis shows capital use (C) and the horizontal axis shows energy consumption (E). As is visible from the graph, it is possible to produce the same amount of energy services (ES_1) using a new and more energy-efficient technology which consumes less energy and more capital. The old optimal input combination is represented by point A, whereas the new combination that corresponds to the use of the new technology is represented by point B. From the graph, it is also clear that switching to the new technology reduces the total cost paid for producing the energy service (point B lies on a lower isocost line than point A). As a result, the unit price of the energy service decreases. This decrease in the unit price

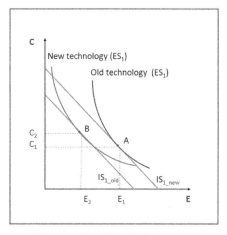

Figure 5.10 Simple rebound effects

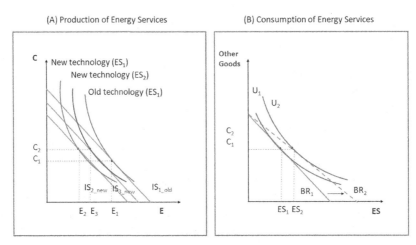

Figure 5.11 Rebound effect and production and consumption of energy services

can, depending on the value price elasticities, lead to an increase in the demand for energy services. In Figure 5.11, we illustrate this phenomenon in more detail.

Figure 5.11A shows the change in energy demand due to the new energy-efficient technology, whereas Figure 5.11B illustrates the change in the demand for energy services. The graph on the left is similar to the one in Figure 5.10, with capital (C) plotted on the y-axis and energy consumption (E) on the x-axis. The second graph, on the other hand, has energy service consumption (ES) plotted on the horizontal axis and consumption of all other goods on the vertical axis.

As in the Figure 5.10, Figure 5.11A shows that the newer technology initially results in lower energy consumption and higher capital consumption for the same level of energy service (ES_1), compared to the old technology. This change constitutes a decrease of energy consumption from E_1 to E_2 with an increase in capital from C_1 to C_2. However, this is not the end of the story. This is because lower levels of energy consumption will also decrease the unit production cost of the energy service (since energy is an input in the production process for energy services).

This may have an impact on the demand for energy services, which is best explained using Figure 5.11B. In this figure, the household is initially consuming ES_1 level of energy services produced using the older technology. Through the mechanisms put in force when the new technology is adopted, however, the budget restriction (BR_1) in Figure 5.11B rotates outwards because of the reduction in the unit cost of the energy service. This leads to a flatter slope for the budget restriction represented by BR_2. Thus, energy service consumption increases from ES_1 to ES_2, and therefore, energy consumption increases. This increase in energy consumption after the adoption of the new technology is illustrated in Figure 5.11A, by the shift from E_2 to E_3. The distance between E_2 and E_3 shows the rebound effect. In conclusion, the adoption of new technology leads to a final decrease in the energy consumption in this example (from points E_1 to E_3); however, this decline is lower than what would have been in the absence of a rebound effect (to point E_2).

The rebound effect and its size are commonly disputed among economists. Some economists argue that these effects are likely to be quite minor, given the inelasticity of demand for energy services and the small share that energy costs constitute of the total living expenses of a household. Other scholars maintain that the rebound effect might, in fact, offset a part of the energy savings gained from increasing energy efficiency.

5.7 Issues in Developing Countries

There are several challenges to achieving energy efficiency improvements in developing countries. In Chapter 2 as well as earlier in this chapter, we discussed the role of market failures in impeding energy efficiency improvements, and how some of these barriers are likely to be more prominent in low and middle-income countries (LMICs). In this section, we will discuss three of these factors again that are relevant for energy efficiency, especially in developing countries, credit/liquidity constraints (or capital market imperfections), and two behavioural anomalies, present bias as well as limited attention. We will then touch upon the notion of poor power quality as well as revenue losses of electric utilities in developing countries also serving as a barrier to energy-efficiency investments. Identifying and evaluating these barriers is important for policymakers to design future interventions.

5.7.1 Market Failures

Capital market imperfections may contribute towards individuals or households being credit-constrained, and thus unable to borrow easily. This situation is particularly salient, and strong, in developing countries. Credit constraints hinder the ability of low-income households from purchasing more energy-efficient technologies, which are likely to be more expensive, even if they are privately optimal. Limited attention, on the other hand, can make it difficult for individuals to be attentive to the operating cost savings from using an appliance, and to factor them in when making investment decisions. It is important to keep in mind that these two barriers are also interlinked: the impact of extending credit to purchase more energy-efficient technologies is plausibly dependent on how inattentive individuals are to future costs (since taking a loan involves postponing costs).

Role of credit provision and enhancing attention in facilitating adoption of energy-efficient technologies

In a study, Berkouwer et al. (2022) [85] used the setting of a field experiment among urban households in Kenya to evaluate the barriers towards the adoption of energy-efficient cook stoves. They found that an intervention that increased the salience to the energy savings from using this stove had no effect on the willingness to pay for these new stoves while extending access to credit (through loans) doubled the willingness to pay for them. The weak result on enhancing attentiveness to the cost savings may be due to the high value of savings that households would have experienced in this case. Thus, in this case, credit constraints served as the more critical barrier towards the adoption of more efficient technologies. However, the authors also articulated that there are challenges towards simply increasing the availability of credit to increase energy efficiency, such as adverse selection in credit markets and the associated information asymmetries.

Myopia or present bias is yet another important factor that may hinder the adoption of energy-efficient technologies. As we discussed in Chapter 2, present-biased individuals de-emphasise future energy (or cost) savings and weigh immediate costs more heavily. Since investment in energy efficiency involves trading off between short-run costs and long-run benefits, myopic or present-biased individuals are likely to experience time-inconsistent decision-making. A repercussion of this behaviour is that these individuals have high short-term discount rates, but a decrease in discount rates over the long run. Thus, these individuals have a tendency to procrastinate with respect to long-term investments (such as in energy-efficient heating systems). This is a relevant phenomenon in many developing countries.

Role of present bias in determining under-investment in energy efficiency

Using data from Delhi, India, Fuerst and Singh (2018) [86] evaluated whether present bias influences the decision of individuals to purchase more efficient appliances. They find that more patient (i.e., less present-biased) individuals are more likely to invest in certain types of energy-efficient appliances (such as refrigerators), but not in other appliances that are relatively cheaper, such as light bulbs. Thus, the authors argue that present bias, in turn, is also linked to credit constraints: in the purchase of relatively larger appliances such as fridges, time preferences are likely to play a larger role.

5.7.2   Poor Power Quality

In large parts of the developing world, power supply is either absent or irregular, at best. Many developing countries frequently experience outages, brownouts, and blackouts, as well as load-shedding, sometimes for several hours a day. This unreliability in power can significantly reduce the utilisation of electric appliances as well as households' incentives to invest in energy efficiency, given that operating cost savings may be less than what may be achieved with full-time use of the appliances (i.e., with continuous power supply).

This situation is described in Equation 5.7. The inequality condition that needs to be satisfied for agents to purchase energy-efficient appliances helps us to understand why.

$$P_e^D + \sum_{t=1}^{T} \frac{P_t^E \cdot C_{et}}{(1+r)^t} < P_I^D + \sum_{t=1}^{T} \frac{P_t^E \cdot C_{it}}{(1+r)^t} \tag{5.7}$$

It is clear that in order for the above inequality to hold, it must be the case that the difference in discounted operating costs between energy-inefficient appliances and energy-efficient appliances should be greater than the difference in their purchase prices, P_e^D-P_I^D. However, an irregular power supply (or poor power quality) is likely to reduce the effective usage of appliances, which implies that households may not be able to recover the operating cost savings that are possible from switching to a more energy-efficient appliance (i.e., the difference in operating costs between the less efficient and more efficient appliance may not be higher than the difference in purchase prices). This risk may disincentivise households from investing in energy efficiency in the first place.

5.7.3   Revenue Losses and Investments in Efficient Electricity Networks

In many developing countries, utilities are not always able to recover their costs because of theft, or suboptimal metering or billing. This implies that households will not pay the full cost of electricity that they consume, and therefore the price they face will be lower than the official tariff. This low price will reduce incentives to make efficiency investments in the network. Policymakers often use different strategies to mitigate such losses, such as replacing a fixed monthly electricity fee with metered consumption, using smart metres, or using prepaid electricity metres. It is understood that some of these measures may increase the cost of electricity for poor households. However, these steps are critical to reducing inefficiencies in transmission and distribution, while low-income households should be compensated through other means (such as through receiving benefits from environmental tax reform).

Policy considerations for limiting electricity theft in the developing countries
Jamil and Ahmad (2019) [87] theoretically analysed the case of electricity theft in developing countries. They studied the impact of policy variables such as electric utility wage rates, tariff rates, conviction and fine rates, and the involvement of civil society on the outcome variable of electricity theft. The authors examined both the aspect of consumers involved in electricity thefts and the role of electric utilities. They found that individuals resorted to electricity theft and misreported electricity consumption either to reduce the cost of electricity consumption or to generate illegal incomes for private benefits and that they chose to steal electricity if they felt that the benefits from the activity exceeded the costs (e.g., the fines). They argue that corruption in society may also promote theft, as such activities often go undetected and are not fined. Electricity theft can lead to significant financial losses for utilities and create unattractive investment conditions for the sector. Thus, there is a need for greater involvement and intervention of civil society to help curb corruption and theft in the electricity sector.

Positive spillovers from improvements in energy efficiency in developing countries
Can energy efficiency improvements in developing countries lead to an increase in the reliability of supply? This is the question that Carranza and Meeks (2021) [88] investigated in their study, by implementing a randomised controlled trial in the Kyrgyz Republic. The authors provided subsidies to purchase relatively efficient

light bulbs (compact fluorescent lamps (CFLs)) to some neighbouring households connected to each other through the same transformer. They found that a higher share of usage of CFLs at the transformer level (compared to the relatively inefficient incandescent bulbs) led to fewer outages for all households connected to that transformer, as well as a reduction in overall energy consumption. This study provides yet another example of the positive externalities that can materialise from improvements in energy efficiency.

Evidence on the rebound effect in developing countries

As shown in a study by Davis et al. (2014) [89], a large-scale appliance replacement programme in Mexico in which old appliances (such as refrigerators and air conditioners) were replaced by energy-efficient models was less effective than predicted by engineering estimates. While the authors attributed this underperformance to several factors (including the fact that appliances were not as old and inefficient as predicted in the engineering forecasts), one of the main factors was increased usage of energy-efficient air conditioners, given their lower operating costs, which also increased total energy consumption. Policymakers need to keep in mind that this form of rebound effect may mitigate the effectiveness of energy efficiency improvements in some cases.

5.7.4   Review Questions and Problems

The online question bank contains review questions and problems for this chapter, including solutions (see https://wp-prd.let.ethz.ch/exercisesfortextbookeep/).

6   Energy-related Market Forms

Several markets are associated with the production and consumption of energy sources and energy services. On the one hand, we have classical energy markets, including wholesale markets for energy sources such as oil and gas, or retail markets for gasoline and electricity; on the other hand, there are also a number of energy-related markets such as the market for durable goods such as electrical appliances, heating systems, or cars, the market for energy-saving houses and the market for energy consulting. Traditional textbooks in energy economics generally propose specific chapters for each energy source, for example, a chapter discussing the organisation of the oil market in detail.

In this chapter, we follow another approach. We propose to shortly present the most relevant market forms to understand the functioning of energy markets, along with some examples. For some of these market forms, the presence of economies of scale and economies of scope plays an important role, as we will see. For these reasons, before discussing each single market form, we will introduce these two concepts.

6.1   Introduction

The market forms that can be observed in the energy and energy-related sectors are natural monopolies, monopolistic competition, oligopolies, and perfect competition. Monopolies and oligopolies occur when only one or a few firms, respectively, are present in the market. An example of a monopoly is a firm managing the distribution of gas and electricity to the end consumers. On the other hand, the market for oil is often characterised as an oligopolistic market.

When many firms are present in a market, the market form is either monopolistic competition or perfect competition, depending on whether the products are differentiated, or identical. Durable energy goods are often sold and purchased in markets of monopolistic competition, while the market for wholesale electricity is close to being perfectly competitive, that is, it is reasonably competitive. Figure 6.1 summarises the main characteristics of the four market forms observed in the energy sector.

As mentioned earlier, the type of market form observed in the energy market is also determined by the firms' cost structure. For instance, in some energy markets, the average cost level is strongly influenced by the firm's size. In fact, the production

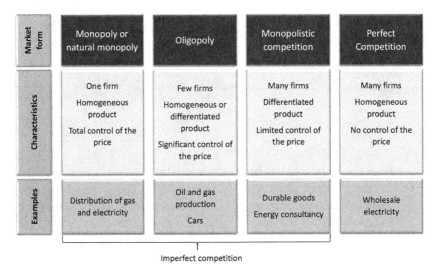

Figure 6.1 Market forms

and distribution of energy are generally characterised by making large-scale invest-ments that have a long lifespan. For instance, the construction of a gas pipeline, or of an electricity transmission line requires making a significant initial investment. More-over, the lifetime of this infrastructure is long, that is, around 40–50 years. Also, the construction of power plants such as hydropower plants, nuclear or coal power plants has similar characteristics, that is, the presence of high initial investment costs and a long lifespan.

Moreover, the share of fixed and variable costs across different technologies is quite heterogeneous. For example, some technologies such as nuclear, hydro, wind, and solar power plants exhibit low variable costs but high fixed costs, whereas gas power plants have relatively low fixed costs but significant variable costs. The presence of sunk costs, that is, expenditures that have been made and cannot be recovered, is also another characteristic of the cost structure of several firms operating in the energy sector. For instance, the expenditures to build a gas pipeline or a dam to produce electricity with a hydropower plant can be considered as sunk costs. Finally, the cost structure of several firms operating in the energy sector is characterised by the presence of external costs, that is, social costs arising due to pollution.

The firms that produce durable goods used for the production of energy services such as electrical appliances, heating systems, and cars also incur high investment costs. Therefore, many energy and energy-related sectors are distinguished by the presence of cost advantages related to the size and volume of production. This cost advantage is an important factor that influences the level of competition that can be observed in these sectors. For this reason, in Section 6.2, we will discuss the concepts of economies of scale and economies of scope in detail.

6.2 Economies of Scale and Scope

6.2.1 Economies of Scale

Economies of scale arise when long-run average total costs (ATCs) fall as the quantity of output increases. This implies that increasing the level of production leads to a reduction in the ATC. Diseconomies of scale, on the other hand, represent a situation in which the long-run ATCs rise as the quantity of output increases. In Figure 6.2, we can observe three typical average cost curves for firms operating in competitive and non-competitive markets. A natural monopoly is characterised by an L-shaped average cost function. Firms operating in a competitive market or in a monopolistically competitive market are characterised by a U-shaped average cost function, whereas firms in an oligopolistic market are characterised by a L/U-shaped average cost function. Note that the optimal size of a firm is determined at the point where the average cost function reaches the minimum. This implies that in a natural monopoly situation, only one very large firm will reach or be close to the optimal size, whereas in an oligopolistic market, only a few firms will reach the optimal size. However, in a perfectly competitive market, the optimal size is relatively small, and therefore attained by several firms.

Traditionally, the magnitude of economies of scale (ES) is measured as the increase in total cost resulting from an increase in output, while holding all other variables constant (*ceteris paribus*). When Equation 6.1 is greater than 1, this indicates that economies of scale exist. In this case, the average costs of a firm decrease as the cumulative output increases. A value below 1 indicates diseconomies of scale, implying the opposite.

$$ES = \frac{1}{\frac{\partial TC}{\partial Y} \cdot \frac{Y}{TC}} = \frac{1}{\frac{\partial \ln TC}{\partial \ln Y}} \tag{6.1}$$

Where:

ES: Economies of scale

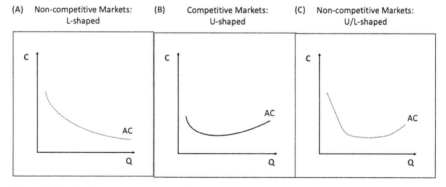

Figure 6.2 Typical average cost curve shapes

TC: Total cost

Y: Output

Equation 6.1, to compute economies of scale, is 1 divided by the cost elasticity with respect to output. Remember that this cost elasticity is equal to the partial derivative of the total cost with respect to output, multiplied by the output divided by the total cost.

The definition of economies of scale defined by Equation 6.1 is relevant for firms with a production structure that is centralised in space, such as firms that produce heating systems or electrical appliances, and not for production structures characterised by a network. The definition of economies of scale needs to be differentiated for network industries, that is, for industries with a production activity based on a spatial network. In the energy sector, we can identify some activities such as the transport and distribution of gas, oil, and electricity that are based on a spatial network composed of pipelines, or high- and low-voltage electricity lines. In this case, as described in Figure 6.3, the increase in the size of a firm can take place along two dimensions: an increase in the output or an increase in the size of the service area or network. For instance, an electricity distribution firm may increase its size either by increasing the volume of electricity distributed, extending the size of the network, or both. Therefore, for network industries, it is necessary to make the distinction between economies of density and economies of scale. While measuring the economies of density, we assume that the size of the network remains constant, whereas while measuring the economies of scale, we assume that both output and network size vary.

The degree of economies of density (ED) is measured as the increase in total cost (TC) determined by an increase in output (Y), while holding all other variables and the network size constant.

A value of economies of density (defined in Equation 6.2) greater than 1 indicates that economies of density exist. In this case, the average costs of a firm decrease as the output increases. A value below 1 indicates diseconomies of density, which implies the opposite.

$$ED = \frac{1}{\frac{\partial \ln TC}{\partial \ln Y}} \tag{6.2}$$

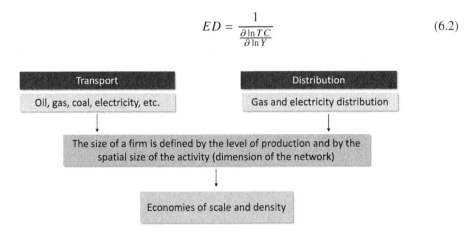

Figure 6.3 Economies of scale and density

Where:

ED: Economies of density

TC: Total cost

Y: Output

Economies of density in networked industries are calculated as one divided by the cost elasticity with respect to the output. Note that this formula is identical to that used to compute the economies of scale in non-networked industries.

Information on the level of economies of density is important for policymakers to decide whether a local monopoly or local competition is the most efficient market form for the distribution of gas (or electricity). In the presence of economies of density, a solution based on a franchised local monopoly would be the most efficient. With diseconomies of density, local competition is the most efficient market form.

The economies of scale (ES) for a networked industry are measured as the increase in total costs (TC) resulting from a proportional increase of output (Y) and network size (AS) while holding all other variables constant.

$$ES = \frac{1}{\frac{\partial \ln TC}{\partial \ln Y} + \frac{\partial \ln TC}{\partial \ln AS}} \tag{6.3}$$

Where:

ES: Economies of scale (for a network industry)

TC: Total cost

Y: Output

AS: Network size

Similar to the classic definition of economies of scale, a value greater than one means that economies of scale are present. The presence of these economies of scale implies that the average costs of a firm decrease as physical output and area size proportionally increase. This measure is important for analysing, for example, the cost impact of merging two gas or electricity distribution firms operating in two different but adjacent regions. In the presence of economies of scale, the merger of the two firms would reduce the ATCs. On the contrary, in the case of diseconomies of scale, a solution based on two firms operating in two different but adjacent regions would be optimal.

6.2.1.1 Application: Estimation of the Values of the Economies of Scale and Density

Generally, for estimating the values of the economies of scale and density, researchers follow the simplified steps described later.

First, researchers must define a total cost function including the factors that determine the cost. Here is a possible example of a cost model used to estimate the value of the economies of density and scale for a sample of electricity distribution firms:

$$TC = f(Y, AS, PL, PC) \tag{6.4}$$

Where TC represents total cost, Y is the output, AS is area size, and PL and PC represent the price of labour and the price of capital, respectively. This model specification doesn't consider the price of electricity, because the firms considered in the analysis are just distributing electricity, and not buying and selling it.

In the second step, researchers need to choose a functional form. The most used functional forms for the estimation of a cost function are linear, log-log, and trans-log functional forms. Adopting a log-log functional form for Equation 6.4, as an example, yields:

$$\ln TC = \alpha_0 + \alpha_Y \ln Y + \alpha_{AS} \ln AS + \alpha_{PL} \ln PL + \alpha_{PC} \ln PC \qquad (6.5)$$

Following this, data collection can be administered to collect information on the dependent and independent variables and the coefficients can be estimated using econometric methods.

Finally, the computation of economies of density and scale is performed using formulas presented earlier (Equations 6.2 and 6.3).

In Table 6.1, we provide the results obtained from the estimation of the cost function represented by Equation 6.5 using data from a sample of Swiss electricity distribution companies and using STATA as the econometric software. The computation has been conducted on data collected by the Centre of Energy Policy and Economics at ETH Zurich.

The regression output of Table 6.1 originates from a simple analysis performed using a data sample with 179 observations. Most of the coefficients are statistically significant. The value of the coefficient of determination (or R-squared) for this model is 0.96. This indicator provides information on the goodness-of-fit measure for linear regression models and denotes the percentage of the variance in the dependent variable that can be explained by the explanatory variables. The value of 0.96 indicates a strong model fit. The F-statistic for this model is 1268.24, which indicates that the model with these four explanatory variables provides a better fit than a model that contains no independent variables.

The coefficients estimated for computing the impact of these variables on the total cost can be found in the 'Coef'. column of the table. We must remember that in the log-log functional form, the interpretation of the estimated coefficients is straightforward in terms of cost elasticities. For instance, the coefficient of 0.629 for the output variable indicates that a 1 per cent increase in output is associated with a total cost increase of about 0.63 per cent. Applying Equations 6.2 and 6.3, we can compute the value of the economies of density and economies of scale for network industries. The value of the measure of economies of density is equal to 1.58, whereas the measure of economies

Table 6.1 Estimated coefficients

ln(TC)	Coef.	Standard Error	t	$P > |t|$	[95 Confidence Interval]	
ln(Y)	0.63	0.03	20.79	0	0.57	0.69
ln(AS)	0.32	0.03	9.49	0	0.25	0.38
ln(PL)	0.08	0.11	0.72	0.48	−0.14	0.29
ln(PK)	0.26	0.03	7.83	0	0.19	0.32
Constant	−1.29	0.67	−1.93	0.06	−2.6	0.03

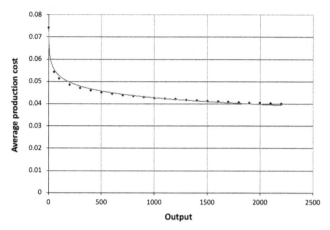

Figure 6.4 Average distribution cost

of scale is equal to 1.06. In line with the theory, we can conclude that the electricity distribution companies in this example exhibit economies of scale and density, which leads them to operate in a system of natural monopoly.

Using the estimated coefficients reported earlier, it is possible to derive the average cost function, and this is depicted in Figure 6.4, which aids us in understanding economies of density. As expected, the average cost of distributing electricity is decreasing with an increase in the output, as shown by the dotted curve, while the service area is kept constant.

6.2.2 Economies of Scope and Economies of Vertical Integration

Another important concept to better understand the cost advantages in the energy sector is the notion of economies of scope. Economies of scope are observed when costs can be decreased by the joint production of several outputs. For instance, in the energy sector, it is important to know whether it is better to organise electricity and gas distribution by two separate firms, or just by one firm. The degree of economies of scope in the production of two products is calculated as the ratio of the difference between the separate production costs and the cost of joint production, to the cost of joint production of all products.

$$ESC = \frac{C(Y_1, 0) + C(0, Y_2) - C(Y_1, Y_2)}{C(Y_1, Y_2)} \tag{6.6}$$

Where:
ESC: Economies of scope
C: Cost
Y_i: Output of firms 1 and 2

where $C(Y_1, 0)$ is the total cost when the level of production of output 2 (Y_2) is zero. In the same way, $C(0, Y_2)$ is the total cost when output 1 (Y_1) is zero, and $C(Y_1, Y_2)$ is the total cost when both outputs are produced. A positive (negative) value for the above expression suggests the economies (diseconomies) of scope, that is, it is more efficient for both firms to produce together.

A variant of the concept of economies of scope is the measure of economies of vertical integration. This concept is relevant to the discussion of the organisation of the electricity market. Economies of vertical integration (EVI) are observed when the costs of jointly producing a product across different production stages are lower than the costs of producing the product across different stages. For example, in presence of economies of vertical integration, organising the production and distribution of electricity in one firm, and not in separate firms, will lower the average production costs. The level of EVI across both stages of production can be calculated as the ratio of excess costs of separate production to the costs of joint production in one firm:

$$EVI = \frac{C(Y_1,0) + C(0,Y_2) - C(Y_1,Y_2)}{C(Y_1,Y_2)} \tag{6.7}$$

Where:

EVI: Economies of vertical integration

C: Cost

Y: Output across different stages

where $C(Y_1,0)$ is the total cost when the level of production of product 2 (Y_2) is zero, for instance, the firm is only involved in energy production. Similarly, $C(0,Y_2)$ is the total cost when the level of production of product 1 (Y_1) is zero, that is, the firm only operates in the distribution stage. A positive (negative) value of EVI implies economies (diseconomies) of vertical integration. The difference between Equations 6.6 and 6.7 is that Y_1 and Y_2 in the latter equation refer to the production and distribution of the same product, and not to two different products, such as electricity and gas.

In general, the empirical literature on the estimation of the economies of scope in the distribution of gas and electricity and the economies of vertical integration in the electricity sector confirms the presence of these economies across different settings.

Economies of scale and scope in Multiutilities

Farsi et al. (2008) [90] conducted an empirical analysis of the economies of scale and scope using data on a sample of Swiss utilities distributing electricity, gas, and water. The results showed that there existed considerable economies of scope and scale overall, but that there was also significant variation in scope economies across firms due to unobserved heterogeneity. These results suggest that, at least in Switzerland, an unbundling of the activities (distribution of gas, electricity, and water) across separate firms may have led to an increase in costs.

Economies of vertical integration in the Swiss electricity sector

Fetz and Filippini (2010) [91] empirically analysed the prevalence of economies of scale and vertical integration in the Swiss electricity sector. The empirical analysis is based on a sample of seventy-four firms during the 9-year period between

1997 and 2005. Thirty-six firms were integrated, and involved in both electricity distribution and generation; nine firms were only electricity distributors, while twenty-nine firms were only generating electricity. They used different econometric specifications for the estimation of the cost functions of these firms, and the results suggested the existence of economies of vertical integration and economies of scale in the Swiss electricity sector.

6.3   Monopoly

6.3.1   Monopolies in the Energy Sector

A monopoly is a market form in which a firm is the sole seller of a good that doesn't have close substitutes. In this situation, the monopolist has control over the price and the output. The main cause of monopoly is the presence of barriers to entry for other firms, such as:

1. An important natural resource is controlled by a single firm or by the state.
2. The government provides one firm with the exclusive right to produce a good or to exploit a natural resource.
3. Due to the presence of economies of scale, production by a single producer is less costly than the production of the same level of output by a large number of producers, that is, it is natural and more efficient that only one firm operates in the market.

The last situation is called a natural monopoly and is characterised by the presence of decreasing average costs, that is, the presence of economies of scale beyond the market demand curve. Therefore, the production costs of satisfying the market demand will be minimised by having only one firm in the market.

A monopoly has the following characteristics:

- There is only one firm in the market.
- There are no close substitutes for the product.
- Entry into the market is not possible because of state intervention or because of economies of scale.
- There is perfect information on prices, quantities, and characteristics of the product.
- The firm faces a downward-sloping demand curve.
- The firm can influence the price, that is, it is not a price-taker as in perfect competition.
- Economic agents are rational (firms are profit-maximising, whereas consumers are utility-maximising).
- There are no external costs or benefits.

In the energy sector, we can observe a situation of monopoly because of the presence of economies of scale and/or economies of density, or because the state owns a natural resource such as water, or land with gas or oil reserves.

If the state owns a natural resource, it can exploit it directly, or assign the right to a firm to exploit it. For instance, the state can assign a hydropower plant the right to exploit the water to produce electricity or the right to an oil company to drill in an oil field. The right to exploit a natural resource is generally assigned with a franchise agreement. For instance, a negotiated contract between the state and the energy company for the use of the natural resource is defined. The contract often specifies the period of service and a fee to be remitted back to the state. In the case of extraction of oil or gas from public lands, this fee is called a royalty, whereas in the case of hydropower plants, the state charges a water fee.

6.3.2   Application: Resource Rent in the Hydropower Sector

Economically speaking, the fee charged for the use of a natural resource should be calculated on the basis of the concept of resource rent, that is, the difference between the total revenues and the total production costs that include a normal return on capital. Resource rent is mainly determined by natural differences between production sites that imply different production costs.

As discussed by Ricardo (1817) [92], the resource rent in the agricultural sector is the surplus value, that is, the price minus the average production costs of a crop. The resource rent is determined by the heterogeneity in the levels of productivity at different sites. A site with less favourable characteristics will – *ceteris paribus* – experience higher production costs and, thus, with an exogenously given price, make lower economic profits. In the hydropower sector, we can observe plants with different production costs due to different environmental conditions. For instance, some plants have been constructed in remote areas. Therefore, the investment cost per installed kW was higher than the one needed to construct a plant at a favourable production site. This implies that, with an exogenously given price, the operators of the plants located in favourable sites earn a higher resource rent in comparison to the operators of the plants operating in less favourable environmental conditions. The concept of resource rent can be shown in a graph. Figure 6.5 illustrates the production situation of four different hydropower plants that produce in different locations. To simplify the presentation of this concept, we assume that for each firm, the level of total average cost and marginal cost (MC) is the same and constant. Plants A, B, C, and D show different total average production costs. The price P_m is yielded by the intersection of the aggregate demand and supply curves.

In Figure 6.5, plant D is the marginal producer. This producer, given the market price P_m, just covers the average cost. The other producers receive a resource rent since their average production costs are below the market price. The resource rents RR_A, RR_B, and RR_C are obtained by multiplying the quantity with the difference between the market price and the respective production costs.

From an economic point of view, the fee for the exploitation of the natural resource should be based on the level of the resource rent. Some governments use a so-called resource rent tax (RRT), that is, the value of the resource rent will be taxed at a rate

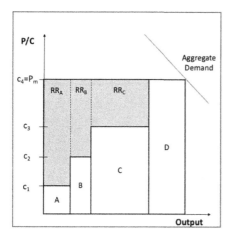

Figure 6.5 Different producers and resource rents (marginal costs = average costs)

that is generally lower than 100 per cent to keep incentives to the firms to produce in a cost-efficient way. For instance, in Norway, the RRT on hydropower is 45 per cent.

6.3.3   Application: Natural Monopoly

In the case of a natural monopoly, the cost structure of the sector is characterised by decreasing long-run average costs. For example, the gas and electricity distribution sectors are considered natural monopolies. In fact, as already discussed, these sectors are depicted by the presence of economies of density and scale. Figure 6.6 presents the typical situation of a natural monopoly with decreasing average cost (AC) and negative sloped downward demand function (D). The monopolist can apply several pricing strategies. Point A (P_1, Q_1) represents the combination that gives the monopolist the possibility to maximise the profit. The optimal quantity to maximise the profit is obtained where the MC is equal to the marginal revenue (MR). Given this optimal quantity, the monopolist sets the price based on the demand function. In this case, the price is higher than the average cost and, therefore, the monopolist is making an economic profit and producing a quantity of electricity or gas, for instance, that is lower than the optimal combination represented by the point C (P_3, Q_3) where MC is equal to the marginal benefit represented by the demand function. Of course, the optimal combination of price and quantity (point C) is not attractive for the firm because the price (P_3) is lower than the average cost and, therefore, the firm would make a loss. An alternative to these two pricing strategies is to set the price at the level of the average cost, that is, the combination of price and quantity defined by point B (P_2, Q_2).

In general, to prevent a natural monopolist from exploiting market power and adopting an inefficient pricing policy, such as the one described by point A, the government often intervenes in the market and regulates the price set by the monopolist. The regulation is usually organised through a regulatory agency that could use traditional as well as relatively modern regulation methods.

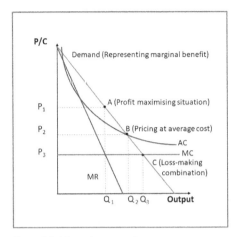

Figure 6.6 Natural monopoly

6.3.4   Regulation Methods

A regulatory agency might apply two different kinds of regulations to influence the prices and outputs of a monopoly firm, that is, traditional methods such as rate of return (RoR) regulation, or modern methods based on incentive regulation schemes such as price-cap regulation, revenue-cap regulation, or yardstick competition. Currently, many regulatory agencies around the world use modern incentive regulation schemes, while some still adhere to traditional regulation methods. In the following discussion, we briefly present these methods.

6.3.4.1   Rate of Return Regulation

With RoR regulation, the regulatory authority limits the RoR on capital invested, instead of directly regulating the price. Note that the direct regulation of the price is often very difficult because precise information on the production costs of the firms is not easily obtainable.

The objective of RoR regulation is to force the company to set the price at the average cost level as a response to the fixed RoR. For instance, this type of regulation is still used to regulate gas and electricity distribution firms in some states in the United States and in Switzerland. In Figure 6.7, the price implied by RoR regulation corresponds to point B.

In mathematical terms, the RoR on the capital invested in a company is represented by the ratio of the accounting profit (revenue minus operational and non-operational costs) to the value of the stock of the company (K). Consider a firm that uses only three inputs: capital (K), labour (L), and energy (E), in this case, the formula to compute the RoR on investment is:

$$RoR = \frac{P_Q Q - P_L L - P_E E - \alpha K - I}{K} \tag{6.8}$$

Where:

RoR: Rate of return on investment

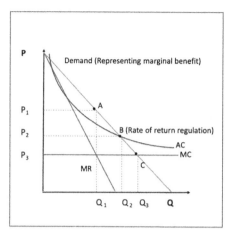

Figure 6.7 Natural monopoly and rate of return regulation

P_Q: Price of the product
Q: Quantity
P_L: Price of labour
L: Labour
P_E: Price of energy
E: Energy
α : Rate of depreciation
K: Capital (assumption only equity capital)
I: Tax

A regulation that focuses on the RoR intends to put a ceiling on the maximum permissible RoR.

$$RoR = \frac{P_Q Q - P_L L - P_E E - \alpha K - I}{K} \leq RoR_m \qquad (6.9)$$

Where:
RoR: Rate of return on investment
RoR_m: Rate of return permitted by regulatory authority
P_Q: Price of the product
Q: Quantity
P_L: Price of labour
L: Labour
P_E: Price of energy
E: Energy
α: Rate of depreciation
K: Capital (assumption only equity capital)
I: Tax

One important issue with regard to the RoR regulation is to find the maximal allowed RoR. Many regulatory authorities fix the rate on the level of the average return on capital obtained in similar non-regulated markets.

Table 6.2 Calculation of rate of return

	Initial	Tariff and tax adjustment	After
Revenues	12,000,000	1,000,000	13,000,000
Expenses			
(1) Purchased gas	7,000,000		
(2) Labour	2,000,000		
(3) Depreciation	1,000,000		
(4) Taxes	500,000	50,000	550,000
Total expenses	10,500,000		10,550,000
(5) Accounting profit	1,500,000		2,450,000
Rate base			
(6) Capital	20,000,000		20,000,000
(7) Rate of return = [(5)/(6)]	7.50%		12.25%

Table 6.2 presents a simple example of how a regulatory authority can calculate the RoR for a firm before and after a tariff adjustment by the firm. In this case, the task of the regulatory authority is to verify if the new RoR after the introduction of the tariff adjustment is not higher than the maximum allowed RoR.

6.3.4.2   Example: Rate of Return Regulation for a Gas Distribution Company

As shown in the table, the RoR is computed by dividing the accounting profit by the total value of the capital stock. In this example, the RoR is initially 7.5 per cent. Then the firm decides to propose an increase in the tariff (tariff adjustment). With the new tariff, the RoR becomes 12.25 per cent. The regulatory agency will judge whether this adjusted RoR complies with the maximum allowed level of return. Assuming that the maximum RoR defined by the authority is 8.5 per cent, then the tariff adjustment proposed by the firm and illustrated in Table 6.2 would not be approved.

It is important to keep in mind that the level of the maximum allowed RoR should be sufficiently high to still attract new investments in the sector. If the permitted RoR is too low, firms might not be able to finance new investments and, therefore, cannot guarantee the expected production and quality of service. A problem associated with the RoR regulation is the absence of strong incentives to minimise production costs. In fact, firms can easily reduce the RoR simply by performing some unnecessary investments, or by increasing the salaries of the employees.

In order to solve the inefficiency problem associated with the RoR regulation, economists have developed alternative regulation schemes that are incentive-based. The most utilised incentive-based regulation models are price- and revenue-cap-based, as well as yardstick competition. The general mechanism behind incentive regulation is to separate the price-setting process from the level of production cost of the firm. Instead of the dependence of the price on the own cost, as in the RoR regulation, the price that can be applied by a firm under these incentive schemes depends on the production cost of other firms or on the productivity of other firms.

6.3.4.3   Price-cap and Revenue-cap Regulation

In the case of price-cap regulation, the price-cap, that is, the maximum price that can be applied by a firm, is generally equal to the price of the previous year multiplied by one plus the annual change in the gross domestic product price index minus an adjustment for a change in productivity. A simplified formula used in price cap regulation is:

$$PC_t = PC_{t-1} * (1 + IPC - X) \tag{6.10}$$

Where:

PC_t: Price in year t (Price-Cap)

PC_{t-1}: Price in year $t - 1$

IPC: Annual change in the gross domestic product price index

X: Adjustment for productivity

A key element of Equation 6.10 is the variable X. The regulator can decide to fix the level of X at the level of the average productivity growth rate of the sector, or of the economy. If a firm has a lower productivity growth rate than the sectoral growth rate, then the price adjustment for the firm will be lower than the one that would consider individual productivity. In this case, the firm will not be able to cover the production costs. For example, if a firm has a productivity growth rate of 3 per cent, whereas the sectoral growth rate is 6 per cent, then after the adjustment of the price by the regulator, the firm will not be able to cover all the costs. Therefore, the firm will have a strong incentive to improve the level of productivity. On the other hand, if a firm has a higher productivity growth rate than the sectoral growth rate, then the price adjustment will be higher than the one that would be based on the firm's productivity. This would give the firm the possibility to obtain an economic profit. In this case, the firm has strong incentives to maintain a high level of productivity. Instead of considering the productivity growth rate as the value of X, the regulator can also use the level of cost inefficiency of the firms. In this case, the regulator can use an average value of inefficiency observed in the sector as the value for X. The level of cost inefficiency can be obtained by estimating a cost frontier function using econometric methods. The revenue-cap regulation method is very similar to the price-cap regulation, but in this case, the price cap will be substituted in Formula 6.10 with the revenue cap. This implies that revenue in period 't' is based on revenue in period '$t - 1$', adjusted for inflation and productivity growth rate.

6.3.4.4   Yardstick Regulation

In yardstick regulation, the price that a firm can apply depends on the average cost of other firms. This implies that if the firm is producing in an inefficient way, that is, if it is not minimising the average cost, then its production costs are higher than the production costs of other similar firms. Therefore, the price that the firm can apply would not be high enough to cover its production costs. In this case, the firm will have a strong incentive to introduce measures to produce more efficiently and to reduce its production costs in order to be able to avoid losses. The regulators can estimate the production cost of similar firms by econometric methods, that is, by estimating a total cost function and using the estimated results to obtain the reference costs for each firm.

Role of Rent-seeking or Technological Progress in Maintaining the Monopoly Power of Energy Enterprises: An Empirical Analysis Based on Microdata from China

Du et al. (2020) [93] discussed the prevalence of monopolistic structures among Chinese energy enterprises. Their empirical analysis suggests that this monopolistic behaviour can be attributed to their rent-seeking behaviour in the energy industry, and the authors argue that it also inhibits the technological progress of these enterprises. Incurring expenses on rent-seeking activities is a common approach for state-owned enterprises to keep their monopoly power. However, these tend to be non-productive expenditures. The authors argue that the negative impact on technological progress can be addressed by undertaking research and development activities. Based on their findings, Du et al. (2020) suggest the implementation of policies which can:

1. Reduce factor market distortions, and thereby rent-seeking behaviour to foster technological innovation.
2. Encourage research and development by improving market competitiveness.
3. Increase the role of private capital to improve the management of the industry.

6.4   Perfect Competition

Perfect competition is an important model in economics, although it is not often observed in real-world economic systems because of its restrictive assumptions. In the energy sector, only some markets, such as the wholesale and retail electricity markets, the gasoline market, the heating oil market, and the market for wood pellets, possess many, but not all, of the characteristics of a perfectly competitive market, which are:

- There are many buyers and sellers of the product.
- The sellers offer an identical product.
- There is perfect information on price, quantity, and the characteristics of the product.
- A single firm cannot influence the price, that is, the firms are price takers.
- Firms can enter or exit the market without restriction.
- The cross-price elasticities of demand are infinite.
- Economic agents are rational (firms are profit-maximising, and consumers are utility-maximising).
- There are no external costs or benefits.

Figure 6.8 represents the short-run equilibrium of a firm functioning in a perfectly competitive market, such as a gasoline station located close to several other stations. The firm maximises profit by producing the quantity at which the MR (which is constant in this market form and equals the market price) is equal to the MC. In the figure, the optimal output is Q^*. Because the market price P is higher than the ATC, the firm realises an economic profit represented by the shaded area.

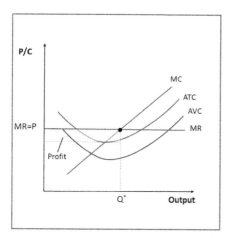

Figure 6.8 Short-run optimal situation of a firm operating in perfect competition

We must note that short-run economic profits stimulate new firms to enter the market. For instance, the presence of economic profit in the short run will increase the number of gasoline stations in the market. This increase will then shift the supply function on the market to the right, reducing the equilibrium price and, therefore, the price for the firm and its level of economic profit. In the long run, the firms operating in a perfectly competitive market cannot realise a positive economic profit, that is, long-run economic profits are equal to zero. As another example, we could think of the market for energy sources used in heating, such as oil and pellets. Let's assume that unexpected technical or political issues introduce supply problems in the heating oil market. In this situation, households equipped with an oil heating system, which is the primary source of heating, as well as a wood pellet stove, will probably begin to use their pellet stoves more intensively to heat the house. This will lead to an increase in demand for wood pellets, and will shift its market demand function to the right, with the consequence of a price increase that will enable the suppliers of wood pellets to realise an economic profit in the short run. However, after a while, new wood pellet suppliers will enter the market, and therefore, these profits will be reduced to zero.

Another important fact to keep in mind when we are discussing firms operating in perfectly competitive markets is that in the short run, the level of the market price should be equal to or higher than the variable costs, otherwise, the firm will cease operation. For instance, in the electricity market, some power plants that are characterised by relatively low variable costs such as hydropower plants will continue to operate in the short run, even with relatively low market prices, as long as the prices are higher than the variable costs. On the other hand, power plants having high variable costs, such as gas power plants, will cease operation during periods of low electricity prices.

6.4.1   Application: The Electricity Market

The importance of electricity markets will increase with the energy transition process. This is due to the fact that in the future, energy systems will be largely electrified.

Figure 6.9 Electricity functions

Therefore, we discuss the electricity sector in further detail in this subsection, given its significance.

As illustrated in Figure 6.9, the electricity sector mainly comprises four activities – generation, transmission, distribution, and sales. In the generation function, electricity is produced with different energy sources and types of plants such as hydro, gas, and solar power plants. The transmission and distribution of electricity are organised through high-, middle-, and low-voltage network lines. Finally, electricity is sold to final consumers in the retail/sales market.

Generally, the electricity sector can be organised using two different approaches:

- The traditional approach, which is characterised by vertically integrated firms performing all four functions (generation, transmission, distribution, and sales).
- The modern approach, where the four functions are separated across different firms (or at least performed by separate units of the same firm), and an electricity market is created. The separation of the firm is also known as the 'unbundling' of the monopoly functions (transmission and distribution) from the competitive market functions (production and sales).

Using the modern approach, electricity is bought and sold on wholesale and retail markets, whereas in the traditional approach, electricity is sold directly by the vertically integrated firms to final consumers. Note that the transmission and distribution functions play an important role in the definition of the level of the final price because these functions account for approximately 50–60 per cent of the final costs per kWh of electricity generated. Of course, this value depends on the organisational form of the utility and the characteristics of the serviced region.

Figures 6.10 to 6.12 illustrate both the traditional and modern versions of the organisation of the electricity sector in a stylised form. In the traditional model depicted in Figure 6.10, we have one vertically integrated electricity company that produces, transmits, distributes, and sells electricity to final consumers. In this model, the final consumer is obliged to enter into a contract for the delivery of electricity with the vertically integrated monopolist. There is no possibility to change or choose another supplier. Some advantages of this model are the possibility to exploit the economies of vertical integration due to lower transaction costs, improved coordination of the operational activities, improved coordination of the investments, and reduced level of risk of the commercial activities. Conversely, this model, based on the presence of a monopoly, also has some drawbacks. For instance, if not well regulated, the vertically integrated monopolist could have inefficiencies in production, suffer from overcapacity, apply non-optimal pricing strategies, and cause delays in the adoption of innovations, such as the exploitation of renewable energy sources.

Vertically integrated company

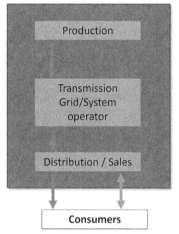

Consumers have to buy electricity from the vertically integrated monopolist (no choice).

Figure 6.10 Traditional market organisation

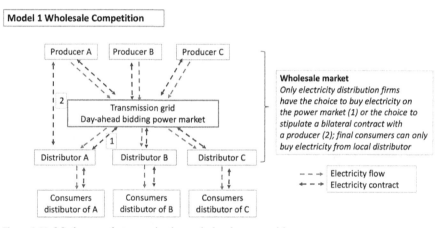

Figure 6.11 Modern market organisation: wholesale competition

The modern organisation of the electric power sector (Figures 6.11 and 6.12), which has been introduced in several countries during the last 30 years through important reforms, is characterised by:

- Consumers' freedom of choice (the consumer can choose the supplier from which to buy electricity);
- Competition in the production and sale of electricity;
- New regulation methods for the functions that remain a natural monopoly, that is, transmission and distribution.

In order to introduce more competition and new regulation methods, the reforms are generally distinguished by the following four main elements:

1. Separation of production and sale functions from the transmission and distribution functions that remain a natural monopoly.

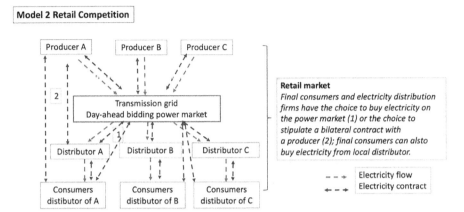

Figure 6.12 Modern market organisation: retail competition

2. Creation of independent firms operating in the production, transmission, distribution, and sale functions.
3. Creation of a power market (day-ahead power market).
4. Creation of a regulation authority.

Generally, as shown in Figures 6.11 and 6.12, a modern electricity sector can have several economic agents and institutions: producers, a company that owns and operates the transmission grid, a power market, electricity distribution companies, a regulatory authority, and consumers. Of course, we should note that there are several variants of the modern organisational form of the electric power sector. Here we describe two simplified versions of a modern organisation of this sector, that is, a market with wholesale competition and a market with competition also in retail sales.

In Figure 6.11, we illustrate the wholesale market model. In this model, competition is incorporated in the wholesale electricity market and not in the retail market. The wholesale model involves buying and selling electricity through an organised market, that is, the day-ahead bidding power market, only to electricity producers and distributors. The final consumers are still obliged to buy electricity from the local electricity distribution company. In this type of market organisation, the level of competition among producers is very high. Moreover, in this model, producers can also sell electricity through bilateral contracts to electricity distribution companies. In the retail competition model, represented in Figure 6.12, final consumers can buy electricity from the local distributors, on the power market, or directly through a bilateral contract from a producer. In all cases, the transmission and distribution companies will charge the consumer for transporting the consumed electricity. In this model, competition is incorporated in the wholesale electricity market and in the retail market. This implies that the level of competition is high among producers as well as among distribution companies.

The day-ahead power market has several, but not all, characteristics of a perfectly competitive market. Before describing how this central market functions, it is important to recall some characteristics of electricity:

1. The supply of electricity needs to be continuous, reliable, and have a stable frequency and voltage.
2. Electricity demand has cyclical, seasonal, and random variations.
3. Electricity supply from renewable energy sources has seasonal (solar, wind, and hydro), cyclical, and random variations (solar and wind).
4. In general, electricity cannot be easily stored. Currently, the most common technology used for storing electricity (indirectly) is the storage hydropower plant. Electric batteries and hydrogen produced with renewable energy sources are also becoming interesting technologies for storing electricity.
5. Equilibrium entails that suppliers keep excess capacity to meet peaks in demand.
6. Electricity can be produced using centralised production units (e.g., nuclear, gas, coal, and hydro power plants) as well as decentralised production units (e.g., wind and solar power plants).

On a day-ahead power market, producers make bids for prices and quantities for a period of the day, based on their marginal production costs, and consumers make bids for electricity purchases. Given this bidding, demand and supply curves are derived. For each hour, a so-called 'system marginal price' is set. In this market, the 'merit-order' principle is applied on the supply side. This implies that there is a sequence in which power plants are asked to produce, and this order is based on which power plant is able to produce at the lowest MC.

Figure 6.13 shows the quantity of electricity on the horizontal axis (Q), and the MC (C) and prices (P) on the vertical axis. The demand function (D) has the usual downward slope, while the supply curve is made up of the bids of the individual producers. The intersection between demand and supply marks the equilibrium, at which the price is equal to the system's marginal price and the MC of the respective producer. Generally, it is assumed that the MC is equal to the variable cost. In this example, the graph shows that the producer marked in the middle (plant 2) as being the marginally

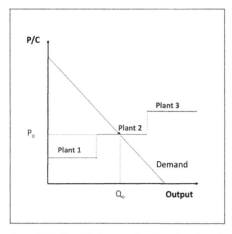

Figure 6.13 Equilibrium on the day-ahead market

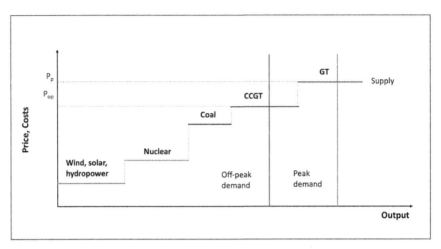

Figure 6.14 A typical merit order curve

producing firm, and it defines the final price and quantity of the product available in the market defined by Q_o and P_o.

Figure 6.14 shows a typical merit order that can be observed on a European day-ahead market. We have five firms that use different production technologies. Wind, solar, and hydro power-based energy types are characterised by low marginal production costs. Nuclear and coal power types often have slightly higher MCs, and combined cycle gas turbines as well as conventional gas turbines exhibit higher variable costs. When demand is high during peak hours, gas turbines produce electricity, while during off-peak hours, gas turbines are not used. Accordingly, system marginal prices for peak hours (P_p) and system marginal prices for off-peak hours (P_{op}) differ. When the system price is higher than the MC of a company (e.g., for wind power during peak and off-peak demand), the company is able to cover parts of its capital costs. Such contributions to the fixed costs are called infra-marginal rents or scarcity rents and are necessary for the long-term survival of the company.

The day-ahead power market possesses many of the characteristics of a perfectly competitive market, such as the presence of many buyers and sellers, a homogeneous product, and a high level of information. However, this market can be characterised by some market failures. For instance, gas and coal power plants do not generally cover the pollution costs during production. Second, there are often entry and exit barriers to the market. Third, these electricity markets are generally earmarked by the presence of very large firms that, in some contexts, may be able to influence the prices. Finally, the price of electricity can also be influenced indirectly by a significant supplier of energy sources such as oil or gas. Large and dominant oil or gas producers such as Saudi Arabia and Russia can directly affect the price of oil and gas and, therefore, indirectly also influence the electricity price. In an electricity market in which the marginal plant is a gas plant, an increase in the gas price due to the reduction of the supply of a large producer will increase its production cost and therefore also lead to an increase in the electricity price. Therefore, the producer of gas can indirectly influence the price of electricity by changing the supply. For these reasons, it is apparent that this type of electricity market is not meeting all the conditions required to be a perfectly competitive market.

In the description of the modern organisational form of the electricity market, we have only considered one power market, that is, the day-ahead power market. However, some reforms have also introduced other types of markets and contracts. For instance, contracts related to the future delivery of electricity are exchanged on the electricity futures market. A future contract ensures the buying and selling of a commodity or financial instrument at a pre-agreed price and time in the future. The electricity futures market can accommodate hedging, a practice that reduces investment risks. Finally, as the name suggests, capacity markets may be established to encourage electricity companies to build new capacity. However, these types of markets in which utilities or other electricity suppliers offer to have reserve capacity available to meet peak electricity demand in exchange for a payment are not always necessary.

6.4.2 Goals and Trade-offs of the Reforms

Until the end of the 1980s, in most countries, the electricity sector was generally organised according to the traditional model, that is, with the presence of vertically integrated companies operating under a monopoly and, therefore, regulated by the state. Given the production and investment inefficiency that characterised this sector at that time, several governments decided to introduce important reforms in the organisation of the electricity sector. These reforms, as discussed previously, included on the one hand the introduction of more competition in the production and trade of electricity, and on the other hand the introduction of new methods of regulation in the transmission and distribution of electricity. The reforms were aimed to improve the level of production efficiency, to promote technological innovations, and the exploitation of renewable energy sources such as solar and wind. Of course, an alternative strategy to try to reach the same goals would have been to introduce new incentive-based regulation instruments for the vertically integrated monopolist.

Both strategies, that is, on the one hand, the introduction of more competition in the production and sale functions and a partial introduction of new regulation methods for the transmission and distribution, and on the other hand, the introduction of new regulation methods for the vertically integrated firms, have advantages and disadvantages. The reform based mainly on the introduction of competition has the clear advantage of stimulating an improved production efficiency of the firms through more competition, as well as innovation in production technologies and in the use of renewable energy sources. However, the cost of this approach is the loss arising due to the lack of exploitation of the economies of vertical integration. The reforms based on enacting new regulations without the introduction of competition in the production and sale activities have the clear advantage of exploiting the economies of vertical integration, but the possible disadvantage of not being effective in promoting productive efficiency, innovation, and a decentralised production of electricity based on renewable energy sources.

6.5   Monopolistic Competition

The model of monopolistic competition is interesting because it can be used to analyse several markets related to energy services as well as durable goods such as heating systems, the installation of solar photovoltaic panels, energy consulting services, consulting for adaptation-based investments, and insurance policies against extreme weather. This model is characterised by several assumptions of perfect competition, but it also incorporates an element of monopoly. A monopolistically competitive market has the following characteristics:

- There are many buyers and sellers of the product in the market.
- The sellers offer similar but not identical products, that is, each product is slightly differentiated from that of all other firms.
- There is perfect information on prices, quantities, and characteristics of the product.
- Each firm faces a very elastic downward-sloping demand curve.
- Each firm can partially influence the price, that is, no firm is a price taker unlike in perfect competition.
- Firms can enter or exit the market without restriction.
- The cross-price elasticities of demand are large, but not infinite.
- Economic agents are rational (firms are profit-maximising and consumers are utility-maximising).
- There are no external costs or benefits.

Since the products offered by a firm in monopolistic competition are not homogeneous, the selling prices may not be the same as in perfect competition. In this market form, the firms use the slight differentiation in the product to exploit some market power as in a monopoly situation, although with some limits. The limitation of the market power is due to the presence of alternative and similar products in the market. A firm operating in a monopolistic competition chooses its quantity and price, just as a monopolist would.

An interesting example is the market for the installation of solar photovoltaic panels for the residential sector. Product differentiation arises in this market from two sources: the first is the difference in the panels themselves and the second is in the installation and maintenance service provided.

Initially, in several countries, the number of firms offering solar panels and providing their installation was low, and this created the possibility to realise short-run economic profits. In addition to this, the possibility of influencing the price to increase profits in this monopolistic competitive market was also facilitated by two factors:

1. The information and technical knowledge of households regarding solar panels was generally limited.
2. Solar panels can be considered a credence good, that is, a good with qualities that cannot be observed, or can only be observed on exerting effort, by the consumer after purchase, making it difficult to judge their value.

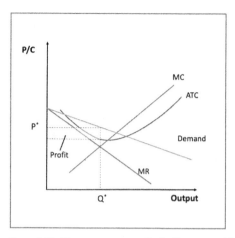

Figure 6.15 Short-run monopolistically competitive firm

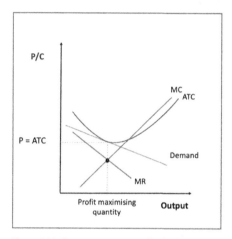

Figure 6.16 Long-run monopolistically competitive firm

Figure 6.15 represents the short-run equilibrium of a firm installing solar panels. Similar to a monopolist, the firm maximises profit by choosing the quantity at which the MR is equal to the MC. In the figure, the optimal combination of price and output is (P^*, Q^*). Because the price P^* is higher than the ATC, the firm realises an economic profit represented by the shaded area.

We must note that the presence of short-run economic profits stimulates new firms specialised in installing solar panels to enter the market. This phenomenon increases the number and type of panels offered in the market and reduces the demand faced by the incumbent firms. The reduction of the demand shifts the demand curve of incumbent firms installing solar panels to the left, and this reduces profits. Thus, the possibility of the firm charging a markup is reduced, and this also lowers the level of economic profit. In the long run, as depicted in Figure 6.16, the solar panel-installing firm will earn zero economic profits. One should keep in mind that in the long run, the possibility of charging a markup is also mitigated by the fact that households gained more information about solar panels and their functioning.

6.6   Oligopoly

Oligopoly is an interesting market form that can be used to analyse some important energy markets such as the fossil fuel markets and, in particular, the oil market. It is important to know that there are several models that try to describe the behaviour of firms in an oligopolistic market. These models differ based on the assumptions used to describe the reaction of the firms in the market. A basic oligopolistic market has the following characteristics:

- The sellers offer homogeneous or differentiated products.
- There are only a few sellers of the product, and the decision of one firm has an effect on other firms.
- Each firm can partially influence the price, that is, firms are not price takers as in the case of perfect competition.
- There are some barriers to entry into the market.
- Economic agents are rational (firms are profit-maximising and consumers are utility-maximising).
- There are no external costs or benefits.

One important characteristic of oligopoly is that firms are interdependent, that is, the decisions taken by one firm regarding the quantity, price, or level of differentiation of the product in order to maximise the profit also depend on the choices made by other firms in the market.

In this section, we present and discuss two models that we think are important to understand the functioning of the fossil fuel markets: the cartel model and the dominant firm model. These models are relevant because fossil fuel markets, especially the oil market, are characterised by the presence of cartels and dominant producers. For instance, the oil market is influenced by the organisation of the petroleum exporting countries (OPEC). Of course, the outcome of these markets in terms of price and quantity is also importantly influenced by geopolitical and demand-side factors. For instance, a war or economic sanctions that involve a producing country will have an important effect on the supply of oil, and therefore on the price and quantity of oil sold on the market. Furthermore, monetary, fiscal, and environmental policies in consuming countries also indirectly influence the oil market through changes in aggregate demand. Since, in addition to economic factors, geopolitical factors also influence certain energy markets, the models discussed in this section can help us to understand some of the price trends that we have observed over this time.

6.6.1   Cartel Model

Firms that operate in an oligopolistic market can decide to create a cartel to increase profits and stabilise revenues. A cartel is a formal organisation created by firms in order to jointly define prices, quantities, and market shares. A well-organised and functioning cartel will give the sellers the possibility to maximise the industry profits and behave as a monopolist would. In general, at the level of countries or cross-border

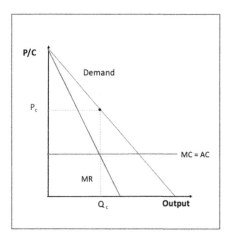

Figure 6.17 Cartel behaviour

institutional settings, such as in the European Union, the creation of formal cartels is prohibited by law. In fact, most countries around the world have adopted antitrust laws, and authorities prevent the creation of formal cartels. However, there is no such law and authority at the global level. Therefore, as in the case of the oil market, it is possible that some firms or producing countries create a cartel. OPEC is one of the most famous cartels in the world. One must remember that there are certain conditions that favour the formation of a cartel, such as the presence of few sellers in the market, significant barriers to entry, inelastic demand for the product, and the lack of substitutes for the product.

A cartel may behave as a monopolist, that is, it may choose the same price and output as a monopolist would. In such a situation, the cartel behaves as a multi-plant monopolist. Figure 6.17 represents the situation of an organised cartel which acts as a single firm that faces the aggregate demand curve (D) for the sector. Assume now that firms that are a part of the cartel have the same constant average cost equal to the MC. In this case, the aggregate MC is also constant, as shown in the figure. We also plot a sectoral aggregate demand curve (D) and a derived marginal revenue curve MR in this figure. The optimal quantity that maximises the profit is obtained where MC is equal to MR, that is, the cartel will choose quantity Q_c and the price P_c. Of course, the cartel can set the price (P_c), only by restricting the total production of the sector to Q_c.

In case each firm independently decides to maximise its profits, the final price and quantity would not be the same ones as the one that maximises the profit from a cartel point of view and will tend to be similar to that of a competitive market. Therefore, an important task of the cartel is to limit the output and distribute production among the cartel members. In this context, the cartel could organise the allocation of the production using three strategies:

1. Adopt the strategy of a multi-plant monopolist.
2. Base the allocation of the production on the situation before the cartel was formed.

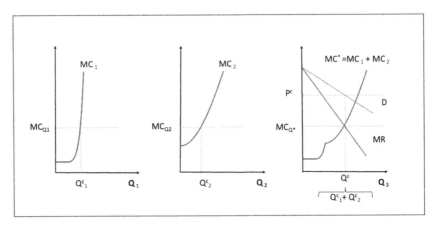

Figure 6.18 Multi-plant monopolist strategy of cartel operation

3. Leave the decision to a bargaining process, which is likely to depend on the bargaining power of each member.

Figure 6.18 illustrates the first strategy, that is, a strategy based on the optimal behaviour of a multi-plant monopolist. Figures 6.18A and B represent the MC of two firms producing oil (MC_1 and MC_2). Firm 1 has a lower MC than Firm 2, and both firms have a limited capacity for production. Figure 6.18C represents the choice of the cartel that maximises the profit, given the aggregate demand (D) and the MC curve (MC^*) obtained by horizontally aggregating the MC functions of the two firms. The optimal solution for the cartel is given by the combination P_c and Q_c. Given the total production Q_c, each firm will produce a share of this output, in this case, Q_1^c and Q_2^c respectively, with MCs MC_{Q1} and MC_{Q2}.

Of course, this model assumes that all producers on the market agree to create a cartel. In reality, it is rare to observe markets where all producers adhere to a cartel. For example, the oil market is characterised by the presence of a cartel, OPEC, but also by the presence of many other producers who have not joined OPEC. In this situation, it may be useful to use another oligopolistic model that can help us understand oil price evolution, namely the dominant firm model.

6.6.2   Application: OPEC

The supply of oil is naturally influenced by oil-producing companies. At the beginning of oil exploration and extraction, the oil market was mainly dominated by the western oil companies such as Shell and British Petroleum (BP). From the 1960s onwards, a wave of nationalisation occurred in the oil industry of non-OECD producers. This resulted in large national oil companies (e.g., Saudi Aramco and the National Iranian Oil Company) in these countries, where the majority of global oil reserves are located today. Additionally, the decision to nationalise oil industries was linked to the creation of OPEC by the five leading oil-producers countries, namely Iran, Iraq, Kuwait, Saudi

Arabia, and Venezuela, in 1960. Today, the organisation has fourteen members, including Qatar, Indonesia, Libya, the United Emirates, Algeria, Nigeria, Ecuador, Gabon, Angola, Equatorial Guinea, and the Congo as well as the initial five members. The goal of OPEC is to coordinate the petroleum policies of member states to control prices. In OPEC countries, national oil companies dominate crude oil production, while both national and international companies operate in non-OPEC countries. As OPEC member countries together produce a large share of global crude oil (~40 per cent) at a relatively low cost and own the majority of the global oil reserves (~80 per cent), the decisions of the organisation can influence the world oil price. The OPEC economies strongly depend on the revenues from their oil production. For this reason, they aim to have a situation in the oil market characterised by stable oil prices and revenues.

A dynamic network analysis of the world oil market: Analysis of OPEC and non-OPEC members

In their work, Al Rousan et al. (2018) [94] looked into the network structure, connectedness, and coordination of the oil-producing countries (seventeen non-OPEC, and thirteen OPEC) over time. Using network analysis, the authors found significant changes in the influence of OPEC and non-OPEC countries over time, with the impact of non-OPEC countries on all countries increasing, contrary to OPEC countries, whose influence decreased significantly after 2012. Nonetheless, the authors found that the OPEC production changes still had a significant impact on non-OPEC countries. Over time, the influence of Russian and American oil production increased, whereas the impact of Saudi production decreased significantly.

6.6.3 Dominant Firm Model and the Oil Market

Another model that can explain the behaviour and development of a large company is the dominant firm model. In this model, a large producer sets the price which other firms take as a given. As a result, all other firms produce quantities based on their MC and the price level chosen by the dominant firm. The large company is considered a residual firm monopoly, and other firms act as fringe firms according to this theory. In other words, the large company might be called the swing producer, absorbing supply and demand fluctuations in order to keep its monopoly price. Fringe firms are accordingly assumed to operate as competitive price-taking firms.

Figure 6.19 presents the price set by a firm in the dominant firm model. Price and cost are indicated on the vertical axis, and quantity is shown on the horizontal axis. This model includes a market demand curve (D) as well as a demand curve of the dominant firm (D_D) that results from the difference between the market demand and the supply by the fringe firms (S_F). As the form of this demand curve shows, at higher prices (e.g., P_1), the dominant firm does not supply any goods or services, as the supply of fringe firms captures the whole demand. Given the demand of the dominant firm (D_D), the dominant firm can calculate its MR function (MR_D). Moreover, its MC function (MC_D) helps the dominant firm to identify the price that maximises its profit. As is usual in monopolistic markets, this price is found by setting the quantity to

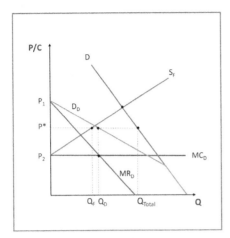

Figure 6.19 Dominant firm model

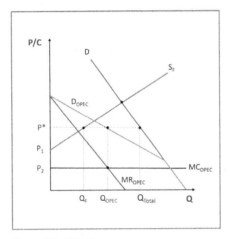

Figure 6.20 OPEC

the level where the MC and marginal revenue are equal. This quantity projected onto the demand curve of the dominant firm (D_D) yields the profit-maximising price P^*. At this price level, the total production Q_{Total} is split between production by fringe firms equal to Q_F and by the dominant firm equal to Q_D.

In the oil market, we can apply the dominant firm model by assuming that the OPEC cartel functions as a single firm. In this case, the outcome of the dominant firm model is very similar to the general case presented in Figure 6.20. P^* is the price set by OPEC, which leads to the outputs Q_{OPEC} for OPEC and Q_F for the fringe companies, respectively. P_2 indicates the price that would have been established in a competitive market. To also note that when the prices are lower (P_1 or lower), only OPEC is supplying and the fringe firms do not supply the goods. This is due to the fact that typically OPEC countries have lower MCs than non-OPEC countries.

Some important characteristics of the oil market

Energy systems thus far have been largely based on fossil fuels and particularly on oil. In this box, we summarise some important characteristics of this market.

- Oil from different locations has different characteristics, such as colour, density, composition, and weight.
- The common classifications of crude oil are: Brent Blend (oil found in the North Sea), West Texas Intermediate (WTI) (a blend of several US domestic light sweet crude oils), OPEC Reference Basket (ORB), and Dubai-Oman Crude.
- Oil is either light or heavy. Light oil either flows easily to the surface, or can be extracted from the ground using pumps.
- We can distinguish non-conventional oil (e.g., oil sands and oil shale) from conventional oil. The extraction of non-conventional oil is more expensive.
- The cost of oil extraction and production varies a lot between regions and types of oil (conventional and non-conventional). The cost of conventional oil varies from around 10 dollars per barrel (Middle East) to around 20–50 dollars per barrel (Europe and North America). These are approximations. The cost of unconventional oil is higher.
- The production of oil is concentrated in the Middle East and in the non-OECD European and Eurasian countries.
- Oil reserves are concentrated in the Middle East and in Central and South America.
- The market is heavily influenced by the strategy adopted by OPEC and by the large and private OECD oil companies, as well as by geopolitical issues.
- Oil is transported by pipelines, as well as small and large tankers, can be stored and is produced in several countries. Therefore, the level of security of supply is relatively high.
- Oil refineries take crude oil and refine it to produce diesel, jet fuels, LPG, heating oil, gasoline, and other products.

Some important characteristics of the gas market

Natural gas also plays an important role in the current energy system. In this box, we summarise some important characteristics of the gas market.

- Natural gas is composed primarily of methane, along with ethane, butane, and propane.
- Through a cooling process, it is possible to obtain liquefied natural gas (LNG). In this form, natural gas can be stored in a safer way and transported by ships and tankers.
- We can distinguish between non-conventional gas (e.g., shale gas) and conventional gas. Conventional natural gas is extracted from the Earth by pumping processes or through naturally occurring pressure. The extraction of unconventional natural gas requires novel technologies to unlock the gas from the shale formations.

- The cost of gas extraction varies between regions and types of gas (conventional and non-conventional). The cost varies from around 3 dollars per MMBtu to around 6 dollars per MMBtu. The cost of LNG is higher (by approximately 2–3 dollars per MMBtu) because of the liquefaction and re-gasification processes that need specific infrastructure. These are approximations.
- The production of gas is concentrated in OECD countries, especially in the United States, in the Middle East, and in the non-OECD European and Eurasian countries, especially in Russia.
- Gas reserves are concentrated in the non-OECD Europe and Euroasia countries, especially in Russia, in the Middle East, and in North America (particularly in the United States).
- Natural gas can be transported by pipelines, whereas LNG can be transported by ships and tankers. Transportation with pipelines is easier and cheaper than the transport of LNG.
- While the transport of natural gas is easier and less expensive via pipelines, this situation has the disadvantage of giving great market power to the producers that extract and sell the gas using the pipelines.
- Transformation of natural gas into LNG gives the possibility to have more suppliers on the market and, therefore, to decrease the market power of producers that use pipelines. However, LNG has a higher cost than non-LNG.
- For countries that are importing natural gas mainly from pipelines, the level of security of supply is lower than for countries that consume LNG. The reason is that LNG can be imported from several producers, whereas natural gas can be imported only from a few producers.

Oil price shocks and renewable energy transition: Empirical evidence from net oil-importing South Asian economies

Murshed and Tanha (2021) [95] investigated the relationship between the consumption of renewable energy and the prices of crude oil by looking at the cases of Bangladesh, India, Pakistan, and Sri Lanka. For their empirical analysis, the authors used data between 1990 and 2018; they found that the increase in crude oil prices did not lead to a rise in the consumption of renewable energy, until a certain threshold. However, upon reaching the price of USD 135 per barrel, significantly higher than the prevalent oil prices at the time of the study, there was an increase in the consumption of renewable energy. The renewable energy shares of both total final energy consumption and aggregated output of electricity confirm this result. Based on their findings, the authors emphasised the importance of reducing the dependence of these net-oil-importing economies on imported crude oil.

6.7   Issues in Developing Countries

In this chapter, we discussed energy markets and the role of market structure and market power. Closely related to this is the notion of electricity market reform, to ensure the security, affordability, and reliability of the supply of electricity. In Subsection 6.7.1, we provide a comparison of the electricity market reform process in industrialised and developing countries, highlighting some important differences between them. In Subsection 6.7.2, we discuss the role of the 'resource curse', which has implied that many developing countries are heavily reliant on oil markets and on oil extraction, and the consequences of this resource abundance on their environmental and economic performances.

6.7.1   Electricity Market Reform: A Comparison of Industrialised and Developing Countries

Many countries have adopted some form of electricity market reform in the recent past, which normally comprises similar measures, such as introducing privatisation (in some cases), unbundling of production, and retailing from the transmission and distribution functions, as well as introducing a market for electricity that is regulated by independent agencies. In many developing countries, this has also meant the dismantling of the natural monopolies of state-owned utilities.

As Kessides (2012) [96] argues, the experience of developing countries, in this regard, has been quite different from the industrialised countries, where the need for reform was felt with the inception of excess capacity and productive inefficiency after the oil crisis of the 1970s. In developing countries, on the other hand, high investment needs were precipitated by an increase in demand as well as load-shedding (or blackouts and brownouts). Moreover, there were important differences in the performance of electric utilities in both sets of countries (developing countries were plagued with problems such as poor service quality and infrastructure, theft, nonpayment for electricity services, etc.). Last, as in other sectors, formulating effective regulation was a difficult process in many developing countries, given weak institutions and generally weaker regulative capacities for natural monopolies.

Important components of electricity reform in developing countries have been raising prices to recover costs (which would eliminate the cost recovery challenge of electric utilities in developing countries), creating regulatory institutions, and eventually privatisation. Moreover, allowing independent power producers (IPPs) to facilitate investments in the generation is a step towards greater private sector participation. However, it is important to note that several developing countries may lack the institutional framework and regulatory capacity to undertake this type of reform. As introducing competition in generation and retail has not always been easy in developing countries, many countries have now adopted hybrid market forms, that are not completely unbundled. Having said that, electricity market reform has also been shown to lead to efficiency improvements in some developing countries (such as Argentina, India, Colombia, and Peru).

Another important hurdle towards electricity market reform in developing countries remains pricing reform, as the reversal of subsidies for electricity often faces public opposition. Given equity concerns and high social acceptability for subsidies, it is challenging for policymakers to align prices with costs. From this perspective, it is important for policymakers to balance the objectives of meeting efficiency improvements while maintaining social equity. When industrialised countries began the transformation to competitive electricity markets, they were already in a situation of excess capacity. During the previous vertically integrated monopoly phase, electric utilities and policymakers in these countries had prioritised ensuring universal access. In many developing countries, on the other hand, the privatisation phase is coming on (or has come) before universal access has been extended. This can have implications for social equity as well.

Blackouts and interruptions in electricity supply are prevalent in many parts of the developing world. This has previously been attributed to limits in the generation capacities of plants, as well as the poor quality of transmission and distribution infrastructure, which leads to significant power losses. However, as shown in a recent study on India by Jha et al. (2022) [97], another reason may also be that the utilities in developing countries respond to increases in procurement prices, that is, wholesale market prices, and purchase less power during such periods. Since storage remains costly, this implies that utilities may end up reducing the supply for end-users of electricity. This is in contrast to developed countries, where strict regulations ensure that utilities satisfy all the electricity demand, regardless of costs. Reducing frictions between the wholesale and retail electricity markets in developing countries thus has the potential to improve the reliability of electricity supply.

In conclusion, some of the industrialised countries introduced electricity market reform to improve economic efficiency and reduce excess capacity, after having achieved universal access, and with strong institutions. On the other hand, some developing countries adopted similar electricity market reforms without having entirely the same initial conditions (i.e., universal access to a reliable supply of electricity and effective institutional conditions). Experience has shown that these differences have created additional problems and challenges in some cases, and therefore produced mixed results.

6.7.2   The Resource Curse

Developing countries that are rich in fossil fuels such as oil and gas (such as Nigeria, Venezuela, and the Democratic Republic of the Congo) face a double-edged sword; on the one hand, these resources are an important revenue opportunity. However, ample evidence suggests that oil-abundant poor countries face several problems because of this endowment too. For example, they experience low rates of economic growth (particularly in manufacturing and services). The main reasons for this phenomenon include weak linkages of the oil industry with other sectors, constant exposure to oil price fluctuations, and oil booms that in some cases give rise to conflict, political upheaval, and increased arms imports in these countries. This phenomenon is called the 'Resource Curse'.

While the importance of macroeconomic fiscal and financial policies in addressing some of these problems (particularly those related to oil price variability) is fundamental, it is equally important to enable these countries to reduce their economic reliance on extractive industries, by diversifying energy sources and investing in renewable energies. This has important repercussions for energy and climate-related domains, both within these countries and abroad. For example, industrialised countries could support renewable energy projects in these countries (using the clean development mechanism (CDM), for instance). It is, of course, clear that financial support would entail significant risks, and thus it is also important to develop monitoring and institutional mechanisms to ensure transparency and compliance. Moreover, it is important to ensure that the development of renewable energy does not engender a resource curse of its own (due to land use, diverting of resources away from human capital development, etc.).

6.7.3 Review Questions and Problems

The online question bank contains review questions and problems for this chapter, including solutions (see https://wp-prd.let.ethz.ch/exercisesfortextbookeep/).

7 Market-based Economic Instruments

The underlying goal of policymaking is to ensure improvements in the well-being of all its citizens. In the context of energy or climate-related issues, the goal of policy design is largely to address some of the problems that we illustrated in Chapter 1, and determined by the market failures, including behavioural anomalies that we described in Chapter 2.

In this chapter, we first provide an overview of energy and climate policy goals, a discussion that we introduced in Chapter 2 and continue upon in this chapter, and then we will present and discuss the most important policy measures using a microeconomics-based approach. As we will discuss in more detail, these two categories of policies (energy and climate) share one goal, namely the protection of the environment, and thus many policy instruments can be classified into both categories. This is why we think that it is important to discuss these two policy categories in tandem. Moreover, in most countries, energy and climate policies are defined by different laws. This can create coordination problems in defining the policy instruments because while they may share a common goal, they are not always discussed and implemented at the same time in the political decision process.

We discuss the relevance of these policies and categorise policy instruments based on whether they operate through the market mechanism, that is, whether they are market-based instruments or non-market-based instruments. While this distinction need not be watertight, market-based instruments incentivise economic agents to adopt efficient behaviour, whereas non-market-based instruments tend to operate by obliging agents to follow some behaviour or adopt some standards. Market-based instruments (what they are, how they work, and their strengths and limitations) will then be discussed in detail in this chapter, whereas non-market-based instruments will be the subject of Chapter 8.

7.1 Energy and Climate Policy: Goals and Instruments

7.1.1 The Purpose of Energy and Climate Policy

States intervene in the energy and climate realms using policy instruments to address market failures including behavioural anomalies that may prevent economies from reaching welfare-maximising (or equitable) outcomes. In doing so, the general objective of energy and climate policy instruments is to improve the well-being of society and promote sustainable development.

As already introduced in Figure 2.4 in Chapter 2, Figure 7.1 illustrates the specific goals of policymakers when designing energy and climate policies. Energy policies seek to meet three objectives: ensuring the security of energy supply, warranting economically efficient and affordable energy supply, and last, addressing ecological and environmental concerns, in broad terms. The last objective involves ensuring that the energy supply is ecological and thus likely to minimise local (e.g., air pollution or waste generation) and global (e.g., greenhouse gas (GHG) emissions) environmental damages, an objective that is also shared by climate policy. The current emphasis is on transitioning societies from positive tons of GHG emissions (such as CO_2) to zero net emissions, a goal that is best captured by the Paris Agreement signed in 2015. Climate policy is also designed to meet another goal, namely to make sure that adaptation strategies are implemented to minimise climate damage during the transition to a sustainable energy system. Therefore, ultimately, climate and energy policies only share one policy goal.

To achieve the three energy policy goals, a policymaker can potentially employ several kinds of strategies, as Figure 7.2 illustrates. For example, diversifying the group of countries from whom energy is imported, as well as the promotion of domestic renewable energy sources can be strategies towards achieving energy security. Policymakers who are interested in making energy more affordable might consider adopting policies that introduce reforms in energy-sector markets to improve economic efficiency, and therefore decrease prices, or to introduce subsidies. Of course, the introduction of subsidies (e.g., subsidies for gasoline), as we will discuss later on, can have a negative impact on economic efficiency, while having a positive effect on equity. Note that in some institutions, the goal of providing affordable energy is listed under the goal of security of supply, and not considered under the goal of economic and affordable supply, as we do. Ensuring the ecological supply of energy can be achieved through the

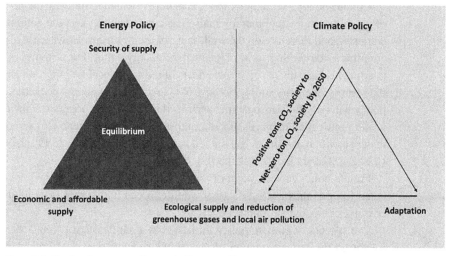

Figure 7.1 Goals of energy policy and climate policy

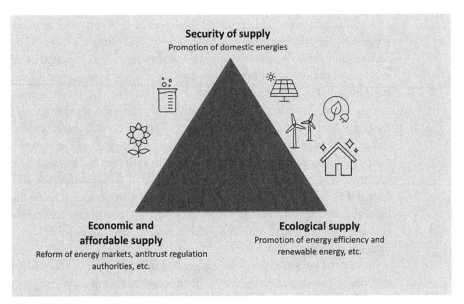

Figure 7.2 Strategies of energy policy

promotion of energy efficiency in consumption, as well as through the increased use of renewable energy sources.

Another important difference that arises between energy policy and climate policy is that energy policy is mostly designed to cater to national interests and, therefore, to maximise the well-being of citizens of a country, but it also has positive spillovers in mitigating global warming. For instance, energy policy involves implementing measures to reduce fossil fuel consumption to improve the security of supply and to reduce local air pollution, so it also has an effect on GHG emissions, and therefore on the sustainable management of a global resource, that is, the atmosphere.

Climate policy, on the other hand, is mainly oriented to mitigate the negative effects of global warming, and thereby it also has a positive effect on the national climate of countries, and therefore on the well-being of their citizens. However, it also indirectly contributes to reaching some of the goals of energy policy. For instance, climate policy instruments have the positive side effects of reducing local air pollution and increasing the security of energy supply because of the reduction in energy consumption. Climate policy will only fulfil its potential benefits if all countries cooperate at the international level in mitigating damages. To summarise, energy policy tends to be more domestic in scope, whereas climate policy tends to be more global (except adaptation-based strategies that are locally oriented).

From a policymaker's point of view, given that energy policy is more directly oriented towards maximising national welfare, it can find higher favourability from the citizens, compared to climate policy.

The success of climate policy initiatives at a national level would then need to be reliant on the implementation of clearly defined international agreements that elaborate on mitigation goals and instruments. Moreover, it also depends on providing financial support to developing countries that are facing the brunt of climate change, and that, as discussed in Chapter 1, did not contribute as much to creating the problem in the first place. Thus, if we recognise this, then from an equity point of view, it is important that industrialised countries not only implement domestic energy and climate policy to reduce their own GHG emissions but also help developing countries in mitigating and adapting to climate change. There are several approaches to do this; one approach is to directly transfer financial resources to developing countries, and the other approach is to realign development cooperation policy and aid, for instance by promoting investment in new sustainable technologies for mitigation and adaptation, or a combination of the two. In this manner, the financial burden of climate policies is shared, and the commitment to achieve sustainable development can be strengthened.

7.1.2   Types of Energy and Climate Policy Instruments

There are two main groups of measures to address energy and climate issues: public measures that are designed and implemented by the state, and private measures that are implemented by non-state entities such as firms or associations. Public measures, also called policy instruments, can further be divided into market-based and non-market-based policy instruments, while private instruments can either be voluntarily implemented by firms or by civil society (Figure 7.3).

7.1.2.1   Public Energy and Climate Policy Instruments

The distinction between market-based and non-market-based instruments is not always unambiguous. One approach is to consider all measures that improve the functioning of the market, including monetary-oriented measures such as taxes and subsidies, as well as information campaigns and nudges that enable economic agents to take better decisions, as market-oriented instruments. The other approach is to count only monetary measures as market-oriented instruments and to consider the other non-monetary measures that improve the functioning of markets as non-market-oriented instruments. In this text, we opt for the former approach. This implies that market-based approaches will comprise monetary policy measures as well as other measures to improve the functioning of markets (such as informational policies and nudges).

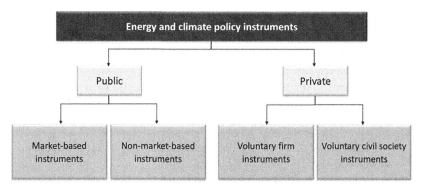

Figure 7.3 Types of energy and climate policy instruments

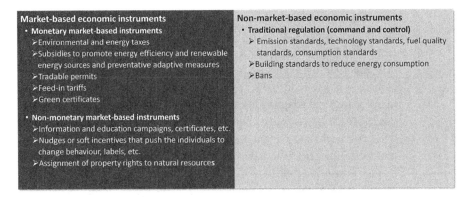

Figure 7.4 Public energy and climate policy instruments

Figure 7.4 includes some examples of public energy and climate policy instruments. Typical market-based economic instruments are environmental and energy taxes, subsidies, tradable permits, feed-in-tariff (FiT), and environmental or 'green' certificates. Non-market-based instruments include traditional regulatory policy instruments (such as standards and direct control measures) and voluntary agreements or negotiated approaches between industries and the government (to reduce fossil fuel consumption). Policies to promote educational or information dissemination programmes, as well as nudges, namely interventions that steer individuals to change behaviour, facilitate effective functioning of markets, and thus can be conceived of as market-based instruments as well. An example of an information-based policy is an energy-efficiency label on durable goods (such as appliances or vehicles) to make consumers aware of their energy performance.

The last non-monetary market-based instrument is the assignment of property rights for the use of natural resources. This instrument can be used to address the market failures of negative externalities and common resources. For instance, if a firm pollutes a lake, and therefore produces a negative externality for the population dependent on it, assigning the property rights to the lake among the population would eliminate the problem. In this case, the firm may, on the one hand, invest in technologies to reduce pollution and, on the other hand, transfer money to the affected population and acquire the rights to pollute. It is important to keep in mind that the practical implementation of this instrument is challenging and cumbersome because it involves reaching an agreement among different parties at the local as well as global levels, on who has the right to the resource. In this chapter, we will not emphasise this policy approach.

The energy and climate policy instruments described in Figure 7.4 can be implemented at different institutional levels:

- Local (i.e., at the level of municipalities, districts, states, cities, etc.)
- National
- International (i.e., at the level of the European Union, the United Nations (UN), etc.)

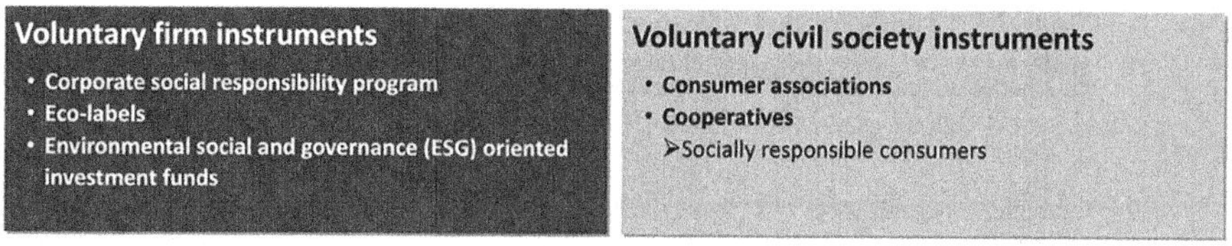

Voluntary firm instruments	Voluntary civil society instruments
• Corporate social responsibility program • Eco-labels • Environmental social and governance (ESG) oriented investment funds	• Consumer associations • Cooperatives ➤Socially responsible consumers

Figure 7.5 Private energy and climate policy instruments

The UN system encourages international agreements to promote sustainable development as well as sustainable energy consumption, and to address climate change. Agreements can be either legally binding or non-binding. A binding contract represents a legally enforceable voluntary commitment by states to take specific actions, whereas a non-binding agreement does not entail legal obligations. A strong legally binding agreement is, in practice, very difficult to negotiate across heterogeneous parties, such as countries. International treaties generally contain a mix of binding and non-binding elements, such as clauses using obligation-related language (e.g., shall) and passages meant to convey a guiding principle (e.g., should).

7.1.2.2 Private Energy and Climate Measures

Some energy and climate policy instruments can also be voluntarily promoted and implemented by private agents, such as firms and civil society groups, as shown in Figure 7.5. Firms, for example, can incorporate notions of corporate social responsibility (CSR) into their business as well as production processes. Alternatively, producers can also contribute towards sustainable development through the adoption of eco-labelling and eco-certification practices, and financial institutions can complement these activities by offering sustainable investment funds such as ESG (environmental, social, and governance-related) funds. Civil society programmes, on the other hand, can guide socially responsible behaviour through the launch of campaigns and initiatives, either through consumer associations or cooperatives.

7.1.3 Market Failures and Policy Instruments

Policy instruments are meant to address market failures, including behavioural anomalies, and thus promote sustainable development. Tables 7.1 and 7.2 provide an overview of some policy instruments for addressing several common market failures related to the energy sector. The policy instruments mentioned in these figures will be discussed in this chapter, as well as in Chapter 8. For instance, if positive externalities can arise from learning-by-doing, as is the case in the research and development (R&D) of energy-sector technologies, R&D subsidies and tax credits might be helpful. Likewise, several policy instruments (such as taxes, permits, and standards) can be utilised to address negative externalities that may arise from air pollution.

Similarly, each behavioural anomaly related to energy consumption might also be counteracted using suitable policy instruments. As discussed in Chapter 2, behavioural anomalies represent systematic deviations of behaviour from assumptions of the rationally self-interested model, namely *homo economicus*. Some of these anomalies that

Table 7.1 Classical market failures and possible policy instruments

Type of market failure	Damage / benefit	Main instruments
Negative externalities: • Local air pollution and global GHG emissions • Public goods and common resources	• Harmful to health • Property damages • Environmental damages • Insufficient provision of public goods • Tragedy of the commons • Insufficient investment in adaptation infrastructure	• Environmental taxes • Tradeable pollution permits • Standards • Subsidies for the provision of public good
Fossil fuel import dependence	• Harm to national energy and economic security	• Energy import tax • Subsidies for Indigenous energy production
Positive externalities: • Learning-by-doing spillovers • R&D spillovers • First adopters of new technologies	• Insufficient investments in R&D, energy efficiency ('energy-efficiency gap') and renewable energy technologies	• Subsidies for R&D • Subsidies for adopters • Tax credits • Standards
Consumers' lack of information: • Asymmetric information • Principal–agent problems	• Insufficient investments in energy-efficiency ('energy-efficiency gap'), in renewable energy technologies and in adaptation strategies	• Information campaigns • Subsidy for consultancies/audit • Nudges (public information campaigns) • Labelling • Standards

Table 7.2 Market failures in the form of behavioural anomalies

Type of behavioural anomaly	Damage / benefit	Main instruments
Bounded rationality	• Insufficient investments in energy efficiency ('energy-efficiency gap'), in renewable energy technologies, and in adaptation technologies • Imperfect decisions related to consumption and investment choices	• Standards • Default options • Nudges in form of information • Social norms • Educational programmes • Information campaigns
Bounded willpower (weakness of will, impulsiveness, and myopia)	• Insufficient investments in energy efficiency ('energy-efficiency gap'), in renewable energy technologies, and in adaptation technologies	• Standards • Default option • Subsidies • Tax credits • Rebates • Loans

have been found to be relevant to the energy or climate realms are described in Table 7.2. An example of a behavioural anomaly is the limited use of information by agents, which might arise because of the limited attention paid to energy consumption, or the limited salience of this information. It could also arise due to incorrect prior beliefs about a product, or about which pieces of information are relevant in making energy consumption decisions. This may result in agents making imperfect consumption decisions, and this can be countered through standards or information campaigns.

In Tables 7.1 and 7.2, we listed the policy instruments that the government can use to address market failures. In this discussion, we are implicitly assuming that the choice, design, and implementation of the policy measure are completely oriented to address effectively the market failure and, therefore, to increase the welfare of the society. However, as discussed in the public choice theory, in some situations, government intervention may not correct market failures. The reasons for the ineffectiveness of government intervention mentioned in the public choice theory are several. For instance, the presence of special interest groups that try to influence policy decisions in their favour rather than towards the broader society interest, lack of alignment between the goals of part of the policymakers and society, or the presence of inefficient government agencies. Further, in some cases, the corruption of the bureaucrats responsible for implementing interventions can also determine the ineffectiveness of policy measures. For this reason, policymakers should promote analysis of the effectiveness of a policy measure to identify the presence of potential problems and correct them. More generally, as we will discuss in more detail in Chapter 9, the choice of a policy instrument should be based on several criteria, such as economic efficiency, the effectiveness of the instrument, its impact on equity, etc.

7.2 Monetary Market-based Instruments

7.2.1 Pollution Taxes, Product Taxes, and Energy Taxes

The next subsection explains the uses of environmental and energy taxes, which are among the important policy instruments to address energy and climate issues.

7.2.1.1 Types of Environmental and Energy Taxes

There are different types of taxes that can be used to internalise the negative externalities due to energy use that arise from environmental damage or climate change. A product tax is levied on the output of polluting firms, while a pollution tax is imposed directly on the pollution/emissions of firms. An energy tax is one that is imposed not on the output, but on the energy inputs used by firms and households in the production of goods and energy services. Figure 7.6 provides brief descriptions of these three taxes.

From an economic point of view, the pollution tax is the most efficient type of tax to address negative externalities that are generated by burning fossil fuels. The level of a pollution tax is set equal to the MEC of local and global pollution, which results in an efficient solution to tackle negative externalities, as the problem is addressed directly, unlike with the use of a product tax. Pollution taxes provide firms with incentives to

Pollution tax	Product tax	Energy tax
• It is a 'Pigouvian tax' – tax equals the marginal external cost of pollution	• A product tax involves taxing the output of polluting firms	• An energy tax involves taxing the bad input (e.g., fossil fuels) and indirectly the emissions
• Efficient solution because the pollution is taxed directly and firms can also decide, at some cost, to reduce the amount of pollution produced per unit of output	• Like a 'simple Pigouvian tax'	• It is an efficient solution if it is possible to reduce the amount of energy used per unit of output
	• Fully efficient only if the amount of pollution produced per unit of output cannot be changed	
• Firms can substitute among inputs → substitution of inputs to reduce pollution	• Firms cannot substitute among inputs (using a fixed proportion production technology) → only way to reduce the level of pollution is to reduce the output	• Substitution of inputs to reduce ENERGY and therefore indirectly pollution

Figure 7.6 Types of environmental taxes

replace polluting inputs and technologies with more environmentally friendly alternatives, and therein reduce their tax costs. However, this is not the case with all types of taxes.

The product tax is less efficient, as the level of taxation is not directly tied to the level of pollution. Accordingly, the only way for a firm to decrease its burden from a product tax is to reduce its output, and no appropriate incentives exist for them to substitute old technologies with new, more efficient ones that produce the same output but cause less pollution. Product taxes, however, can be efficient in the case where the pollution produced per unit of output cannot be changed. As an example, consider fixed-proportion production technologies, where firms are forced to use inputs in pre-determined proportions, due to a lack of substitutability between inputs (such as energy and capital).

Last, the energy tax, especially an energy tax on fossil fuels, is another relevant form of environmental taxation, and it is a useful policy instrument to reduce pollution if it can be concluded that there is a constant ratio between the use of fossil fuels (or energy) and the level of pollution. In this case, the level of the energy tax is determined by the level of pollution, and the instrument offers firms the possibility to substitute away from using fossil fuel-intensive inputs. Adoption of energy taxes might, therefore, lead to the use of more sustainable inputs (substitution of energy with capital) and technologies, and in that sense, it is like a pollution tax.

From an economic point of view, the best type of tax to address market failures such as negative externalities is a pollution tax, followed by an energy tax, and last, a product tax. Even though this has been theoretically shown, note that from an energy policy point of view, the energy tax has several advantages. The introduction of an energy tax on all energy sources will reduce levels of energy consumption and, therefore, will decrease pollution (if the energy supply is dependent on fossil fuels), as well as increase the security of supply. This positive effect on the security of supply is due to the fact that by reducing energy consumption, indirectly one is also likely to reduce the imports of energy, and this augments energy supply security. Of course, a pollution tax will also tend to reduce the energy consumption up to the extent that economic agents do not use filters, scrubbers, or sequestration technologies that enable reducing pollution while continuing to burn fossil fuels. An energy tax can also be introduced only on imports to encourage the development of indigenous production and thus also strengthen the security of domestic supply. Another advantage of an energy tax with respect to the pollution tax is that it is more salient to consumers: for example, a gasoline tax is likely to be noticed by consumers whenever they refill, and it is also more easy to implement compared to a pollution tax.

Note that generally, with the introduction of environmental and energy taxes, we will observe two behavioural changes. On the one hand, economic agents will reduce consumption due to the price increase. On the other hand, these taxes can promote a change in investment behaviour, such as encouraging economic agents to make investments in energy efficiency or pollution abatement technologies.

Generally, the revenues from collecting these taxes can be used by the state in the following ways: to fund R&D in new technologies, provide subsidies for the adoption of energy-efficient or renewable technologies, or a per capita redistribution of revenue based on income, etc. For instance, in Switzerland, the government introduced a CO_2 tax on heating oil and natural gas in 2008, and the revenues are used both for R&D funding and for promoting measures for enhancing energy efficiency, as well as redistributing to the people on a per capita basis.

We will now discuss each of these types of taxes in more detail.

7.2.1.2 Product Tax

As discussed previously, a product tax is added to the price of pollution-generating output to correct negative externalities. The tax, therefore, follows the polluter-pays principle. The graph in Figure 7.7 depicts a case in which a product tax is imposed on a market for a product derived from livestock, such as meat. We choose this as an example, because as mentioned in Chapter 1, the agricultural sector (including the management of livestock) is responsible for a large share of the emissions of GHGs, particularly methane. The price level is shown on the vertical axis and the quantity on the horizontal axis. The demand function for meat is represented by the marginal private benefit (MPB) function, which in this case is considered equal to the marginal social benefit (MSB), and it slopes downwards, as consumers will demand less meat as prices increase. The upward-sloping marginal private cost (MPC) curve represents the supply and captures the increase in the quantity of meat supplied by producers, as prices increase. However, each additional kilogram of meat produced also has an external cost (in terms of emissions), due to feed production and processing, as well as enteric fermentation. This is captured by the upward-sloping marginal external cost (MEC) curve. Of course, we could also imagine a MEC curve that is constant, but also in this case, the analysis will follow. The marginal social costs (MSCs) of meat production, thus, equal the sum of the MPC and MEC, at each quantity.

If the external costs (i.e., negative externalities) are not considered in the output decision, the competitive equilibrium quantity of meat will be given by the intersection of the MPC and the MPB curves, namely at Q_C. At this quantity, Q_C, however,

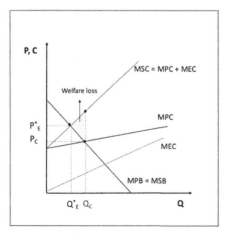

Figure 7.7 Welfare loss without considering externalities of meat production

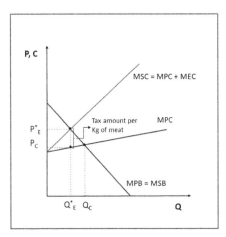

Figure 7.8 Product tax on meat produced

the MSC from the consumption of meat is higher than the consumers' marginal willingness to pay (which is given by the MPB and MSB curves). Therefore, a welfare loss manifests from output level Q_C, shown by the shaded triangle, due to the overconsumption of meat. To reach the socially optimal equilibrium Q_E^*, that is, where the MSB curve intersects the MSC curve, a tax per kilogram of meat, namely a product tax, can be levied.

Figure 7.8 illustrates the introduction of a product tax. Both axes in this graph remain the same as before. The product tax is in our example the tax charged per kilogram of meat that is produced, and it is set equal to the difference between the MSC and MPC at the desired quantity, that is, it should be set equal to the marginal environmental cost MEC. For example, to achieve the optimal equilibrium represented by the point (P_E^*, Q_E^*), the tax should be set equal to the amount shown in the diagram. The imposition of this tax will ensure that the equilibrium quantity is determined by the intersection of the MSB and MSC curves because firms will respond to this tax by reducing their output such that their supply curve will align with the MSC curve.

Generally, the use of a product tax can create two problems. First, it is difficult to identify the value of the MEC at output level Q_E^*. Second, the use of a product tax in a situation in which firms can substitute inputs and therefore invest in abatement technologies to reduce the use of fossil fuels is not efficient because it doesn't provide incentives to reduce pollution. Therefore, with a product tax, the only way to reduce pollution is by reducing the output. In general, this is an unrealistic assumption. However, in a situation characterised by a fixed-proportion production function, implying that no input substitution is possible, a product tax is efficient. Input substitution is, in most circumstances, possible. For example, a producer of meat could reduce the level of emissions, by improving energy efficiency, feed quality as well as cattle diets, or by using improved management practices such as rotational grazing. However, even in case the producer can reduce the pollution by investing in new production processes, with a product tax imposed per unit of meat produced, the producer will continue to pay the same amount of taxes, even though it has reduced the amount of emissions per unit produced. Therefore, even with the possibility to substitute inputs, there is no significant incentive to reduce emissions.

7.2.1.3 Pollution Tax

In the case of a pollution tax based on emission levels, the tax is imposed directly on the pollution instead of being imposed on the output produced by the firm. This is more efficient, as the output is not directly affected, and the polluting firm's response is not restricted to an output reduction. Producers can reduce pollution by changing the combination of inputs used, through investments in abatement technologies or in energy efficiency, for example. The cost of reducing the amount of pollution produced (through these investments) is called an abatement cost. Alternatively, firms might choose to continue to pollute in response to the tax and decide to pay the tax instead of investing in abatement equipment. The decision regarding which costs will be taken on, and how much taxes are paid, depends on the marginal abatement cost (MAC) curve; the MAC is defined as the incremental increase in abatement costs due to incremental increases in abatement levels. At the firm level, these MACs are increasing in the levels of abatement, and are graphically represented by an upward-sloping curve in the space with abatement (A) on the horizontal axis and cost (C) on the vertical axis as depicted in Figure 7.9.

To understand how an emissions-based tax works, consider a simple example of an economy with a coal power plant that produces a constant quantity of electricity. This scenario is shown in Figure 7.10. The maximum level of abatement that can be achieved in this society is given by the level A_{E0}, that is, this is the amount of abatement needed to reach zero emissions from the coal power plant for a given level of output (for instance, using a carbon capture and sequestration (CCS) technology). However, from society's point of view, the optimal amount of abatement is reached at A_{E*}, and not necessarily at A_{E0}. The reason for this is that the reduction in the level of pollution to zero is too costly relative to the benefits of this reduction. The level

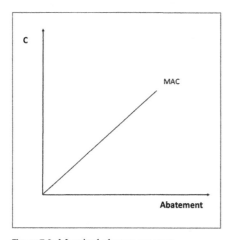

Figure 7.9 Marginal abatement cost

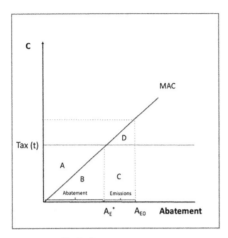

Figure 7.10 Emission tax

of optimal abatement is determined at the aggregate level (as we will discuss next) and reflects a situation where the MACs of all polluters are equal to the MSB from reducing pollution.

Now, consider the introduction of a pollution tax, set at the level 't' shown in the graph. In the situation that the firm decides to undertake zero abatement after the introduction of the tax, it would need to pay the full tax burden to the state, and this is given by the sum of areas A, B, and C in Figure 7.10, that is, the areas under the tax curve, up to the level of total emissions released by the firm (which is the horizontal quantity A_{E0}, in the zero abatement case). However, the more likely scenario is that the firm abates some pollution, right up to the point where each additional unit of abatement just starts to become more expensive than paying the tax, that is, the firm will choose to abate at the level A_{E^*}. In this case, the total abatement cost is given by the area under the MAC up to the level of abatement (area B in the graph), and the total tax burden is given by the area under the tax curve, corresponding to the total emissions (area C). Thus, it becomes clear why it is in the firm's interest to invest in abatement, as total costs are lower (total costs = $B + C$) than if the firm were to choose to not abate at all (total costs = $A + B + C$). Consequently, the firm abates this portion of its emissions (until A_{E^*}), but not more. This is due to the fact that for an additional unit of abatement to the right of this point A_{E^*}, the cost of abatement (the area $C + D$) is higher than the tax cost (C), so this portion of pollution will not be abated by the firm.

In Figure 7.11, we now explain how the optimal level abatement A_{E^*} is determined at the aggregate level. As shown, we can plot price or cost on the vertical axis and abatement levels on the horizontal axis. The curve MAC_{AGG} is the aggregate MAC function, and it is obtained by horizontally summing the firm's individual MAC curves. This is the curve which captures the abatement costs of all firms in society, which are increasing in levels of abatement. The downward-sloping MSB_{AGG} curve is the aggregate marginal benefits function, and it represents society's demand for environmental quality. It is measured as the value of damages or costs associated with

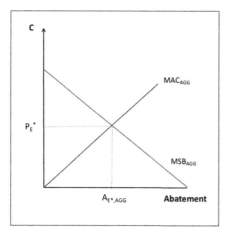

Figure 7.11 Emission tax at the aggregate level

pollution, and this can be expected to decline as levels of abatement increase. When abatement is low and emissions/pollution levels are high, society's marginal benefit from a unit reduction in pollution is high, but it decreases with increased abatement. The optimal level of abatement at the aggregate level is thus reached at $A_{E^*,AGG}$, where the curves for the two functions (MAC_{AGG} and MSB_{AGG}) intersect, and this represents the allocative efficient equilibrium for the economy.

Assuming that all firms have the same MAC curves, then the optimal level of abatement illustrated in Figure 7.11 can be reached by equal abatement, defined by $A_{E^*,AGG}$ divided by the number of firms (n), that is, $A_{E^*} = A_{E^*,AGG}/n$. This is the approach to derive the value of A_{E^*} that we plotted in Figure 7.10.

The model can also be extended to include more than one firm with different abatement costs. Consider the simplest case of two firms. In Figure 7.12, two distinct MAC curves for the two individual firms, MAC_1 and MAC_2, are shown. The primary vertical axis represents the costs and benefits for Firm 1, corresponding to the origin point a. Thus, MAC_1 represents increasing MACs for Firm 1, as total abatement levels (with respect to origin a) increase. Likewise, MAC_2 is drawn with respect to the origin for Firm 2, which is denoted by point b, and the secondary vertical axis denotes the costs and benefits for Firm 2.

Now assume that the total emissions by these two firms are 20 units of pollution. If the government finds, after doing a cost–benefit analysis, that the environment can assimilate no more than 10 units of pollution, a total abatement of 10 units would be needed in the economy. These 10 units are shown in the graph as the distance between a and b, that is, the total emissions required to be abated. Assume once more that output levels shall not be changed to reduce emissions. If the state wants to achieve minimum costs of abatement for the 10 pollution units, it should not ask the firms to each abate 5 units. Instead, the most efficient solution is the introduction of a tax set at level t, where MAC_1 and MAC_2 intersect.

Firm 1, with a relatively flatter MAC curve, experiences smaller increases in abatement costs than Firm 2, for each additional unit of abatement. Its total abatement cost,

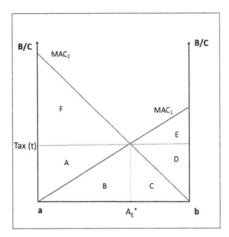

Figure 7.12 Equilibrium abatement with an emission tax

if it were to abate the maximum of 10 units in the absence of a tax, would be the sum of areas B, C, D, and E, or the area under MAC_1. This is lower than the total abatement cost of Firm 2 (which is $F + A + B + C$, or the area under MAC_2). Therefore, societal costs are minimised if Firm 1 abates more than Firm 2. The optimal tax level to achieve this goal is set at the price level given by the intersection point of the two MAC curves (A_{E^*}).

The principle that helps us to identify the appropriate tax level is known as the equi-marginal principle, which states that at an allocative efficient equilibrium, MACs must be equalised across all firms. At this tax rate, the total abatement cost of Firm 1 is given by area B, whereas it pays area $C + D$ as tax. Likewise, the total abatement cost of Firm 2 is given by area C, while the tax revenue obtained from it is given by $A + B$. Thus, total tax revenue in this simple economy is $A + B + C + D$, while the total abatement costs are $B + C$. The total costs to society, in this case, are lower than if the firms would have abated 5 units each with no tax introduced.

So far, the discussion about the introduction of a pollution tax has concentrated on the abatement strategy and costs to the firms determined by the introduction of the tax, assuming that the level of production remains the same. It is likely, that the introduction of a pollution tax, as we illustrated in Figure 7.10, leads to an increase in the production costs for firms, because of investment in abatement, as well as the payment of the tax. Note that this increase may also be neutralised if the investment in new abatement and production technology gives the firm the possibility to produce the same amount of output at the same cost, or at a lower cost. In case of an increase of the production cost due to the pollution tax and abatement costs, we can expect a shift of the supply function on the market of the good produced by the firms to the left. This shift will then increase the price, similar to the effect of the product tax, and reduce the demand and supply of the good. On the other hand, if the increase in cost is mitigated by investment in new and less polluting technology, the supply function need not shift, and the output will remain at the same level.

For instance, in the case of meat consumption, if the producers are able to adopt better management practices, implement improved diets for cattle, etc. without incurring significant costs, then the MECs represented in Figure 7.7 will have a lower slope, and the MPC function will remain the same. In case of an increase in costs, the MPC function will shift upwards.

7.2.1.4 Energy Tax

Some countries have introduced a tax on fossil fuels, that is, a so-called energy tax, based on the assumption that there is a roughly proportional relationship between the quantity of the fuel used and the corresponding emission levels. The tax is imposed on each unit of polluting fuel (fossil fuels) used, with the tax rates varying according to the type of fuel. Fuels that pollute more per unit used are taxed higher; this implies higher tax rates for coal and oil, with lower rates for natural gas and uranium. Non-polluting renewable energies are either taxed at very low tax rates or tend to benefit from tax exemptions.

An energy tax is thus a type of policy that incentivises economic agents to reduce energy demand by consuming less due to behavioural changes, and by investing in more energy-efficient technologies. In the latter case, the energy tax incentvises the economic agents to change the combination of inputs and adopt new energy-efficient technologies. In this regard, the economic analysis of the effects of an energy tax is similar to that of a pollution tax. However, an energy tax, as discussed previously, by inducing a reduction of energy consumption, will promote the security of supply. Furthermore, some countries have introduced an energy tax on gasoline and diesel to finance the construction and maintenance of highways and roads. This last type of energy tax is not a direct energy policy instrument, because it is not oriented to any energy policy goal. However, such a tax can indirectly help in reaching these goals.

In Figure 7.13, we will present how an energy tax can promote investment in energy efficiency that implies a substitution of energy with capital. The figure shows the mechanisms driving the adoption of energy-efficient technologies for an economic agent. We can use this to think about investment in energy-efficient cars energy-efficient cars (EECs), buildings, or in heating systems.

The graph plots the level of energy efficiency (EE) (and equivalently, the decline in energy consumption) on the x-axis and the costs and benefits of investing in energy efficiency on the y-axis. The two downward-sloping lines represent the MPB and the MSB curves. The MPB curve represents the private benefits from the reduction in energy consumption (which also implies a reduction in private energy expenditures) obtained by increasing the level of energy efficiency by using more efficient technologies. This curve represents the demand function for the level of energy efficiency. The MSB additionally considers the presence of a positive externality in improving energy efficiency levels, thus is represented as the sum of the MPB and marginal external benefits (MEB). The positive externality of investing in energy efficiency takes into account the reduction in air pollution and the resulting improvement in energy supply security. In this graph, we also plot the upward-sloping marginal energy reduction cost (MERC) curve. The MERC curve indicates the increasing marginal costs of improving

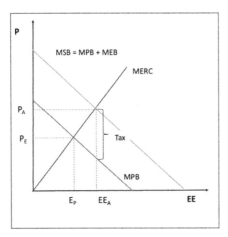

Figure 7.13 Introduction of an energy tax on the market for energy-efficient technologies

energy efficiency and reducing energy consumption. If no positive externalities are considered, the private optimum is reached at the level of energy efficiency denoted by E_P. However, since there are positive externalities associated with any type of energy efficiency improvements, economic efficiency is reached at EE_A where the MSB curve intersects the $MERC$ curve.

To reach an efficient level of energy efficiency, the state could introduce an energy tax that will shift the MPB curve to the right, as the benefits from adopting energy-saving behaviour increase due to the imposition of this tax. A unit reduction of energy implies lower energy expenditures as well as lower tax expenditures.

Of course, the introduction of an energy tax will also have an impact on the market for the energy source that is taxed and not only on the market for energy-efficient technologies. In this case, an energy tax that the producer will pay will shift the market supply function upwards and to the left. Therefore, the equilibrium price on the market for the energy source, for instance, heating oil, will increase and the quantity will decrease, as we described earlier for the product tax.

7.2.1.5   Benefits and Challenges of Environmental and Energy Taxes as Policy Instruments

Economists tend to favour environmental and energy taxes over other instruments, as they tend to promote economic efficiency more than other instruments. Some benefits of these types of taxes are:

- They maintain the freedom of economic agents to allocate their resources as they wish.
- The overall cost of achieving pollution and energy use reduction is minimised.
- Polluters pay for the damages incurred or the negative externalities (polluter-pays principle).
- Incentives for the development and adoption of less polluting and less energy-consuming products and technologies are created.

While many governments have adopted environmental and energy taxes as policy instruments, there are some challenges with the use of taxation to address market failures:

- It is difficult to know the MAC of pollution, the MERC, and the MSB of reducing pollution or energy use for economic agents.
- In the presence of MSBs that are heterogeneous across economic agents and regions, the introduction of a uniform tax can lead to economic inefficiency.
- Implementing taxes based on environmental performance (for example, the pollution quantity) needs to introduce a system to monitor the emissions and enforce the regulation, both of which can be difficult and costly, especially in developing countries. This is not relevant in the case of the energy tax, because it is more straightforward to measure energy consumption.
- Political pressure by large firms as well as general public dissatisfaction with paying taxes may dissuade policymakers from adopting taxes as instruments, and lead to a lack of will to implement taxation policies.
- Due to their distributional implications, taxes are generally less acceptable than other policy instruments. An additional challenge is related to deciding how to use the tax revenue. There are several possibilities to recycle this revenue, such as financing direct transfers to reduce other taxes, promoting innovation in green technologies, as well as compensating people affected by the externality.

7.2.1.6 Environmental Tax Reform

Environmental taxes may be introduced in an economy through a reform of the tax system. Consequently, several countries around the world have implemented the so-called environmental tax reform (ETR). The European Environment Agency defines an ETR as a 'Reform of the national tax system where there is a shift of the burden of taxes from conventional taxes such as labour to environmentally damaging activities, such as resource use or pollution' [98]. In practice, this means that taxation is shifted from goods such as labour (e.g., by a reduction in income taxes or in social security contributions) or capital (e.g., by a reduction in corporate taxes) to bads (e.g., implementing taxes on fossil fuels, air pollution, etc.). These reforms are said to be revenue-neutral, that is, governments do not retain any of the tax revenue earned from taxing the bads. In addition to reducing income taxes and social security contributions, as discussed previously, governments might use additional revenue to compensate affected groups and introduce incentives for achieving both environmental improvements and technological change. This reform can also be partial, that is, only some bad resources such as specific fossil fuels may be taxed. For instance, a government could decide to introduce a reform that foresees the introduction of a CO_2 tax on gasoline with redistribution of the revenues.

The benefits that can materialise out of such reforms can take different forms. The double-dividend hypothesis suggests that environmental tax reform can produce:

- A first dividend: an improvement in environmental quality, due to lower emissions

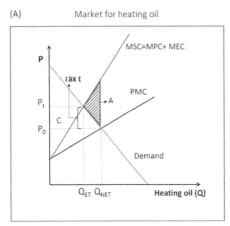
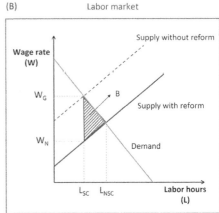

Figure 7.14 Environmental tax reform

- A second dividend: an increase in overall economic efficiency through the reduction of distortionary taxes such as income taxes that may manipulate labour and savings decisions

Figure 7.14A and B illustrate the notion of the double-dividend hypothesis associated with environmental tax reforms, using a simple example. Figure 7.14A, the market for a polluting good (for example, heating oil) is shown with output levels on the x-axis and price levels on the y-axis. On this graph, we also see the marginal private cost curve (MPC) and the marginal social cost curve (MSC) that are obtained by adding the MEC to the MPC. Figure 7.14B represents the labour market with total hours worked on the x-axis and wages on the y-axis. On this graph, we observe the individual labour supply function, as well as the demand of the firms for labour. The dotted labour supply curve that is shifted up takes into account the social security contributions that employees have to pay. The payment of social security creates a deadweight loss represented by area B.

If an environmental tax 't' is introduced in the market for heating oil, the optimal output-price combination, from a societal point of view, is reached (P_t, Q_{ET}). By implementing the tax, the policymaker effectively eliminates the dead-weight loss associated with the negative externalities (shown in the figure by triangle A) and achieves a reduction in heating oil use from Q_{NET} (the quantity without any environmental tax) to Q_{ET} (the quantity with an environmental tax). This also represents the first dividend of environmental tax reform.

The introduction of an environmental tax generates revenue (shown by rectangular area C in Figure 7.14A), which then allows the government to reduce individual social security contributions in the labour market (represented by the difference between W_G (the gross wage) and W_N (the net wage) in the diagram). Therefore, employees have the incentive to increase labour supply from L_{SC} (their labour supply when they had to pay social security contributions) to L_{NSC} (the labour supply without having to pay for these social security contributions). The lowering of these contributions on labour implies that the dead-weight loss area B in Figure 7.14B will also be eliminated, as workers increase their labour supply to L_{NSC}. This constitutes the second dividend of environmental tax reform. Thus, both sources of dividends can be effective in improving economic efficiency in the energy transition.

Environmental taxation and the double dividend hypothesis
in CGE modelling literature: a critical review

Within the economics literature, there is a general consensus that environmental tax reform results in an improvement in environmental quality, whereas evidence on the second dividend is slightly weaker. Gonzalez (2018) [99] provided a meta-analysis of some economic studies that have tested the double-dividend hypothesis, and argued that while almost all the studies in the sample found that environmental taxation improved environmental conditions, an augmentation of economic efficiency was only observed in about 55 per cent of the cases, whereas it was not observed in the remaining 45 per cent. Thus, while there is some evidence to suggest that the double-dividend hypothesis may materialise under some conditions, it still remains ambiguous whether there are economic efficiency improvements in response to environmental taxation.

On the distributional impact of a carbon tax in developing countries: the case of Indonesia

Yusuf and Resosudarmo (2015) [100] analysed the distributional impact of a carbon tax imposed on energy sources such as kerosene, natural gas, coal, gasoline, and automotive diesel oil using a computable general equilibrium model. The authors conducted the analysis for highly disaggregated groups of households in Indonesia. They found that the carbon tax in Indonesia was likely to be a progressive instrument because the allocation of resources and structural changes arising from the carbon tax favoured low-income and rural households. This progressivity arises due to the fact that currently, households living in rural areas and belonging to the agricultural sector are less likely to consume gasoline, diesel, kerosene, etc., due to underinvestment in durables. This underinvestment also explains the low sensitivity of these households to price variations. The progressive impact of the carbon tax was also shown by the expansion of the service and agriculture sectors and the contraction of the manufacturing sector, which is highly energy-intensive.

7.2.2   Subsidies

Another pivotal instrument used to address both energy and climate-related issues is subsidies. Section 7.3 will provide an overview of how subsidies can be used in the framework of energy and climate policy. In general, such subsidies are implemented to encourage the adoption of energy-efficient technologies, to promote the use of renewable energy, or public financing of investment in adaptation to climate change that has a local public good character (public financing would be equivalent to a 100 per cent subsidy). Subsidies can also be used to make energy more affordable. Some examples of subsidies are:

- Subsidies to buy energy-efficient electrical appliances or cars
- Subsidies to build energy-efficient houses
- Subsidies to renovate houses with the installation of energy-efficient technologies
- R&D subsidies to promote innovation in new environmentally friendly and energy-saving technologies, for example, in renewable energy technologies
- Subsidies to promote the adoption of solar panels and wind turbines, etc.
- Subsidies to finance adaptation measures that have a local public good character, such as storm surge walls to prevent flooding, green shading of areas in urban localities, etc.

Such subsidies, by effectively reducing costs and prices, can lead to higher levels of adoption of energy-efficient technologies, renewable energies, or supply of local public goods that would otherwise be underconsumed or underprovided in a free market economy. Governments can also introduce subsidies to make energy consumption more affordable, especially for low-income households, which is a goal of energy policy.

7.2.2.1   The Justification for Using Subsidies

From an economic point of view, the introduction of subsidies can be justified as a means to improve economic efficiency in one of three cases. First, subsidies are justifiable in the presence of positive externalities linked to the adoption of new sustainable technologies (that can help with air pollution reduction, or in increasing the security of energy supply) as well as of potential positive spillovers of knowledge from first adopters of this sustainable technology to later adopters. Second, the presence of behavioural anomalies such as bounded rationality and bounded willpower related to the use of energy-efficient technologies or renewable energy might also warrant the use of this policy instrument. The third justification for using subsidies is related to climate policy objectives and, more specifically, to promote investment in adaptation measures. These measures tend to have the characteristics of local public goods. For instance, consider dikes to reduce the risk of flooding. In this case, a subsidy could promote the construction of such projects.

As previously mentioned, governments can also introduce subsidies to make energy consumption more affordable, that is, they can use this instrument for equity-related reasons, and not necessarily as a means to improve economic efficiency. For instance, due to the substantial increase in energy prices in Europe in 2022, mainly due to the war between Russia and Ukraine, several European governments decided to subsidise gasoline and diesel (by reducing the taxes on these fuels that were previously collected to finance the maintenance of the road systems or to fund other public expenditures). From an economic point of view, this approach may be inefficient for two reasons. First, the price will no longer equal the marginal cost and this is a source of economic inefficiency. Second, given that all households that own a vehicle receive a discount on gasoline and diesel prices, irrespective of their income or wealth, this creates an inequitable outcome. A better solution could be to introduce a direct subsidy to make energy consumption more affordable only for households that belong to the low-income classes.

7.2.2.2   How Subsidies Work: An Illustration

Figure 7.15 represents the market for investment in energy-efficiency technologies, and is similar to Figure 7.13. In this case, we represent the market for efficient cars with the quantity of EECs plotted on the horizontal axis and the price plotted on the vertical axis. This market is illustrated with the help of the MERC function, an MPB function, and an MSB function which reflect the benefits from the society's point of view. In this context, MEB is the marginal external benefits function. The external benefit is arising mainly because of the reduction in pollution due to the higher level of energy efficiency of EECs, the sharing of experience in using new and relatively unknown technology, and an improvement in the security of supply. In the absence of a subsidy for EECs, equilibrium is denoted by the combination (P_E, E_P). In this case, consumers are underpurchasing EECs because the optimal number of cars from the society's point of view (that considers the external benefits) is higher than E_P.

Now, consider the situation in which a policymaker decides to implement a subsidy to increase the adoption of EECs. The introduction of this subsidy has the intended effect, as shown in the figure, of moving the equilibrium point to (P_A, EE_A), also known as the allocative efficient equilibrium, by shifting the private demand curve to the MSB curve. If the subsidy is set to equal the MEB (as is the case at EE_A), an efficient equilibrium from the society's point of view is achieved, and this level of subsidy is called a Pigouvian subsidy. Thus, the introduction of a subsidy results in the internalisation of the positive externalities. Unfortunately, it is often difficult to measure the benefits to society from the use of a good (the MEB, as illustrated in Figure 7.15), which is a necessary first step to determine the optimal level of the subsidy.

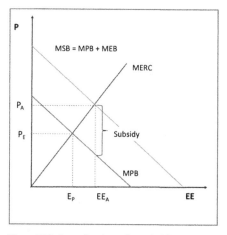

Figure 7.15 Introduction of a subsidy

The impact of policy awareness: evidence from Vehicle
choices response to fiscal incentives

Switzerland is a federal state, with twenty-six provinces called cantons. These cantons are relatively independent in terms of the energy policies they implement. Some cantons have developed policies to promote the use of EECs and have introduced a so-called 'bonus-malus' system for the annual vehicle registration tax. This system consists of an adjustment of the annual registration tax, depending on the environmental impact (or fuel efficiency) of the car that is calculated using a specific metric. Owners of relatively inefficient cars need to pay a higher tax (a malus), whereas owners of relatively efficient vehicles receive a subsidy or bonus on this tax, that is, they need to pay a lower tax. In some cantons, thresholds on CO_2 emissions of cars are used to determine whether a vehicle is eligible for a bonus. In other cantons, vehicles that have received a high-efficiency rating, based on the energy label, receive a bonus.

Energy labels for vehicles typically provide energy-efficiency ratings for different models, that vary from A (most efficient) to G (least efficient) based on the fuel consumption of the cars. The bonus-malus system is an example of a policy instrument to enhance the adoption of EECs, and it works by providing a rebate on the owed registration taxes for relatively more EEC models. Naturally, its effectiveness as a policy tool depends at least partially on the level of awareness of economic agents about the policy and what it entails. A study by Cerruti et al. (2023) [101] has shown that consumer awareness of the existence of the bonus-malus system is relatively low. Accordingly, the effectiveness of such policies may often be hampered. Therefore, the authors of the study conclude that communication, as well as education on the presence of the bonus-malus system, is important to ensure its success, as economic agents may otherwise be oblivious to these benefits while making their investment decisions.

7.2.2.3   Subsidies to Promote the Adoption of Renewable Energy

As we discussed in Chapter 1, the promotion of the production of electricity using renewable energy sources (such as solar and wind) is an important pillar of the energy transition. In this context, several countries have introduced a subsidy policy to encourage investment in these renewable sources. In this subsection, we briefly present two types of subsidies, that is, initial grants and the FiT, which are used to promote the installation of solar photovoltaic (PV) panels.

- Initial subsidies/investment grants can be provided to producers of renewable energy, which may depend on the capacity of the renewable installation. This type of subsidy is particularly useful for households or firms that are more responsive to the upfront costs, rather than the lifetime costs, of technologies.
- A FiT is another form of subsidy which ensures that renewable energy producers receive a fixed price for the extra electricity that they produce (over and above the energy used for self-consumption) and feedback to the grid (which is known as a net FiT), or a fixed tariff that is paid for the total amount of electricity generated

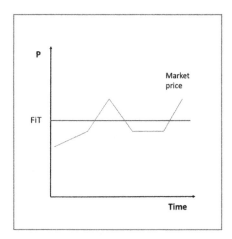

Figure 7.16 Fixed price feed-in-tariff

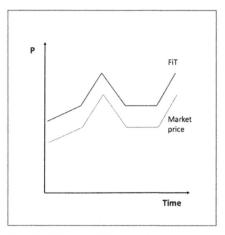

Figure 7.17 Non-variable premium price feed-in-tariff

and sent to the grid if they are obliged to sell all of it to the local distributor (gross FiT).

There are three main types of FiTs, that are illustrated in Figures 7.16 to 7.18:

1. Fixed-price FiT – the total FiT payment is fixed and remains independent of the market price as shown in the first graph (normally, it is also guaranteed for a long time, even up to 15–20 years, depending on the life-cycle of the technology). In this graph, we present time on the horizontal axis and prices on the vertical axis. The fixed tariff is set at the level shown (FiT). On the same graph, we also plot the market price, which on average is lower than the FiT. For example, the German government implemented a fixed price FiT in 2000 that guaranteed energy producers a payment per kilowatt hour for all quantities of electricity generated from renewable energy for a fixed period (generally 20–25 years). Other countries, such as Canada and France, and developing countries such as Ghana, have also implemented this system.

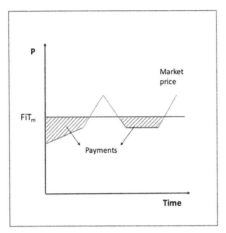

Figure 7.18 Variable premium price feed-in-tariff

2. Non-variable premium FiT model – in this model, an additional payment ('premium') is paid on top of the spot market electricity price to developers. The developer then receives payment for the total electricity generated (at market prices) and, in addition, a constant FiT payment, as is illustrated by the two parallel lines in the second graph. Examples of countries that have implemented this policy are Spain, Slovenia, Czechia, and the Philippines (although these countries have also offered a fixed price FiT).

3. Variable premium price FiT model – projects are guaranteed to receive a minimum total payment (shown in the third graph below as FiT_m). When the prevailing spot market electricity price is lower than this minimum threshold, the developer receives the difference between FiT_m and the market price. If the price is higher than this threshold, the developer will just receive FiT_m. In the figure, we can see the level of FiT_m, the evolution of the market price over time, and the shaded regions represent the total payments received by the developer when the spot price is lower than FiT_m. This type of FiT has been used in the Netherlands and in Finland.

7.2.2.4   Challenges with Using Subsidies as Instruments

Subsidies are a very popular and well-accepted policy instrument (understandably so, more than taxes). However, there are some issues that should be considered in the choice of this instrument. For instance, subsidies may tend to bias a consumer's decision on how best to reduce their energy consumption. This might result in a sub-optimal deployment of economic resources, with the possibility of consumers getting locked into certain technologies, and not shifting to newer ones. This might lead to inefficient solutions, depending on how the market for energy efficiency or renewable technologies develops. Finally, there is also the possibility that governments hand out subsidies to producers or consumers who would have adopted the technology anyway, even without being given the subsidy. This is yet another example of an inefficient market outcome that may arise with the use of subsidies as a policy instrument.

To conclude, subsidies are attractive policy measures that can be used to reach various goals. However, the design and implementation of these policy measures should be done carefully, to avoid reducing their effectiveness and to bring out the economic advantages of using these instruments.

7.2.3 Pollution Permit Trading Systems

In this section, we present the last monetary market-based policy instrument, namely the market for pollution permits, also known as a cap-and-trade pollution permits system. In this framework, the government decides to regulate the level of emissions, for instance, the level of GHG emissions (mostly CO_2), by issuing and allocating pollution permits across polluters and allowing them to buy and sell unused permits among each other. Such a pollution permit trading system establishes a market for the rights to pollute, with the help of tradable pollution allowances. A well-known example of a permit trading system is the EU Emissions Trading Scheme (ETS) for CO_2. Note that this policy instrument can also be used to promote the adoption of renewable energy sources, or to promote energy efficiency. In this case, for example, the state can define a general target for the number of renewables produced by electricity companies, and assign individual targets for these companies. Firms have the flexibility to deviate from this target, by buying or selling renewable energy certificates on a market. The functioning of this market for renewable certificates is similar to that of the market for pollution permits. In this chapter, we will focus on the latter, because they are more commonly used.

Can carbon emission trading scheme achieve energy conservation and emission reduction? Evidence from the lindustrial sector in China

Hu et al. (2020) [102] explored the impact of the 2011 CO_2 ETS pilot policy in China on emissions reduction and on the conservation of energy. For the econometric analysis, they used province-level panel data on industries between 2005 and 2015. The results of the analysis confirmed that regulated industries achieved a reduction in energy consumption and CO_2 emissions by 22.8 and 15.5 per cent, respectively, when compared to the areas where the pilot was not conducted. These results mainly arose due to industrial structure adjustments and increases in technical efficiency. The authors thus argued that using market-oriented environmental policies to tackle environmental challenges may be effective in developing countries as well, and highlight the importance of monitoring and tracking the sources of pollution and obtaining accurate information regarding pollutant emissions.

7.2.3.1 Functioning of the System

A cap-and-trade system for pollution permits consists of two main components:

- A fixed number of permits that are issued based on a target pollution level/accepted level of emissions, that is set by the government
- A market in which these permits can be traded

The implementation of the system follows several steps. These are:

1. Setting the total pollution allowance (also known as the cap); for example, the total CO_2 emissions target that is optimal for society.
2. Allocating permits between polluters.
3. Allowing the permits to be freely traded.
4. Monitoring individual pollution levels and imposing a (sufficient) penalty for any infraction. No polluter is allowed to emit more pollution than it has acquired permits for.

In step 2, permits may be auctioned off (in an auction-based system) or issued for free (a so-called grandfathering system). In an auction, several allowances based on the total abatement target of an economic system are auctioned to bidding polluters. This process generates additional revenue for the government, unlike the grandfathering approach, in which each polluter receives allowances based on their past pollution levels or based on an egalitarian principle after a share is subtracted to meet the overall emission target. The advantage of assigning the permits through an auction is that the revenue stream obtained with the auction can be used to fund R&D activities, to compensate economic agents affected by the pollution, or to finance policy measures such as subsidies for renewable energy sources or energy efficiency.

The functioning of a cap-and-trade system can be represented in the simplest case of two polluting firms. In Figure 7.19, two distinct MAC for the two individual firms are shown, MAC_1 and MAC_2. The primary vertical axis represents the costs for Firm 1, corresponding to the origin point a. Thus, MAC_1 represents increasing MACs for Firm 1, as total abatement levels (with respect to origin a) increase. Likewise, MAC_2 is drawn with respect to the origin for Firm 2, which is denoted by point b, and the secondary vertical axis denotes the costs for Firm 2.

Now, assume that the total CO_2 emissions by these two firms are 20 units and a total abatement of 10 units is necessary to reduce the negative effects of the CO_2 emissions. In this situation, the government decides to put a cap of 10 units of emissions. These

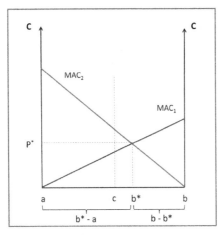

Figure 7.19 A cap-and-trade system

10 units are shown in the graph as the distance between a and b. Suppose now that the state introduces a cap-and-trade system to obtain a reduction of 10 pollution units. As we have seen, in this system, the government can decide to allocate permits either through an auction, or distribute an equal number of permits to firms, or use some other criteria. Assume, for our example represented in Figure 7.19, that permits are distributed equally between the two firms (denoted by point c in the figure).

After receiving the permits, the firms can start producing, and simultaneously making investments to lower emissions. Given the difference in their MACs, Firm 1, characterised by having lower marginal costs, might consider selling some of the permits to Firm 2, with higher MACs. This trade would potentially benefit both firms across all quantities where the MAC of Firm 1 is lower than the MAC of Firm 2. In this case, for Firm 2, it is cheaper to buy permits from Firm 1, as long as the price of the permit is lower than its marginal cost and higher than the marginal cost of Firm 1. As can be seen from the figure, the process of bargaining and trading permits, even after initially distributing them equally, leads to a price (P^*) and quantity equilibrium (b^*) that corresponds to the point where MAC_1 and MAC_2 intersect.

In this situation, Firm 1 will invest in abatement technologies to abate b^*-a units of CO_2, use permits equivalent to the distance (b^*-b) to pollute, and sell (b^*-c) worth of permits to Firm 2. Firm 2 will abate a lower amount of CO_2 emissions (b-b^*) because its MACs are higher than those of Firm 1. It will buy permits from Firm 1 to pollute for the quantity b^*-c, at the price P^*. Note that in this simple example, the most efficient solution could also be reached with the introduction of a tax set at the level of the equilibrium price P^*, where MAC_1 and MAC_2 intersect. This implies that a pollution tax is equivalent to a cap-and-trade system in a very simple economic system. However, these two policy measures are not identical in a more realistic economic scenario, with several sectors and several economic agents, as well as in the presence of uncertainty.

The pollution permit trading system is mainly used to internalise negative externalities due to GHGs by industrial sectors. For the implementation of this system, the government can use an upstream emission source approach, that is, the cap-and-trade system is introduced for fossil fuel producers, transporters, petroleum refineries, and other firms that create emissions, or a downstream approach, which implies that the level of emissions is regulated at the point of emissions (such as at the power plants that use fossil fuels).

The upstream approach is generally easier to implement than the downstream approach because the number of firms is normally fewer at that stage. If one were to consider the inclusion of households into such a system, that would further complicate the implementation and functioning processes and increase the administrative costs (including the cost of organising the market and monitoring/compliance). One important advantage of the downstream approach is that the price increase in fossil fuels brought about by the cap-and-trade system is directly passed on to the economic agents, namely firms and households, when they make investment and consumption choices. The price signal is thus more salient and immediate in the downstream approach than in the upstream approach. Economic literature suggests that consumers and firms tend to react more to price changes arising due to the introduction of an environmental tax, for example, if this were apparent to them. This may be due to the presence of behavioural anomalies.

Role of salience

The role of the salience of policy instruments such as taxes has been explored in different contexts. In a study, Li et al. (2014) [103] showed, using national data from the US, that increasing gasoline taxes were associated with consumers reducing gasoline consumption more than a comparable increase in gasoline prices. For instance, the authors found that a USD 0.05 increment in the gasoline tax led to a reduction in gasoline consumption by 0.86 per cent, which they argued was much larger than the effect found by not separating gasoline prices into tax and tax-exclusive components. Thus, consumers are more likely to respond to tax increases that are visible, rather than to pre-tax price increases. This has been shown in another context (unrelated to energy or climate) by Chetty et al. (2009) [104], who used an experimental approach at a grocery store to highlight the salience of sales tax in consumer purchase decisions. They found that including the sales tax in the posted price of some products, as opposed to consumers only learning about the amount of tax when they later paid at the cashier, resulted in them making correct calculations of the total price of a basket of goods. These studies pinpoint that with policy instruments such as taxes, it is important to make consumers aware of them when they make their choice, in order to distil an optimal response.

7.2.3.2   Advantages and Disadvantages of Tradable Permits Compared to a Pollution Tax

A pollution tax and a cap-and-trade system are similar market-oriented policy instruments. Both introduce a pollution price and, therefore, a monetary incentive to reduce pollution. The main difference between these two methods to internalise negative externalities is in the way that the pollution price is set, and the mechanism used to define the level of emissions reduction. In a cap-and-trade system, the price for emission allowances is determined by the emission trading system, and a limit on emissions is set by the government (the cap), whereas the pollution tax is set by the government, and in this case, no limit on emissions is defined.

Both systems have advantages and disadvantages. For instance, a cap-and-trade pollution permit system allows governments to define and reach a goal in terms of the quantity of emissions reduction. Therefore, there is certainty on the allowed emissions, which also enables easier estimation of the benefits that can be accrued by the emissions reduction. However, the cap-and-trade system provides less certainty regarding the price level of the pollution permits. Pollution taxes, on the other hand, result in a high degree of certainty about the price level, but induce uncertainty about the quantity of emissions that will be reached, because this depends on the reactivity of energy demand to the price change introduced by the tax across all sectors.

Another difference between the two systems is the level of simplicity in terms of the implementation and management of the system, and their administrative costs.

The cap-and-trade system, if applied to all sectors, is rather difficult and complex to implement and manage, and therefore also costly. The pollution tax system is relatively simple to introduce in all sectors of an economic system, with a relatively easy administration as well. If we consider the level of acceptance by the civil society and politicians, we can observe that the pollution trading system has a higher acceptance level than the pollution tax. This may be because the emissions trading system has, thus far, largely been introduced in the industrial sector, which means that the price of pollution may not actually be salient (or even too high) for the final consumers. The introduction of a pollution tax has a direct impact on final consumers and is also more salient. We can conclude by stating that a combination of these two market-based instruments, that takes into account these benefits and disadvantages, may be a prudent approach for policymakers to adopt.

The Weitzman (1974) perspective on price versus quantity instruments

In a seminal paper, Weitzman (1974) [105] proposed a simple framework to evaluate price instruments (such as pollution taxes) and quantity instruments (such as permit trading schemes), in the context of environmental policy. He postulated that under the condition of full certainty of MACs, there is said to be a duality of price and quantity instruments, that is, the two instruments may be equivalent to one another. On the introduction of uncertainty in MAC curves, however, using a pollution tax may be more efficient than a permit trading scheme, when the damages from emissions increase slowly (i.e., the MSB curve is relatively flat compared to the MAC). However, if the MSB curve is relatively steep, that is, if the damages from emissions increase catastrophically (e.g., if we are on the brink of a climate tipping point), an immediate reduction in emissions is more advisable, and thus, a quantity-based instrument such as a permit trading scheme (or a standard, which we will discuss in more detail in Chapter 8) would be better. This study offers an important perspective on the choice of price- and quantity-based instruments, under the case of uncertainty in MACs.

7.2.4 Behavioural Anomalies and Monetary Market-based Instruments

So far, we have considered the introduction of market-oriented monetary instruments in situations where economic agents are rational and well-informed, that is, before taking any decision, they go through an optimisation process and evaluate the costs and benefits of several alternatives. The demand and supply functions drawn thus far in this chapter assume that consumers and firms are rational and that they maximise utility and profits, respectively. This implies that economic agents react in full effect to monetary incentives such as subsidies or taxes. However, as discussed in Chapter 2, some consumers or firms may be characterised by limited rationality, that is, they may exhibit different behavioural anomalies. In this case, the change in consumption from the introduction of a subsidy or a tax may be lower than can be expected from rational consumers.

Consider, for example, the provision of a grant (or subsidy) to promote the adoption of energy-efficient heating systems. Rational consumers will incorporate this subsidy into their investment calculation when computing the savings in energy expenditures throughout the life cycle of the heating system. In this case, the subsidy can be an attractive monetary incentive to convince these consumers to invest more in energy efficiency. The same argument is valid for an energy tax on fossil fuels. In this case, rational consumers will fully consider the increase in costs of using the fossil fuel-based heating system for the next 20–30 years, due to the energy tax. Boundedly rational consumers, on the other hand, tend to lack competency in evaluating the different investment options in heating systems, and they may not completely recognise the potential future benefits of switching to more energy-efficient heating systems. Therefore, these consumers are not likely to fully incorporate either a subsidy or an energy tax in their choice of heating system, which reduces the efficacy of these instruments.

We will analyse this situation using Figures 7.20 and 7.21 representing the market for heating systems that have the same energy source but are characterised by different levels of energy efficiency. Therefore, these figures are similar to the ones we presented earlier in Section 7.2.2 on subsidies. We first illustrate the demand functions for the two types of consumers and then, in a Figure 7.21, present the effect of introducing a subsidy. In Figure 7.20, we can see the MPBs functions of improving energy efficiency that will result in a reduction in energy expenditures. We show this for a rational consumer (MPB_R), as well as for a boundedly rational consumer (MPB_{BR}). On the graph's horizontal axis, we plot the level of energy efficiency (LEE) of the heating system, while on the vertical axis, its benefits. The demand function (MPB_R) reflects the willingness to pay for a rational consumer, whereas, in contrast, the demand function (MPB_{BR}) illustrates the willingness to pay for the boundedly rational consumer. Due to anomalies in the optimisation process, the willingness to pay of the boundedly rational consumer for energy efficiency is lower than that of the rational consumer, at each level of energy efficiency. For this reason, the demand function for energy efficiency of the boundedly rational consumer (MPB_{BR}) is located left to one of the rational

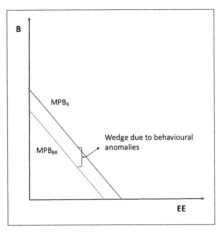

Figure 7.20 Demand for energy efficiency by rational and bounded rational consumers

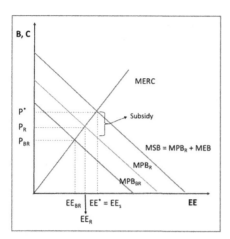

Figure 7.21 Optimal solution considering subsidy

consumers as illustrated in Figure 7.20. The wedge between the two demand functions arises due to a range of underlying anomalies described above (and in Chapter 2).

It is interesting to understand the implications of these two types of demand functions on the effectiveness of market-oriented monetary policy instruments that, generally, are designed assuming that consumers and firms behave rationally.

In Figure 7.21, we plot a graph illustrating the choice of the level of energy efficiency of heating systems. The graph includes three demand functions: the MPBs function demand of a rational consumer (MPB_R), the MPBs function of a boundedly rational consumer (MPB_{BR}) and the MSBs function (MSB) for energy efficiency of heating systems for a rational consumer from a societal point of view. This demand function is obtained by summing the MPB for rational consumers with the MEB, and it represents the MSBs of increasing the level of energy efficiency of the heating systems. The external benefit is due to the fact that an increase in energy efficiency reduces fossil fuel consumption and, therefore, diminishes air pollution and increases the security of supply. The graph also includes the upward-sloping marginal energy reduction cost curve ($MERC$), which indicates the increasing marginal costs of improving the heating system's energy efficiency and of reducing energy consumption.

If no positive externalities are considered, the private optimum for the rational consumers is reached at the level of energy efficiency denoted by EE_R, and the private optimum for the boundedly rational consumers is reached at EE_{BR}. However, since these energy efficiency improvements are associated with positive externalities, economic efficiency is achieved at EE^*, where the MSB curve intersects the MERC curve. To reach this optimum level, the state could introduce a subsidy that shifts the demand function to the right to reach the socially optimal level of energy efficiency EE^*. As can be seen from Figure 7.21, however, a subsidy designed to increase the demand of rational consumers would be insufficient to shift the demand function of the boundedly rational consumers to the right, in order to reach the optimum social EE^*.

The shift in the demand function of boundedly rational consumers would depend on how these consumers react to the subsidy, that is, how they integrate the subsidy into doing an economic analysis of investments in heating systems. In any case, even if we assume that the subsidy is highly effective for this group in increasing demand, it will not be enough to reach the social optimum. To ensure that all types of consumers reach the social optimum, that is, choose the right level of energy efficiency of the heating system, the state could try to reduce the extent of the behavioural anomalies through some non-monetary market instruments that we will introduce in Section 7.3, or by using standards that will be discussed in Chapter 8.

An analogous analysis could be done for the implementation of a pollution or energy tax on fossil fuels. The introduction of the tax would increase the MPBs obtained from investing in energy efficiency. Indeed, increasing the level of energy efficiency will reduce the level of energy consumption and, therefore, the level of energy and tax expenditures. The graph would be very similar to the one for the subsidy, whereby the tax will shift the demand functions of both consumers to the right to reach the social optimum. However, in this case, as well, the tax will not shift the demand function of the boundedly rational consumers to the social optimum bundle.

7.3   Non-monetary Market-based Instruments

In this section, we will shortly present two non-monetary market-based instruments that can increase the level of well-functioning of a market. As we know, in order to take sound decisions, economic agents have to be well-informed about the choices and have to act rationally. Information and educational programmes, as well as nudges, are policy instruments that can help economic agents to make sound and informed decisions.

7.3.1   Information and Educational Programmes

Informational and educational programmes are examples of policy instruments used to address imperfect information and asymmetric information that may prevent individuals from investing in energy-efficient or renewable technologies, or not conserving energy adequately. These policies are designed to enable consumers or firms to make better decisions, while not compelling them to take any particular action. The underlying assumption is that either providing consumers or firms with information, or the right incentive structure, can enable them to realise the benefits of adopting more energy-efficient technologies or of switching to renewable energy sources, and this would lead them to increase their demand towards the socially optimal level.

The following are some examples of informational or educational policies:

- Information campaigns on climate change
- Information campaigns on the implementation of energy and climate instruments
- Educational programmes on sustainable development
- Educational programmes on environmental or general energy-related knowledge
- Educational programmes on undertaking investment analysis with respect to the purchase of energy-consuming durables

- Information campaigns to inform about adaptation measures to climate change and improve resilience

---

The light at the end of the tunnel: impact of policy on the global
diffusion of fluorescent lamps

To study the determinants of energy policy choice in developing countries, and to better understand whether these policies are effective in fostering clean technology diffusion, Srinivasan (2019) [106] used data on the diffusion of compact fluorescent lamps (CFLs) in seventy-two developing countries spanning 1993–2013. She found that in general information provision policies (explaining the benefits of using CFLs, compared to incandescent lamps) had a strong and positive effect on the diffusion of this technology, while subsidies and a ban on the use of incandescent bulbs (a non-market-based instrument) did not have any effects, in this sample of countries. The study also showed that governments that were more 'effective' in terms of implementing policies were more likely to provide information and less likely to subsidise CFLs. This study sheds light on policy choice and effectiveness in developing countries, where very little is known on the functioning of energy policies.

7.3.2   Nudges

Nudges are defined as subtle positive reinforcements that influence a person's behaviour without imposing any prohibitions on them. Proposed by Richard Thaler and Cass Sunstein in their 2008 book 'Nudge: Improving Decisions about Health, Wealth and Happiness', nudges have shown good promise in encouraging individuals to make better decisions.

They essentially comprise suggestions and invitations that encourage people to take decisions that are in their broad self-interest, as well as in the interest of society. They work without providing any explicit economic incentives for behavioural change or establishing any rules or conditions. This is closely linked to the idea of Libertarian Paternalism, defined as '... an approach that preserves freedom of choice but authorises both private and public institutions to steer people in directions that will promote their welfare' (Thaler and Sunstein, 2003) [107].

Nudges designed as energy or climate policy instruments aim to promote sustainable behaviour and encourage individuals to voluntarily contribute to energy and climate goals. Some examples of nudges to encourage sustainable choices and behaviour are:

- Nudges that provide clearer and/or salient information or help in processing information: they work to simplify product information or make certain product characteristics more salient (e.g., smart metres or eco-labels or energy labels).
- Nudges that provide some form of stimulus to follow a behaviour (e.g., messages in hotels to reuse towels).

- Nudges that provide information on the behaviour of peers. They exploit people's inclination to follow social norms, to imitate the behaviour of their peers (e.g., home energy reports, energy consumption comparisons, etc.).
- Nudges that change the choice architecture to enable easier decision-making. For instance, nudges that, in the presence of *status quo* bias or loss aversion, do not require consumers to actively choose something (e.g., setting renewable electricity contracts/green electricity contracts as the default option).
- Nudges that provide information on extreme weather events (such as flooding and heat wave risk) and suggest precautionary behaviour (such as staying home, and minimising outdoor activities)

Nudges are particularly useful to promote the more sustainable behaviour of boundedly rational consumers. For instance, if we consider again Figure 7.21, the implementation of a subsidy is intended to shift the demand functions of both boundedly rational and rational consumers to the right. However, as discussed earlier, a subsidy may not be enough to incentivise boundedly rational consumers to reach their social optimum. In this case, a nudge could help to shift the MPB_{BR} curve additionally to the right for these consumers, over and above the subsidy.

Nudges in the marketplace: the response of household electricity consumption to information and monetary incentives

Sudarshan (2017) [108] studied the impact of various behavioural interventions on the levels of electricity consumption of a sample of households in India based on a field experiment as well as a quasi-experimental analysis. The interventions included peer comparison reports for electricity consumption every week, reports with associated monetary incentives to help reduce consumption, and variations in the prices. The study revealed that peer comparison nudges led to an electricity consumption reduction of 7 per cent in the summer season. The price elasticity was estimated to be -0.56. However, households that received monetary incentives along with the peer-comparison reports increased their electricity consumption, thereby crowding out the non-monetary intervention. The author argued that principal-agent problems, with a lack of trust in the utilities and government, may have led to this unexpected outcome. This result showcases the need of designing policy instruments carefully to ensure that they may have the intended impact on the outcome variable and that they cannot be applied generically.

Table 7.3 is drawn from a report published by the Nordic Council of Ministers, and it provides some additional examples of nudges relevant to the energy and climate domains.

7.3.2.1   An Example of Nudges: Eco-labels and Energy Labels

Eco-labels and energy labels are designed to solve typical information problems related to the use of energy-efficient technologies. Not all consumers are fully

Table 7.3 Types of nudges [109]

Type of Nudge	Examples
Provision of information	• Information on energy use, for example, of household or office units.
	• Real-time displays providing current information on energy consumption and prices, either through green lights or information on prices and quantities.
	• Information on current energy prices through green lights system.
	• Energy labels on housing, household appliances, and products.
	• Information campaigns to households.
	• Social media campaigns.
Changes in the physical environment	• Change in waste-sorting equipment.
	• Changing the plate size.
Changes in the default options	• Change in default for CO_2 offsetting.
	• Change in default temperature in offices.
	• Change in default to accept the installation of smart-grid technology.
	• Green electricity contracts as default.
	• Change in default menus in restaurants to a meat-free version.
Use of social norms and regular feedback	• Feedback on energy and water usage compared to social reference groups, such as similar neighbours.
	• Information campaign focusing on social responsibility to sort waste.

informed about various aspects of energy-consuming technologies, such as their operating costs or the characteristics of a product or energy service. Eco-labels and energy labels can be effective in alleviating imperfect information. Additionally, they might also create better outcomes in the face of the limited attention paid by consumers to critical information (such as energy or fuel consumption).

Eco-labels and energy labels provide consumers with an objective and accurate evaluation of a product's energy consumption and environmental impact. They are often implemented with energy standards, and it may be either mandatory or voluntary for firms to print labels on their products. Energy labels can be either endorsement labels (such as the Energy Star label from the US, which endorses the product as being energy-efficient) or comparative labels (which compare the performance of the appliance or vehicle with that of other similar products on the market).

Labels have been implemented in many industrialised as well as developing countries. For example, the European Commission has a website that lists all eco-labels that member states are obliged to implement in the European Union [110], as well as the corresponding regulations.

Field interventions for climate change mitigation behaviours: a second-order meta-analysis

In their study, Bergquist et al. (2023) [111] provided a meta-analysis of studies involving interventions to promote climate change mitigation behaviour. They found that among the different types of interventions normally studied, field experiments based on social comparisons or financial incentives were likely to have the largest effects on pro-environmental behaviour, while information provision and education-based interventions had the least impact. Thus, comparing an individual's behaviour to that of others has been found, across several studies, to induce consumers to react, in terms of observable behaviour, such as littering, use of sustainable transportation, meat consumption, or saving electricity and water. This study provides some evidence on the types of interventions that can have an effect in influencing certain types of sustainable behaviour.

Boundedly rational consumers, energy and investment literacy, and the display of information on household appliances

Energy labels usually provide information on the energy use of an appliance, light bulbs, or a car, but not on the monetary savings of expenditures. In this study, Blasch et al. (2019)[112] study the effects of providing monetary information on an energy label for electrical appliances and light bulbs. The empirical analysis based on a randomised controlled trial with a sample of more than 2000 Swiss households indicates that individuals provided with labels containing monetary information had a higher likelihood of performing a lifetime calculation, and correctly identifying electrical appliances that minimise these costs. Therefore, this study shows that the type of information included on energy labels can have significant effects on choices.

7.3.2.2 The Limitations of Informational and Educational Programmes and Nudges

A standard criticism levelled against nudges (and more generally, against informational or educational policies) is that they are insufficient by themselves to reach energy and climate policy goals. Policymakers may need to supplement them with other market- or non-market-based instruments that can provide the impetus for consumers and firms to make sustainable decisions. For instance, educational programmes about how to perform an investment analysis or calculate the lifetime cost of an electrical appliance or a heating system can increase the effectiveness of a pollution tax. In fact, if consumers do not consider the lifetime cost in their investment decisions, then the increase in the fuel cost determined by a pollution tax will not be completely considered in the choice. Although information and educational programmes and nudges are unlikely to be capable of bringing about lasting changes, they are relatively cost-effective policies that can have sizeable effects in some cases. Of course, in this chapter, we discussed the use of nudges in order to maximise societal welfare. However, we should not forget that nudges can also be designed, especially by firms, to sell goods and services as well as technologies that are promoting sustainable development.

7.4   Issues in Developing Countries

We discussed several market-based policy instruments in this chapter, including taxes, subsidies, permits as well as information-based policies. In this section, we elaborate on the benefits and weaknesses of some of these instruments in a developing country context, especially pollution and product taxes, permits, and fossil fuel subsidies, which are quite salient in many developing countries. In the last part of this section, we shed light on some unintended effects of market-based instruments that may materialise in developing countries.

7.4.1   A Comparison of Product Taxes and Pollution Taxes in Developing Countries

The implementation of pollution taxes, as we saw in Section 7.3, requires regulators to have an idea of the MACs of average economic actors. If regulators do not know this, they will be unable to accurately predict the responses of economic agents. Moreover, it also requires monitoring of environmental parameters and enforcement, which is costly in developing countries where a higher share of firms belong to the informal sector, and thus they are more difficult to monitor. Other factors that may be important in determining the performance of pollution taxes are the quality of institutions and the enforcement of contracts (which is often substantially weaker in developing countries). An example of a pollution tax in a developing country is South Africa, which implemented an emissions-based pollution tax back in 2019. In this system, the tax is imposed on the use of fuels, based on emission factors.

Product taxes and energy taxes, on the other hand, may be relatively easier to implement in developing countries (since they are imposed on quantities of goods produced or inputs used, and not on actual environmental performance). As we discussed, they are not as efficient as pollution taxes, because they are not explicitly reducing emissions, but they may be the best solution for developing countries, at least in some cases. Product and energy taxes, for instance, have weaker monitoring and enforcement requirements than emissions-based pollution taxes. They also tend to be managed centrally, making them less subject to corrupt practices. Examples of energy taxes in the developing world include fuel taxes in countries such as India, Colombia, and Mexico.

7.4.2   A Comparison of Carbon Taxes and Permit Trading Systems in Developing Countries

As the arguments in Section 7.3 illustrated, in a simple economic setup, taxes and permit trading systems should be equivalent' however, in practice, often differences may arise in their effectiveness as instruments. This is particularly plausible in developing countries. For instance, while permits offer the advantage of certainty with respect to the number of emissions (and no requirement of knowing the MAC of a unit of pollution), in developing countries, their performance may be hindered by the fact that plant-level emissions data is mostly unavailable, and the difficulties of monitoring a large informal sector. In practice, other problems arise due to the illegitimate reporting of emissions.

On the other hand, carbon taxes offer some certainty with respect to the price, and the transaction costs of implementing tax-based policies are also low, even though inadequate regulatory/legal institutions, political pressure by large firms, a lack of political will, and negligence/corruption of enforcement agents may undermine this instrument, particularly in developing countries. As discussed previously, there are some challenges with the implementation of carbon taxes (and product/energy taxes may be better in some cases).

The choice between these instruments, as already mentioned, will depend on which of these (advantages or disadvantages) policymakers choose to weigh more heavily, and on public acceptability, as well as the strength of regulations and institutions in the country. We will touch upon these issues in more detail in Chapter 9.

Another interesting and important permit trading system is the clean development mechanism (CDM) that is still in place and has interesting positive effects for developing countries. The CDM is an international offset programme for carbon emissions that was proposed under the Kyoto Protocol in 1992. It allows countries that have committed to emissions reductions under the Kyoto Protocol to implement an emission-reduction project in developing countries. These projects are eligible to earn Certified Emission Reduction (CER) credits, which can be sold, each equivalent to one ton of CO_2, and these can be counted towards meeting Kyoto targets. In the scope of this project, industrialised countries have invested in both small-scale and large-scale projects in renewable generation, reduction of GHG emissions in industries such as cement and coal, demand-side energy-efficiency projects, and in afforestation and reforestation projects in developing countries.

7.4.3   Inefficiency of Fossil Fuel Subsidies

In general, many countries, particularly developing countries, have spent a lot on fossil fuel subsidies (including petroleum, natural gas, coal, and end-use electricity). A typical subsidy in developing countries is for the use of coal. These subsidies are often designed with the purpose of helping low-income consumers and stifling energy poverty. However, such subsidies are economically inefficient, because not only do fossil fuels contribute to climate change (and thus these subsidies are generating negative externalities), but their presence also implies that private investments in energy efficiency may not reach socially optimal levels.

Fossil fuel subsidies can either be producer subsidies (that reduce the costs for fossil fuel producers, for example, subsidies to produce electricity or transmission and distribution of natural gas) or consumer subsidies (that are applied to reduce the price of energy to end consumers, such as subsidies on cooking fuels such as liquified petroleum gas (LPG)).

There are multiple sources of inefficiency from the use of fossil fuels. This is illustrated in Figure 7.22, depicting the effects of subsidies in a hypothetical market for

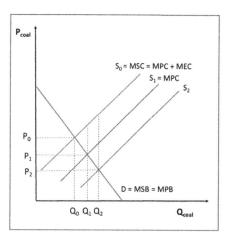

Figure 7.22 Market for coal

coal. As earlier, in this graph, we plot the demand function for coal that corresponds to the MSB curve, which in this case equals the MBP curve. Further, we have several upward-sloping supply functions that correspond to the MSC and the MPC curves, with and without considering the MEC.

The initial social welfare maximising equilibrium is denoted by (P_0, Q_0), where both producer costs and external costs from the use of coal are accounted for (given that it is the point where the MSC curve intersects the demand curve that corresponds to the MSB).

Now, we evaluate how the equilibrium in this market shifts if, first, policymakers were to ignore the negative externality from the production of coal; the new equilibrium point would be denoted by (P_1, Q_1) (where the MSB curve intersects the MPC curve), and this equilibrium gives rise to a dead-weight loss. This is the first source of inefficiency in this market. Furthermore, if policymakers incentivised the extraction of fossil fuels such as coal by subsidising its production, the supply curve for coal further shifts to the right to S_2. Thus, the equilibrium supply of coal increases further from Q_1 to Q_2, whereas the price of coal declines to P_2. Thus, subsidies not only imply lower coal prices and increased production but also lead to an increase in the total dead-weight loss to society.

This simple graphical framework illustrates that fossil fuel subsidies are both unsustainable and economically inefficient. Their presence also hampers investments in energy efficiency, as well as in renewable energy. For these reasons, many countries have taken active steps to phase out fossil fuel subsidies.

7.4.4 Unintended Effects of Market-based Instruments in Developing Countries

Given the low levels of energy access and electricity-consuming durable ownership in many parts of the developing world (such as of electric cook stoves), introducing policies such as taxes on the use of certain kinds of fuels (such as kerosene, or charcoal) can shift households away to sources of fuel that are outside the scope of taxation.

For example, households may switch to using firewood for cooking purposes after the introduction of such a tax. This would stem the effectiveness of the tax and still increase local environmental and health costs due to indoor air pollution. These considerations imply that policymakers need to consider context-specific constraints and changes in behaviour that may lead to unintended consequences from implementing market-based instruments.

7.4.5   Review Questions and Problems

The online question bank contains review questions and problems for this chapter, including solutions (see https://wp-prd.let.ethz.ch/exercisesfortextbookeep/).

8 Non-market-based Instruments

In the Chapter 7, we introduced market-based policy instruments which aim to alter the economic incentives of agents in an economy and thereby influence their behaviour. This chapter will discuss non-market-based energy and climate policy instruments. These can be either regulatory instruments, that is, rules imposed by governments that directly modify or affect the behaviour of households, firms, or organisations, or non-mandatory measures agreed upon by governments and other economic agents. Regulatory instruments, which play an important role in energy and climate policies, tend to impose restrictions or obligations on economic agents that limit their freedom of choice.

Broadly, traditional regulatory policies can be categorised into standards (this includes pollution and energy standards) as well as direct control measures (such as a ban on incandescent light bulbs, or a prohibition from using energy-intensive appliances such as washing machines during certain hours). As mentioned previously, non-market-based instruments can also include voluntary or negotiated approaches. Examples include any voluntary agreements between industry groups and the government or public disclosure programmes for firms, and these have also been found to have important effects in facilitating the shift to a green economy, in some instances. We describe each of the non-market-based instruments in further detail in the following subsections.

8.1 Standards

Standards are important tools of climate and energy policy and are pervasive in terms of their use across both industrialised and developing countries. Standards can be implemented with the goal of reducing energy consumption and/or emissions.

The introduction of an energy consumption standard will, indirectly, reduce emissions if the energy source consumed is a fossil fuel, whereas a pollution standard will directly reduce emissions. Moreover, both of them enhance the security of the energy supply.

Standards are broadly of two types:

- **Technology-based standards:** standards that designate the type of technology/equipment or method to be employed in the production of goods or energy services. For example, a government can impose that households can only use light-emitting diode (LED) technology for lighting.

- **Performance-based standards:** standards that specify a pollution or energy consumption limit to be upheld by economic agents. As an example, the European emission standards for vehicles have been adopted by many countries, and they are designed to limit the amount of pollutants released per kilometre driven by certain types of vehicles (including passenger vehicles). Another example is the use of energy consumption standards in the building sector. For instance, several European countries have introduced a rule defining the 'maximum' amount of permitted energy consumption per square metre for space heating in new buildings. This implies that new buildings have to be designed and constructed with insulation that allows them to meet the energy consumption standard.

Performance-based standards do not specify the kind of technology that should be used in the production and consumption of goods or services. Consequently, these standards allow firms and individuals to choose the best means of achieving their target and expand their compliance options. Technology-based standards, on the other hand, are better suited when there are few technological options available to firms and consumers to produce goods or energy services. Generally, standards in the energy and climate realms are performance-based standards rather than technology-based standards.

As mentioned previously, performance-based standards impose restrictions on the emission of pollution or energy consumption. Thus, by definition, their implementation implies that economic agents such as firms and households are likely to face some restrictions. It thus becomes important to investigate whether an efficient outcome is possible with a particular standard or not. Two questions that then arise with the use of standards are:

- Given some environmental objective (for instance, the reduction of emissions by 100 units), or some energy consumption target, is that objective being achieved by a standard in a cost-effective manner?
- Is the standard being set to achieve allocative efficiency, that is, does it lead to a situation in which the marginal social benefit (MSB) of abatement (or the MSB from decreasing energy consumption) equals the MAC (or the marginal abatement cost)?

It is important to note that standards are not always cost-effective and efficient policy instruments, for several reasons. First, imposing a standard in a situation in which economic agents face different technologies and costs to reduce pollution may be less cost-effective than using market-based instruments. Second, with pollution or energy consumption standards, polluters do not have to pay for the remaining pollution beyond the level set by the standard, which, if the policy is enforced properly, is also the level of compliance. In this case, the state doesn't receive revenue as with an environmental or energy tax. Last, the MSB and MAC of firms and households often vary across geographical regions, as well as at an individual level. Accordingly, a uniform standard will not be efficient when imposed on all firms or households, if abatement costs or benefits differ across agents. We illustrate some of these nuances using examples, as well as demonstrate why standards may be inefficient, in the following subsections.

Note that uniform environmental or energy taxes will also not be efficient if imposed on firms or households that have the same MAC function but different MSB functions. However, as we saw in Chapter 7, the implementation of market-based instruments poses some challenges too, and therefore, there are situations in which standards can be a viable solution, despite these limitations. For instance, in the presence of economic agents characterised by limited rationality, the effectiveness of some market-oriented instruments may be less than expected. With the presence of behavioural anomalies, the introduction of standards can make it possible to achieve goals that probably would be difficult to accomplish, with, for example, a CO_2 tax. Consider the real estate sector, where standards for buildings have been implemented in most industrialised countries over the past fifty years. In the 1970s, buildings consumed in Switzerland about twenty-two litres of oil equivalent per square metre for heating; this number stands at less than five litres today (as can be seen from Figure 8.1), and there are even buildings that produce energy. This is all thanks to the introduction of increasingly restrictive consumption standards that oblige all building owners (even those exhibiting limited rationality) to invest in energy efficiency. Using a market-based instrument such as the CO_2 tax may not have yielded the same outcome with certainty, because of the presence of behavioural anomalies. These anomalies make it difficult for individuals to incorporate price information in making long-term investment decisions in energy efficiency. This is only a hypothesis, not accompanied by an empirical study. Unfortunately, it is very difficult to perform an empirical study to analyse the relative effects of an energy consumption standard and of an energy/environmental tax on reducing the energy consumption per square metre of buildings. To do this, as we discuss in more detail in Chapter 9, we would need to compare the energy consumption per square metre in a region that implemented an energy consumption standard, and in another similar region that implemented an energy or environmental tax, while controlling for several other factors that could also affect policy effectiveness.

From a developing country's perspective, standards have both advantages and disadvantages. Some of their advantages are that they are relatively intuitive and straightforward, and often politically more feasible than other instruments such as taxes. Moreover, they can bring about environmental improvements relatively quickly. Some of their disadvantages are that they are often plagued with challenges related to poor enforcement, weak institutions, monitoring requirements, and so on, which are endemic in many developing country settings. Standards also provide the least incentives for innovation and the adoption of low-abatement technologies. For example, if the standard is satisfied, firms have poor incentives to reduce emissions further.

In this chapter, as in Chapter 7, we emphasise analysing various instruments based on their economic efficiency. That is, we use economic efficiency as the criterion for evaluating an energy or climate policy instrument. As we will see in Chapter 9, the choice of an instrument can also be based on other criteria, such as the practicality of implementation and control, administrative costs, or degree of effectiveness.

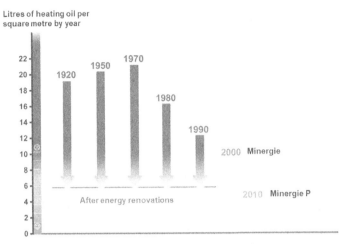

Figure 8.1 Impact of the introduction of energy consumption restriction
Adapted from energie-environment.ch [113]

In the following section, we concentrate on two types of performance-based standards that are relevant for energy and climate policy, that is, pollution and energy consumption standards that impose restrictions on emissions or on the level of energy consumption, respectively.

8.1.1   Pollution Standards

8.1.1.1   Pollution Standards and Efficiency

In this subsection, we will discuss the introduction of a pollution standard and its effect on economic efficiency in three cases. The first one is that of a simple economy with just one polluter, the second one considers the presence of two polluters having different abatement costs, and the last one takes into account two polluters that have the same abatement costs but are located in two different regions and have different marginal social benefit functions. In the first two cases, we present a comparison to a tax.

Case 1: A Single Polluter

Consider a simple economy with one polluting firm. This firm is a thermal power plant that uses coal for generating electricity and thus pollutes. Let us assume that the output of electricity generated in this economy is constant. Graphically, we can represent this simple setup as shown in Figure 8.2. As in Chapter 7, we plot the level of abatement on the x-axis and the benefits and costs on the y-axis. We have an upward sloping MAC curve, which denotes the rising costs per unit of abatement undertaken by the firm, and we have a downward sloping MSB curve, which denotes the declining benefits to society per additional unit of abatement undertaken. The efficient amount of abatement is denoted by A_E^*.

Now, we will use a comparison between a simple Pigouvian tax and a pollution standard to analyse their effects on efficiency. First, we assume that the state introduces

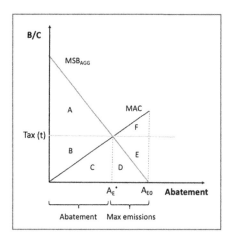

Figure 8.2 Functioning of pollution standards

a tax denoted by 't'. This is the optimal tax for this economy, given that it is set at the price where $MSB = MAC$, and as discussed in Chapter 7, this gives sufficient incentives to the firm to abate and reach the equilibrium allocation A_E^*. In this case, the coal power plant pays a total abatement cost equal to area C, and pays a per unit tax on the amount of emissions that it undertakes; the total amount of tax paid by the firm (and thus total tax revenue) is given by $D + E$.

Next, consider that the policymaker introduces a standard instead of a tax in this economy. Given that the MSB and MAC intersect at the abatement level A_E^*, the policymaker would set a standard that implies an abatement level A_E^*. Once the standard is set, the efficient level of abatement A_E^* is achieved, which again means that the total abatement cost would be the area under the marginal abatement cost up to that point, given by C. However, in this case, the state does not earn any revenue, given that the standard simply caps the maximum emissions in the economy, without assigning a price. This implies that for the quantity of pollution between A_{E0} and A_E^*, the firm is not required to pay anything to the state. Therefore, the polluter-pays principle is not valid. Thus, from a social perspective, the tax would be a better policy instrument compared to a standard.

Case 2: Two Polluters with Heterogeneous Abatement Costs
In the previous case, we discussed a simple situation characterised by the presence of one firm that emits pollution, with the state having information on both the optimal level of abatement and the marginal abatement cost. Let us now use an example to show why a standard might not minimise the cost of firms in the case of non-uniform marginal abatement costs, that is, marginal abatement costs that differ across agents. Consider a case similar to the one proposed in Chapter 7, where two firms initially emit a total of twenty units of emissions or pollution. The policymaker then decides that the environment can assimilate/withstand only ten units of pollution so the two firms need to abate a total of ten units of emissions. Figure 8.3 shows the level of abatement on the horizontal axis and the benefits and costs of the two firms on the two vertical axes. Point a is the origin with respect to Firm 1, whereas point b is the origin of Firm 2.

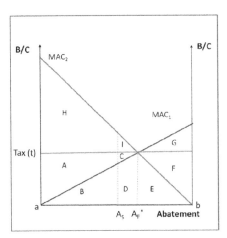

Figure 8.3 Standards and non-uniform MAC

Thus, on moving right from point a, Firm 1's abatement levels increase, whereas its emission levels decrease. Likewise, on moving left from point b, Firm 2's abatement levels increase, whereas its emissions decrease. The horizontal axis ab thus captures the total emissions that are permitted in this economy (which, after the standard is imposed, would be ten units). The primary vertical axis denotes the benefits and costs for Firm 1, while the secondary vertical axis is valid for Firm 2. MAC_1 denotes the marginal abatement cost for Firm 1, and these costs increase as levels of abatement for Firm 1 increase, while MAC_2 denotes the marginal abatement cost for Firm 2.

According to the equi-marginal principle that we discussed in Chapter 7, the efficient abatement level is achieved where the two MAC curves intersect at A_E^*, and at this point, the total abatement cost is also minimised. In this economy, it costs Firm 1 less to abate each unit of emissions than it costs Firm 2, thus Firm 1 abates more (i.e., reduces emissions more) than Firm 2.

As we saw previously, a pollution tax imposed at the level 't' would result in a total abatement cost given by the sum of the areas under both the MAC curves at the equilibrium level of abatement: for Firm 1, this is $B + D$, whereas, for Firm 2, it is E. Thus, the total abatement cost is given by $B + D + E$. The government revenue in this case would be given by the total area under the horizontal tax line, which is equal to $A + B + C + D + E + F$.

Alternatively, the government might implement a uniform standard (A_S) that requires each firm to abate five units. If such a standard is imposed, the total abatement cost would be given again by the sum of the areas under both MAC curves at the level of abatement defined by the standard, now given by A_S. This is area B for Firm 1, and areas $D + C + E + I$ for Firm 2. Thus, the total abatement cost with uniform standards is $B + C + D + E + I$, while no associated government revenue is generated. Consequently, the uniform standard achieves the goal of ten units of abatement at a higher cost than the pollution tax does (i.e., the total abatement costs are no longer minimised), without yielding any revenue to policymakers.

Case 3: Two Polluters in Regions with Heterogeneous Abatement Benefits

As previously discussed, another possible source of lost economic efficiency in the implementation of pollution standards is the presence of two polluters that are located in two regions that have different MSB functions of abatement. This difference may arise due to differences in population density in these regions, for example. Consider two coal power plants, one operating in a rural area and the other one in an urban area. It is clear that the power plant located in the urban area will cause higher social costs (e.g., on health) than the one located in the rural area, where the population density is lower.

Figure 8.4 shows the impact of implementing a standard in this case. The x-axis again represents the levels of abatement, and the y-axis represents the costs and benefits. Consider two coal power plants (X and Y) having the same marginal abatement cost, but located in two different regions of a country. Thus, in this simple economy, $MAC_X = MAC_Y$. Furthermore, assume that their marginal social benefit functions of abatement (MSB_X and MSB_Y) differ, as shown in the diagram. Thus, the marginal social benefits from each unit of pollution abated are higher in region Y, than they are in region X (since MSB_Y is higher than MSB_X). For reasons of simplicity, the graph only shows the MSB curves without the MPB curves. To reduce emissions, the policy-maker implements a uniform standard that applies to both regions, let us assume that this standard is set at the level A_S. As in the previous example, this does not lead to the optimal or efficient level of abatement. For the firm located in region X, the required level of abatement is set too high, whereas, for the firm located in region Y (that has a higher MSB from abating), the abatement level is set too low. The respective efficient levels for both firms are A_X and A_Y. Thus, with polluters located in different regions, setting a uniform standard is not an economically efficient outcome. Note that in this situation, in which the MSB is different in both regions, setting a uniform environmental tax will also lead to an inefficient solution.

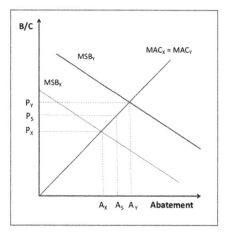

Figure 8.4 Impact of implementing standards

From the presentation of these three cases, it is evident that introducing pollution standards can create some economic inefficiency. In particular, with respect to an environmental tax, a standard in the presence of different pollution abatement functions among economic agents is less cost-effective. Moreover, for the level of pollution that still exists after the introduction of the standard, the economic agents don't have to pay; therefore, the polluter-pay principle doesn't apply and the standard is less efficient than an environmental tax.

8.1.1.2   Enforcement of Pollution/Emission Standards

The enforcement of emission standards can be challenging, given that they require consistent monitoring and enforcement. In this subsection, we illustrate the importance of enforcement in delivering the efficacy of emission standards and argue how poor enforcement might undermine their performance as instruments.

First, consider the scenario where a policymaker is setting an emission standard, and that there exists a single polluting firm in this market. This is illustrated in Figure 8.5, which plots the abatement level on the x-axis and the benefits and costs on the y-axis. As shown in the diagram, the policymaker will choose to set an emission standard that implies an abatement level A, where the MAC intersects the MSB.

Now, imagine that the policymaker decides to impose a penalty on the firm if it abates less than A and that the enforcement of this measure is perfect, that is, the firm that does not comply will be penalised with probability 1. At what level should she set this penalty to ensure that the firm complies with the rule and fully abates at A? Consider the penalty level P indicated in the diagram. If the penalty is set at P, the cost to the firm of abating at level A (i.e., full abatement) will be given by the total area $B + C + D$, which is given by the total area under the MAC up to abatement level A. The firm does not pay any penalty in this case and fully complies with the rule. If instead, the firm decides to violate the rule and abate at any level less than A (such as A'), the cost to the firm would comprise two components: the total abatement cost up

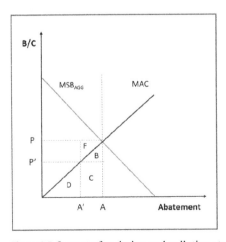

Figure 8.5 Impact of emission and pollution standards

to level A' (indicated by area D), and the total penalty that the firm would then need to pay. This penalty will equal the difference between the target level of abatement and actual abatement multiplied by the per unit penalty, and it is equal to the total area $B + C + F$ in the diagram. Thus, the total cost to the firm equals $B + C + D + F$. Given the perfect enforcement, a firm will then weigh its options and prefer to abate fully at level A, instead of undercutting abatement at A', because it costs the firm less to comply.

This argument suggests that setting the right penalty (i.e., equal to P shown in the previous diagram) is very important. What happens if the policymaker decides to set another penalty level? Let us assume that they set a penalty at a lower level such as P' instead of at the optimal level. Setting the penalty at the lower level will disincentivise the firm from undertaking full abatement in this economy. If the firm chose to abate fully at A, it would incur a total cost equal to $B + C + D$, given that it then does not pay any penalties for under-abating. However, if the firm chooses to abate at level A' shown in the diagram, the total cost to the firm will be the total abatement cost (given by area D), and the total penalty (which will now equal only C, given the lower penalty imposed). Thus, the firm's total cost equals $C + D$, which is less than what it would have incurred if it fully abated ($B + C + D$). Thus, the firm will rationally break the law in this case and under-abate. On the other hand, if the policymaker were to make a mistake and set a penalty higher than P, the firm will not deviate from full abatement, that is, it would still be in their interest to undertake full abatement. Thus, such a penalty will not be very useful (or it would not yield a different outcome).

This reasoning can be extended to understand the significance of the enforcement of standards. Consider that the policymaker puts in place a penalty P for abating any unit less than the level A, but is unable to strictly enforce this policy. This implies that the probability of being penalised is lower than 1, and the expected penalty imposed on the firm will be lower than P, for instance, P' in the diagram. As we saw, with a lower penalty such as P', the firm has the incentive to under-abate (for example, at A') rather than fully abate at A, and society will not reach the optimal allocation. Thus, poor enforcement of a standard (to the extent that it reduces the average penalty paid by the firm) will result in a suboptimal equilibrium.

8.1.2 Energy Standards

Energy standards can also play a pivotal role in reaching energy and climate policy goals.

Energy standards are primarily meant to reduce the consumption of energy through an improvement in the level of energy efficiency. As illustrated in Figure 8.6, the implementation of energy standards has three effects that may be relevant to energy and climate goals. These are (1) the reduction of pollution (if, for example, the energy system is dominated by polluting fuels), (2) an increase in the security of supply, and (3) mitigation of private energy expenditures (due to an augmenting in energy efficiency).

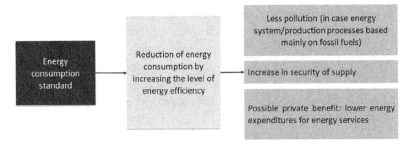

Figure 8.6 Effects of energy standards

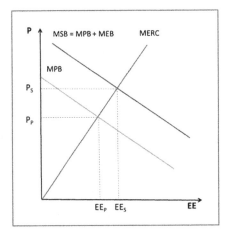

Figure 8.7 Impact of adoption of energy-efficient technologies

8.1.2.1   Energy Standards and Efficiency

The mechanisms driving the adoption of energy-efficient technologies for an economic agent are shown in Figure 8.7, a figure similar to the one presented in Chapter 7. The graph plots the level of energy efficiency (EE) (and equivalently, the decline in energy consumption) on the x-axis and the costs and benefits of investing in energy efficiency on the y-axis. The red and green lines represent the MPB and the MSB curves. The MPB curve represents the private benefits from the reduction in energy consumption (which also implies a reduction in private energy expenditures) obtained by increasing the level of energy efficiency using more efficient technologies. This curve represents the demand function for the level of energy efficiency. The MSB additionally considers the presence of a positive externality in improving energy efficiency levels, thus is represented as the sum of the MPB and the MEB.

The positive externality of investing in energy efficiency takes into account the reduction in air pollution and the resulting improvement in energy supply security. The upward-sloping MERC indicates the increasing marginal costs of improving energy efficiency and, therefore, of reducing energy consumption. If no positive externalities are considered, the private optimum is reached at the level of energy efficiency denoted by EE_P. However, since there are positive externalities associated with these energy efficiency improvements, economic efficiency is reached at EE_S where the MSB curve intersects the aggregate $MERC$ curve. To reach the efficient level of energy efficiency, the state should introduce an energy standard that implies a level of energy efficiency equal to EE_S.

Of course, as with the pollution standard, it can be difficult for the state to identify the right level of the energy standard. This difficulty will increase with heterogeneous economic agents that have different marginal private or social benefit functions or that are located in different regions and, therefore, have different marginal social benefit functions. In these situations, the introduction of a uniform standard will create economic inefficiencies similar to the pollution standard. In this subsection, we discuss a situation characterised by economic agents that have different marginal social benefit functions.

Let us assume that the policymaker wants to implement an energy standard to limit the energy consumption for heating services. We consider a case in which this energy standard is imposed on two households having different marginal social benefit functions as shown in Figure 8.8. This might be the case if households use different energy sources for heating purposes, or are located in two different regions with two different MSB functions. To illustrate the first example, let us now assume that if household 1 lives in an old building with an oil-based heating system, an energy standard imposed on this household would have a different effect than it would on household 2, which we assume resides in an old house that heats using some form of renewable energy (and thus, has a lower MSB curve).

In Figure 8.8, the $MERC$ function is the same for both households, but their marginal social benefits differ. For household 2, abatement (i.e., an increase in energy efficiency) yields a smaller benefit to society, so MSB_{H2} is lower than MSB_{H1}. For reasons of simplicity, the graph only shows the marginal social benefit curves without the marginal private benefit curves. When an energy standard is introduced at a level of energy efficiency given by EE_{H1}, both households are obliged to meet this level of energy efficiency, for instance, 50 kWh/m^2. While this level of energy efficiency

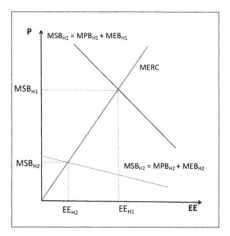

Figure 8.8 Energy standards and heterogeneous market benefits

is optimal for household 1, it is far above the socially optimal level for household 2 (that already uses a renewable energy-based heating system) which would be at EE_{H2}. Accordingly, for the household that uses renewable energy, additional costs are generated by the implementation of this standard. In such cases, the energy standard could be substituted by policy instruments such as an energy tax for fossil fuels or a pollution tax that is more likely to lead to an efficient solution for everyone.

Energy efficiency standards for refrigerators in Brazil: A methodology for impact evaluation

Evidence suggests that standards have achieved significant reductions in energy consumption in some developing countries. In this study, Augustus de Melo and de Martino Jannuzzi (2010) [114] looked into the effectiveness of minimum energy performance standards (MEPS) established in 2007 for refrigerators and freezers in Brazil. The authors used a bottom-up econometric approach to evaluate the potential for energy savings with refrigerators and freezers, using household survey data. Their cost-benefit analysis predicted significant reductions in energy consumption, even in the presence of high discount rates, with the implementation of these standards. From a societal point of view, the energy and cost-saving potential of the MEPS was projected to reach 21 TWh (which was around 25 per cent of the then residential consumption) over 2010–2030.

8.2   Direct Control Measures

Apart from standards, traditional means of regulation also include direct control measures. These are measures taken by governments or companies to directly control the behaviour of firms and households. With such instruments, the freedom of regulated firms and households is curtailed. Examples include limiting the usage of installed appliances during peak load periods (when electricity demand is very high), bans on the circulation of highly inefficient and polluting cars, as well as the ban on incandescent light bulbs, which has been implemented in several countries. An example of an adaptation-based direct control measure is requiring people to stay at home during extreme weather events or putting restrictions on the working hours of construction workers during heatwaves. Yet another example is the enforcement of urban planning requirements to minimise energy consumption as well as damages due to climate change (e.g., green and shading zones, protective infrastructure for extreme weather, zoning to avoid threats from flooding or sliding due to excessive rain, etc.).

In this section, we illustrate the economic effect of a direct control measure that curtails the use of appliances. In particular, we analyse the effect of introducing a limit on the usage of washing machines during peak load periods, using Figure 8.9. On the x-axis of the figure, we plot the electricity consumption (Q_E), and on y-axis, we plot the price (P) and the costs (C). The figure illustrates a step-wise supply function of electricity (S), the electricity demand during the off-peak period (DOP), and the demand curve during the peak period (DP).

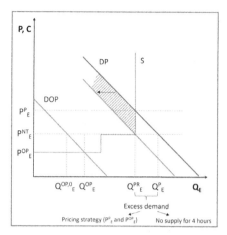

Figure 8.9 Impact of pricing strategy and time restrictions

If a utility imposes a single normal price at the level P_E^{NT}, the electricity demand during the off-peak period would be $Q_E^{OP,0}$ and during the peak period, it would then be Q_E^P. As can be seen from the figure, due to the limited production capacity defined by the level Q_E^{PR}, the utility cannot offer the quantity Q_E^P in the peak period. Therefore, as indicated in the figure, we have a situation of excess demand, that is, a shortage of electricity. To solve this issue, the utility could adopt a direct control measure and introduce a ban on using washing machines during the peak period (e.g., households can be curtailed from using appliances for four hours). In doing this, the demand function is moved to the left, until the level of maximum capacity is reached and, therefore, an equilibrium between supply and demand is achieved (at Q_E^{PR}).

Of course, an alternative strategy that the utility could introduce to reduce this shortfall would be a time differentiation in the pricing structure, that is, a peak and an off-peak pricing scheme, which is a market-based instrument. In this case, consumers would pay a lower price than the normal price during the off-peak period (P_E^{OP}) and a much higher price during the peak period (P_E^P). As can be seen from the figure, these 'time-of-use' rates would guarantee an equilibrium and ensure zero shortages. Furthermore, time-of-use rates would avoid welfare loss by curtailing consumption during the peak period, represented by the dark area between the two demand functions, one drawn with the restriction imposed and the other without this restriction. Thus, it is apparent that the implementation of a direct measure such as a ban on using washing machines would lead to a welfare loss for consumers in this case. We should, however, keep in mind that price differentiation could create distributional issues, because only some households may be able to pay a high price to use their appliances.

Time-varying pricing may increase total electricity consumption: Evidence from Costa Rica

The effectiveness of policy instruments may often depend on socioeconomic as well as behavioural factors that govern how households respond to them. For example, in a study on Costa Rica, Capitan et al. (2021) [115] evaluated the effectiveness of time-varying pricing by a major electric utility. Time-varying pricing implies that electric utilities introduce higher prices during peak demand and lower prices during periods of low electricity demand. The authors found that the introduction of this policy actually increased total electricity consumption: households reduced consumption during peak periods, but increased consumption during off-peak periods significantly, due to lower electricity prices. Since many households in developing countries do not use heating or cooling devices, the scope for technological improvement (that can potentially reduce consumption during peak and off-peak periods) is only limited in these settings. Thus, rebound effects such as the one observed in this study may be prevalent.

8.3   Non-market-oriented Instruments and Behavioural Anomalies

In Chapter 7, we discussed the effects of introducing a subsidy to promote the adoption of energy-efficient heating systems with rational and boundedly rational consumers. In this section, we will analyse the impact of using a standard instead of using a monetary market-oriented instrument considering two types of consumers, boundedly rational and rational. In Figure 8.10, we illustrate the choice of the level of energy efficiency of heating systems. The graph is similar to Figure 7.21 in Chapter 7 and includes three demand functions: the marginal private benefit function which represents the demand of a rational (MPB_R) consumer, the marginal private benefit function of a boundedly rational consumer (MPB_{BR}), and the marginal social benefit function for energy efficiency. The third demand function is obtained by summing the marginal private benefit function (for rational consumers) with the marginal external benefit, and it represents the marginal social benefits of increasing the level of energy efficiency of heating systems, assuming all consumers are rational. The graph also includes the upward-sloping MERC curve, which indicates the increasing marginal costs of improving the heating system's energy efficiency, and therefore the marginal cost of reducing energy consumption.

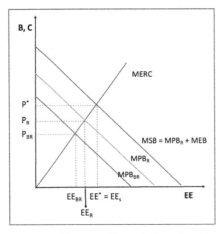

Figure 8.10 The case of boundedly rational households

If positive externalities are not considered, the private optimum for rational consumers is reached at the level of energy efficiency denoted by EE_R, and the private optimum for the boundedly rational consumers is reached at EE_{BR}. However, since energy efficiency improvements are typically associated with positive externalities when these are considered, economic efficiency is achieved at EE^* where the MSB curve intersects the $MERC$ curve. To reach this efficient level of energy efficiency, the state could set an energy efficiency standard for the heating system at the level of energy efficiency $EE^*=EE_S$ where the social optimum is achieved. As can be seen from the figure, the standard would force rational and boundedly rational consumers to adopt an optimal heating system from a societal point of view.

Using an energy standard may become quite relevant in the presence of boundedly rational consumers who tend to under-invest in energy efficiency. Boundedly rational consumers tend to, for various reasons, not undertake investment calculations, and thereby underestimate the future benefits of investments in energy efficiency. As discussed in Chapter 7, the introduction of a subsidy may then not be enough to shift the marginal private benefits function of the boundedly rational consumers towards the social optimum. A standard can force these consumers to reach the social optimum. Direct control measures are also potentially interesting in the presence of boundedly rational consumers who don't respond to monetary measures such as subsidies, taxes, and prices. For instance, let's consider the example from Section 8.2 with a situation of excess demand. In this case, the utility could implement either a time-differentiated tariff or a ban on washing machines during some hours to avoid peak electricity demand. With boundedly rational consumers who don't react to price increases (or only react partially), the introduction of a time-differentiated pricing strategy will likely not be enough to solve the problem. Using a ban on some important electrical appliances could be an interesting solution to this situation.

To summarise some of the main points that we discussed in this chapter about the cost-effectiveness and efficiency of the different policy measures:

1. In the presence of varying MACs or MERCs but the same MSB function across different economic agents, standards can be costly, and do not require agents to cover the social costs for the remaining pollution.
2. With homogeneous MAC functions or MERCs, but different MSB levels, uniform standards and taxes are both creating economic inefficiency.
3. Direct control measures generally create economic inefficiency with respect to market-based instruments.
4. With boundedly rational economic agents, the use of standards and direct control measures can provide a means to ensure that society reaches the optimal equilibrium.

Therefore, from a policymaker's point of view, it is essential in the choice of policy instruments to consider the advantages and disadvantages of market-oriented and non-market-oriented tools in the presence of both rational and boundedly rational consumers.

8.4   Voluntary Agreements

Voluntary agreements are the last form of non-market-based instrument that we discuss in this chapter. These are mostly signed between private parties and governments and serve the purpose of not only meeting certain energy or climate objectives but also of potentially improving performance on these measures beyond the levels required by traditional regulatory instruments. They are popular policy measures among economic agents such as firms that are directly affected by them because firms can have a say in the design of these instruments. Moreover, voluntary agreements are less likely to face political opposition.

By definition, a voluntary agreement does not mandate that any firm participate in it. However, voluntary participation may, in some cases, entail rewards or penalties. Examples include firms agreeing to reduce emissions or to adopt energy-efficient technologies, and in some instances, there are also reporting requirements. Another form of voluntary agreement could be one between firms in an industry, whereby they come together to negotiate on behaviours or technologies that they need to adopt, and then third parties may keep track of the group's progress.

Note that voluntary agreements offer participants some benefits. For example, they are used by firms to augment their reputation both with the public and with shareholders. They may also serve as an important means for other (mostly smaller) firms to gain knowledge on means of reducing emissions (especially if participants agree to public disclosure rules). Last, voluntary agreements are important in engaging firms in meeting climate and energy objectives. Of course, there is an element of self-selection involved in the design of this instrument. Only firms that are either committed to meeting these objectives, or those that are in a capacity to do so, tend to participate in such programmes. Having said that, voluntary agreements are a useful policy to complement other measures.

One example of a voluntary agreement is the Long-Term Agreement on Energy Efficiency for the non-ETS sectors (LTA3) from the Netherlands. Participants in the agreement join on a voluntary basis, and once they join, they are required to make a long-term energy-efficiency plan (LTEEP) detailing the steps that they will take to reduce energy consumption. Among developing countries, many Latin American countries (such as Mexico and Colombia) have been using this policy measure to negotiate voluntary clean production agreements for several years.

8.5   Issues in Developing Countries

We have presented some of the main non-market instruments in this chapter, including standards as well as direct control measures. Below, we discuss some of the merits as well as challenges with the use of these instruments in developing countries, in particular pollution standards and one specific type of direct control measure, license plate-based driving restrictions. We also discuss the role of technology and information provision in determining the efficacy of standards as instruments in developing countries. As we will see, the primary constraints with the implementation of standards are related to enforcement, information, and inequality.

8.5.1   Enforcement of Standards

As we argued in Chapter 1, developing countries are facing the brunt of outdoor air pollution, and as we saw above, while pollution standards may be useful instruments for addressing this problem, enforcement and monitoring may often hinder their effectiveness as instruments in developing countries. A report by the United Nations Environment Programme (UNEP) suggests that only 33 per cent of countries impose obligations to meet legally mandated pollution standards and that at least 37 per cent of countries do not legally require monitoring [116].

With a startling 92 per cent of the population of the world living in regions with pollution levels exceeding the World Health Organisation (WHO) guidelines for ambient air quality, it is critical for policymakers to intervene and treat air quality as a public good. Given that instruments such as pollution standards define the quantity of permissible pollution, in principle, they may be highly effective in improving air quality relatively quickly in urban areas of developing countries, which has significant potential to improve human health outcomes. However, it is important that their implementation is accompanied by legal mechanisms to monitor air quality levels, and improvements in enforcement, which may be challenging in developing countries.

The importance of enforcement is also clear from the implementation of energy standards in developing countries. For example, the Indian government passed the Energy Conservation Building Code (ECBC), which imposes minimum energy standards for new commercial buildings. While the law was developed by the national government (the Bureau of Energy Efficiency), the implementation, and thus enforcement, of the codes varies across Indian states. For example, the state of Telangana adopted the third-party auditor model of implementation, in which a pool of experts at the state level ensures the enforcement of the building codes. This type of enforcement has been found, in some studies, to yield greater reductions in energy consumption and/or lower levels of emissions (with pollution standards).

It is clear that monitoring emissions, and thus enforcement, are also critical elements to ensure the success of policy instruments such as standards. As technological advances make monitoring emissions easier, enforcement of these instruments can also be expected to improve. The development of continuous emissions monitoring systems (CEMS) that continually track emissions from plants is a step in this direction, and as the costs of such technologies drop, policymakers may consider mandating their use by firms.

Role of incentives in enforcement of standards in developing countries

We have learnt that when policymakers cannot enforce standards, the effectiveness of these measures is questionable. Duflo et al. (2013) [117] add an additional perspective to this notion of enforcement in developing countries by considering the role of incentives. The authors argued that the incentives of enforcement agents such as environmental inspectors matter for the success of the policy. If inspectors have incentives to misreport their findings at an inspection site, firms are unlikely to abide by a standard. The article introduced above drew on evidence from energy audits conducted in the Indian state of Gujarat. It found that third-party environmental auditors misreported firm-level emissions when firms chose the auditors that inspected their firms. In line with these findings, randomly assigning auditors to firms resulted in more accurate tracking of emissions by auditors, and subsequently lower emissions by firms. In a wider context, the study indicates that the effects of monitoring and enforcement are substantial.

8.5.2 Role of Information Provision in Facilitating the Effectiveness of Standards

Information provision can also enhance the effectiveness of standards. Individuals in many developing countries have a low willingness to pay for improvements in air quality, because they are unaware of the health effects of air pollution, have cognitive biases that prevent them from understanding the benefits, or there is unclear communication from authorities on health hazards from pollution. In this respect, clear and consistent communication and information campaigns may augment the willingness to pay consumers for improvements in air quality, and this in turn can lead to a demand for regulation and heightened pressure on policymakers to deliver with regulations. This has been argued to be the reason for the effectiveness of air pollution regulation in India, whereas water pollution regulation has largely been ineffective, as highlighted by Greenstone and Hanna (2014) [118].

8.5.3 License Plate-based Driving Restrictions

A form of direct control measure which is quite common in developing countries is the license plate-based driving restriction. In this system, cars can operate only on certain days of the week based on the license plate number (e.g., Beijing, New Delhi, Quito, Mexico City, Bogota, Santiago, etc.).

While this policy is used to reduce congestion as well as exhaust fumes from vehicles, there is mixed evidence to suggest whether they have been effective in reducing air pollution. Moreover, there are costs to these policies, such as inconvenience and the opportunity cost of time, which, in some situations, may affect poor people more. Thus, these measures also create inequalities. For instance, relatively wealthier individuals may be able to buy a second car to circumvent these regulations, while poorer households may not be able to make these investments.

With license plate-based driving restrictions, policymakers need to ask some important questions before deciding to implement them:

1. How binding is the programme, in terms of the areas where restrictions are imposed, and the number of times a day one can use the vehicle?
2. What is the next best alternative? Such policies can only work if a viable and clean public transport system is available.

3. How easy is it for consumers to buy additional cars? Is there a strong second-hand or used car market? Individuals could purchase another car, having a different license plate number.
4. What are the exemptions to these rules? For instance, in many cities in developing countries that implemented these policies (e.g., New Delhi), motorcycles and two-wheelers were still allowed to be driven, even though they comprise the largest share of the vehicle fleet.

Impact of driving restrictions in developing countries

Carillo et al. (2016) [119] analysed the impact of the *Pico y Placa* Programme in Quito, Ecuador. The PyP programme aimed at reducing air pollution and traffic congestion in Quito by restricting motor vehicles on working days. Unlike other countries, where the driving restrictions failed to bring a difference, the PyP programme helped reduce carbon monoxide concentrations in the peak hours by 9–11 per cent. The authors found that this was due to a reduction in vehicle flows and that there was no shifting of traffic to other locations or times of the day. Likewise, Viard and Fu (2015) [120] analysed a similar policy in China. Driving restrictions were imposed in Beijing that led to reductions in pollution. In the short term, based on a driving restriction of one day per week, air pollution is reduced by 21 per cent. However, this restriction also resulted in higher daily commuting costs, which negatively affected discretionary labour supply. The authors argued that the driving restriction scheme was useful in reducing air pollution in the short run, but also emphasised that it was not the most economically optimal means to achieve this reduction, given that the restriction was based on the license plate number of the vehicle.

8.5.4   Review Questions and Problems

The online question bank contains review questions and problems for this chapter, including solutions (see https://wp-prd.let.ethz.ch/exercisesfortextbookeep/).

9   Policy Choice and Evaluation

In Chapters 7 and 8, we discussed several market-oriented and non-market-oriented energy and climate policy instruments. Each policy instrument has specific characteristics, and can thus be used to solve a market failure or behavioural anomaly. For example, in the presence of positive externalities from the use of a new energy-efficient technology, a policymaker might want to introduce a subsidy to promote the adoption of this new technology. Furthermore, in the presence of bounded rationality, the policymaker may also want to introduce nudges or standards. Finally, if market failures and behavioural anomalies both coexist in an economy (as is typical in many cases), a combination of instruments may be needed to address the multitude of problems.

In this chapter, we propose and examine some vital criteria for selecting and implementing either a single policy instrument or a mix of policy instruments.

9.1   Policy Evaluation Criteria

Optimal policy instrument choice and the right balance of policies are not trivial goals for policymakers. Economists have developed some criteria to help policymakers identify the policies to adopt.

From an economic point of view, as mentioned in Chapters 7 and 8, the most important rule for selecting 'desirable' policy instruments is to compare their benefits and costs, that is, to analyse whether a policy instrument increases the level of economic efficiency (productive, allocative, and dynamic) and, more generally, the welfare of society. However, it is also essential to judge policy instruments on other dimensions, such as distributional issues (impact on different socioeconomic income groups and regions), macroeconomic issues (impact on economic growth, inflation, and employment), and the level of acceptance and administrative feasibility of the instruments as well.

The following criteria can be considered when deciding the policy mix:

- **Productive and allocative efficiency**: an economic system achieves productive and allocative efficiency when, given scarce resources, it can produce goods and services by minimising the resources and optimally allocating them given consumer preferences. In such a situation, the welfare of society is maximised. A policy instrument is efficient from an economic point of view if it improves productive and/or allocative efficiency.

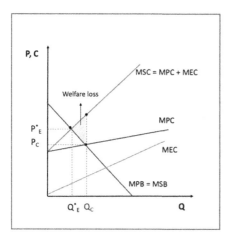

Figure 9.1 Welfare loss without considering externalities of electricity produced by coal plant

To apply this criterion, we first need to estimate the impact of a proposed policy on these two efficiency measures. For instance, in an electricity market dominated by power plants that use fossil fuels such as coal, introducing a CO_2 tax will eliminate the welfare loss, as illustrated in Figure 9.1 (and already explained in Chapter 2). In this case, the CO_2 tax will lead to an improvement in the level of allocative efficiency, as before the introduction of the tax, the price was not set equal to the marginal social cost. Of course, this welfare gain should be compared to the implementation and enforcement costs of a CO_2 tax (discussed later in further detail).

- **Dynamic efficiency**: dynamic efficiency is related to the production processes of energy services and goods by firms and households. In the energy and climate policy context, a firm or household is dynamically efficient if, over time, it can introduce new production methods that contribute towards achieving sustainable development. Therefore, a policy measure is efficient from a dynamic point of view if it provides incentives to invest in research and development that can generate the optimal rate of technological change to reduce average costs, exploit renewable energy sources, improve energy efficiency, and thus ensure sustainable development. For example, R&D subsidies for firms operating in the heating sector may allow them to develop new, more efficient, heating systems based on renewable energy sources that also reduce the production cost of heating services, as depicted in Figure 9.2 (rotation of the heating cost function 1 (HC_1) to heating cost function 2 (HC_2)). Another example is the introduction of pollution or energy taxes, or performance-based pollution standards, that generally provide incentives for advancements in pollution abatement technologies.

- **Effectiveness**: the efficiency criterion assumes that energy and climate policy instruments are effective, that is, that they have a substantial impact on the variable that they are intended to change, such as energy consumption, electric car adoption, or innovation. Empirical evidence, however, suggests that energy and climate policy measures need not always be effective. Therefore, before analysing

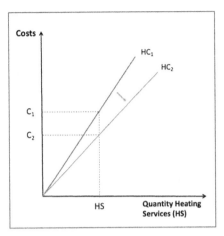

Figure 9.2 Dynamic efficiency and heating costs

the impact of a policy measure on the level of welfare, it is essential to conduct empirical analyses to verify whether there is any effect of the measure on the outcome variable of interest. For example, a subsidy for the adoption of electric cars may not work, because not all consumers may know about the presence of the subsidy. Additionally, some consumers may be boundedly rational, and therefore may fail to consider the car subsidy in the calculation of the life cycle cost, and in doing so, they may end up purchasing less expensive, but also less efficient vehicles. For this reason, the evaluation process is an essential first step to verify the effectiveness or impact of a policy measure using empirical methods, some of which will be discussed in more detail later in this chapter.

- **Macroeconomic effects**: the introduction of energy or climate policy instruments such as taxes or standards can lead to economic effects on the markets directly affected by these instruments, as well as result in economic effects at the economy-wide level such as changes in employment, or in gross domestic product (GDP) growth. Therefore, in choosing a policy measure, it is important to also consider these effects.

- **Fairness**: introducing a policy instrument may engender costs and benefits that vary across geographic regions or segments of the population. It is, therefore, essential to analyse the heterogeneity in the effects of a policy instrument among all economic agents and to judge if these distributional effects align with the general level of fairness and equity that is acceptable to society. Of course, in the application of this criterion, one should also consider the intergenerational equity dimension (namely, the distributional impacts of a policy measure across generations).

- **Acceptance**: generally, it is important that proposed energy and climate policy measures are accepted and supported by citizens. In a direct-democracy system, consideration of an instrument that does not have the support of citizens may lead to a referendum, and thus to a possible rejection, which implies a lengthening of the time frame for policy implementation. In an indirect democratic system, an unpopular instrument may lead to citizens taking to the streets to protest publicly in authorised or unauthorised forms, or to go on strike. In this context, public communication campaigns play an important role in providing information on the introduction of the measure, as well as on its possible distributional effects. For example, suppose that the distributional effects of introducing a CO_2 tax are not adequately communicated, both while levying the tax and while distributing the tax revenue. In such a scenario, the proposal to introduce a CO_2 tax is likely to create significant opposition. For instance, in the case of the introduction of a CO_2 tax where the revenues of the tax are redistributed to the households and firms, it is essential to explain and communicate the re-distributional effects of the system. Due to the importance of this criterion from a practical point of view, we will discuss the relationship between distributional effects and social acceptance in further detail in Section 9.2.

- **Enforceability and administrative practicality**: the identified policy measure should be transparent and easy to implement and administer. Moreover, it should also be feasible to monitor its performance (and check for compliance), while minimising possible evasion and avoidance behaviour.

9.2   Distributional Issues and Acceptance of Policy Instruments

The introduction of energy and climate policies can produce different effects among consumers and firms on the level of negative externalities experienced, on income and wealth, and on the level of access to energy sources.

We know from the literature that air pollution and greenhouse gas emissions generally affect individuals differently, both within a country and across countries. This implies an unequal distribution of the burden across individuals, regions, and countries. For instance, a household living in an urban area close to a road with heavy traffic is generally more affected by local air pollution, compared to a household living in a more suburban area. Given that low-income urban households generally tend to live in areas where land or real estate may be cheaper, but that are likely to be more polluted, air pollution will disproportionately tend to affect these households compared to richer households, who tend to live in less polluted areas. Furthermore, at the international level, we have seen in Chapter 1 that some low-income countries are more affected by climate change than high-income countries. Therefore, we can say that air pollution and climate change are natural sources of inequity. These inequities are more stark at the global level, whereas they are weaker within the urban areas of a city or region.

This implies that the implementation of energy and climate policy instruments can affect individuals both within a country and across countries in different ways. For instance, the implementation of a pollution tax can reduce the level of pollution and, therefore, decrease some inequality in the distribution of pollution. On the other hand, a pollution tax increases prices that may have an impact on income and wealth distributions. For instance, introducing a carbon tax on gasoline without redistributing the revenues will disproportionately affect households that spend a more significant fraction of their income on gasoline, who tend to be, in general, low-income house-holds or households living in rural areas where public transport infrastructure may be lacking. Of course, if the revenue from implementing such a tax is redistributed to the households and firms in a revenue-neutral manner, such as within the frame-work of ecological tax reforms, then these distributional implications may even be absent. Also, keep in mind that the introduction of the gasoline tax will also likely promote the adoption of more energy-efficient cars that can lead to further reduc-tions in air pollution in heavily polluted areas where low-income households tend to reside.

Subsidies are another interesting example of an energy and climate policy instru-ment with income and wealth distributional effects. For instance, subsidies for the installation of solar panels have important distributional effects. Indeed, this type of subsidy will mostly be used by owners of single-family houses belonging generally to the middle- and high-income classes. In this case, the subsidy will tend to be regres-sive. Of course, in an analysis of the distributional effects of this subsidy, we should also consider the financing of this measure, that is, how the government collects funds for the subsidy. For instance, in case the government decides to use general tax rev-enues, then the distributional effects of the subsidy will depend on the progressiveness of the tax system. On the other hand, if the government decides to use a tax on elec-tricity consumption to finance the implementation of the subsidy, then non-owners of houses will subsidise owners of houses, and this has clearly some distributional effects.

In general, some market-based instruments such as pollution and energy taxes do not enjoy high levels of social acceptance (in comparison to subsidies, for example). This is mostly due to their effect on the individual as well as regional income distri-butions, and the increase in the prices of several base products. Moreover, the effects of these types of instruments are salient to economic agents. Therefore, in the design and implementation of these types of taxes, such distributional effects should be con-sidered to both avoid opposition and achieve equitable outcomes in terms of reduction of pollution, as well as in terms of costs.

Non-market-based instruments, on the other hand, can also have distributional implications. For instance, an energy consumption standard in the building sector, defined in terms of energy consumption per square metre, may increase the build-ing cost of a house, due to the increase in the level of insulation. This cost increase, which need not be salient to economic agents, is more likely to affect low-income households, given that high-income households may be more price-inelastic in their preferences for the sizes of their homes.

Direct control measures have been known to exacerbate prevailing inequalities: for example, license plate-based driving restrictions result in a stronger negative welfare effect for lower-income households who may not be able to afford to own more than one car. Another example of a policy that may have had important distributional effects is a ban on using incandescent light bulbs. Poor households are likely to have been affected by this policy much more adversely, especially given that the replacement technologies (such as light-emitting diode (LED)-based bulbs) were more expensive, at least initially. In such situations, combinations of policies (such as providing a subsidy, while imposing the ban) may have important welfare effects, even if they may not necessarily be efficient policies by themselves.

Energy and climate policy measures, both market and non-market-based, are also likely to have vital distributional implications on energy access, particularly in developing countries. A good example to illustrate this is the liquefied petroleum gas (LPG) subsidy that was provided for all households in India. LPG is used as a clean cooking fuel by many households, and the Indian government was heavily subsidising its use to particularly encourage low-income and rural households to switch to it from using firewood. However, setting a uniform subsidy meant that relatively richer households, who could afford to pay more for LPG, received the same subsidy as poorer households and, thus, benefitted relatively more from receiving these subsidies. Many rural households, for whom acquiring firewood was relatively easy, still did not end up using LPG on a regular basis.

On the other hand, economic studies have also shown that carbon pricing can be progressive in poorer countries, particularly due to different patterns of energy expenditure. For instance, in countries where biomass is used extensively by poorer households, poor households will remain relatively unaffected by policies that tax carbon. The implementation of direct control measures such as bans on incandescent light bulbs can also have a positive effect in improving the adoption of energy-efficient technologies such as light bulbs among poorer households in developing countries, as long as they are enforced. However, it remains important to conduct a welfare analysis to understand the full impact of such policy measures on households and firms.

Regional impact of CO_2 tax on gasoline

In a study based on data from Switzerland, Filippini and Heimsch (2016) [52] evaluated the effects of a hypothetical CO_2 tax on gasoline, by estimating a demand function using spatial econometric approaches. The authors found that the short-run elasticity of gasoline demand at the aggregate level was about −0.27, whereas the average long-run elasticity was about −0.82. Regarding the distributional implications, the authors found that the tax burden of a hypothetical CO_2 tax was likely to be higher in rural areas, compared to urban areas. This finding can explain opposition to such taxes, such as the notable protest movement against the introduction of a similar tax in France (called 'Gilets Jaunes'), which was also rooted in this rural-urban divide.

9.3   Policy Evaluation Methods

In Section 9.1 of this chapter, we illustrated the most important criteria to consider in choosing an energy or climate policy measure. For applying the first two criteria, that is, productive/allocative efficiency and dynamic efficiency, it is essential to perform a policy evaluation from an economic point of view. Policy evaluation is an analytical and scientific tool that uses the methods and models of the economic sciences to evaluate the economic effects, that is, the costs and benefits produced by the introduction of a public policy.

Generally, the economic effects of an energy or climate policy instrument are estimated *ex-ante*, that is, before the policy measure is introduced, using different economic and econometric models that we will shortly introduce in Section 9.3.1. In doing this economic analysis, generally researchers implicitly assume that the policy measure has a significant and notable effect on economic variables. For instance, researchers may assume, in evaluating *ex-ante* the economic effects of a subsidy for the adoption of electric cars, that it is likely to be effective, that is, that the adoption rate of electric cars will significantly increase once the subsidy is implemented. However, this assumption may, on occasion, be too optimistic. For this reason, as already mentioned, it is important to perform empirical analysis to understand the level of effectiveness of a policy measure. If it turns out that the policy is less effective than was initially assumed, the *ex-ante* analysis would not have been accurate. In these cases, the policy measure must be reevaluated, that is, the causes of ineffectiveness must be identified and corrected. Therefore, in Section 9.3.2, we present some important empirical methods of policy evaluation.

In conclusion, designing and implementing energy and climate policy measures should be considered an interactive, dynamic process, where the results of studies on the impact of a policy instrument can be used to confirm or reevaluate the effects of a policy measure and to 'update' its economic effects.

9.3.1   Modelling the Economic Effects

In this subsection, we summarise the most important economic models that can be used to evaluate the effect of energy and climate policies. The goal of this summary is to sketch a general preliminary idea of some of the most commonly used models in energy economics and policy. Overall, these models provide a framework for economists and policymakers to take more informed decisions about energy and climate policy. Note that these models can be specified and used to evaluate a policy measure's impact on a society's overall welfare, on the welfare gains/losses in a single market, and/or on other economic outcome variables such as employment or GDP.

When studying economic behaviour, economists often start by building an economic model. This type of model provides a simplified representation of the functioning of markets, economic systems, or the behaviour of economic agents. Therefore, they may not be able to accommodate all the details and context of reality. However, good models can capture and explain economic phenomena in a realistic manner. Once a model is built, economists have a tool that can be used to analyse the effect of policies.

The models that we present are interesting and informative, however, they have some limitations due to the need to represent markets, economic and energy systems in a simplified way. Therefore, in the interpretation of the results provided by these models, it is always important to keep in mind the assumptions and limitations of the models that partially arise because of the need to simplify the representation of the real world. We believe that these models are very useful for economic policy discussions; however, it is important to not use these results at face value.

- **Applied general equilibrium models**: these models represent economic systems by modelling the functioning and interaction of different markets, such as the energy and labour markets. Moreover, this type of model represents the endogenous origin and spending of income. Therefore, general equilibrium models do consider the effects of income flows on the market as well as the effects of price changes on that market. In these models, each market is characterised by consumers and firms whose behaviour is captured through mathematical functions of supply and demand, derived from economic theory. Some of the parameters of these mathematical functions, in particular the price and income elasticities and the elasticity of substitution of production inputs, are generally defined based on the results of empirical studies published in the literature. In contrast, other parameters are calibrated to reproduce the economic equilibrium in the market that was observed in one specific year.

  Researchers have also developed applied general equilibrium models that include a detailed description of the energy system to analyse the economic effects of energy and climate policy measures. This type of model, also called a hybrid model or 'top-down' model, integrates an energy system model, which provides a technology-rich representation of the energy system based on energy technologies and their associated costs. Important hybrid models have been obtained, for instance, by linking the energy system model TIMES with the applied general equilibrium models EMEC and GEM-E3. Hybrid models make it possible to analyse the *ex-ante* economic impact of energy or climate policy measures on both energy markets and other markets. For instance, implementing a carbon tax won't only raise energy costs, but it may also have an impact on the supply and demand of other goods.

- **Partial equilibrium models**: these models generally encapsulate the functioning of a single market. In the basic version of this type of model, the market is represented by consumers and firms whose behaviour is modelled using the mathematical functions of aggregate supply and demand functions. Some of the parameters of these mathematical functions are defined based on the results of empirical studies published in the literature (e.g., elasticities of substitutions and price elasticities). In contrast, as for the applied general equilibrium models, other parameters are calibrated to reproduce the economic equilibrium in the market that was observed before the introduction of the energy or climate policy. Unlike applied general equilibrium models, these models: (1) do not consider the effects of an energy or climate policy measure on other markets; (2) consider the effects of a policy on the price changes on a market but not on the income flows on the market.

  This enables detailed consumer and producer behaviour modelling within this single sector and the technological options available for producing and transforming energy sources. Using partial equilibrium models, it is possible to analyse, ex-ante, the impact of suggested energy and climate policies on economic indicators, such as prices, quantities and consumer surplus, and producer surplus.

- **Energy system models**: energy system models, often also referred to as bottom-up models, offer a detailed representation of the energy system with a special focus on technologies. For instance, these models consider individual energy technologies, such as wind turbines, solar panels, and natural gas power plants, and then aggregate the use of these technologies into a larger energy system to identify the best combination of the various technologies to satisfy a given energy demand. This type of model is based on (linear) optimisation methods and tries to find the optimal mix of energy technologies that satisfy the energy demand while minimising the discounted net present value of energy system costs (including investments in supply technologies, operational expenses, and fuel costs). These models adopt a centralised approach, that is, assume that a social planner decides to identify the cost-minimising technology mix to meet the demand. Therefore, these models do not represent markets and do not capture prices, and the reactivity of demand to price changes. Therefore, they are unable to model decentralised economic behaviour when agents respond to economic incentives or prices.

  These models can also be used to evaluate the ex-ante impact of different energy and climate policies on the cost-minimising technology mix; however, they are not able to provide information on the welfare effects on energy markets or, more generally, wide-scale economic effects. Of course, the advantage of using these models is that they allow us to analyse the costs and feasibility of different energy technology pathways.

  Energy system models, such as the well-known TIMES model, are informative tools that can be used to understand the effects on the system cost of various combinations of energy technologies and the effects on the system cost of energy and climate policy instruments.

- **Microeconometric structural models**: these models are designed to represent the behaviour of consumers or firms by estimating econometric models that are formulated based on the principles of formal theoretical economic models (generally of a neoclassical nature). The parameters of the models are estimated using econometric methods, after collecting the necessary data. For example, a firm's supply curve depends on the parameters of its cost functions. By observing and collecting data on costs and production levels, it is possible to estimate a cost function by adopting a functional form as the trans-logarithmic form and then deriving the parameters necessary to specify the supply function. Given this supply function, it is then possible to simulate the economic effects of the introduction of an energy policy, such as a subsidy for the adoption of energy-efficient production technology.

  Another example of a simple structural model is estimating a system of equations representing the demand for different energy sources in the residential sector, based on the almost ideal demand system model as that discussed by

Deaton and Muellbauer (1980) [121]. This empirical model is derived from an indirect utility function characterised by a specific functional form. Starting from this, it is possible to obtain a set of equations modelling expenditure shares, whose parameters are estimated using econometric methods, after having collected the necessary data. Given the estimated parameters, price and income elasticities are derived, and the welfare impact of a CO_2 tax on the households can be simulated ex-ante. A commonly used approach for modelling demand is the model proposed by Berry, Levinsohn, and Pakes (1995) [122], which is based on using a discrete choice modelling approach. Structural microeconometric approaches can also be used to model the interaction of demand and supply, either in a competitive or a non-competitive market.

- **Economic growth models**: these models analyse the factors that influence long-term production and consumption increases such as technological progress, investment, human capital, and institutional factors, and can be used to assess the impact of energy and climate policies on economic growth. These models represent economic systems with the help of mathematical functions and identities, after making assumptions in a very simple and aggregated way.

  At the heart of these models exists a single aggregate production function for the economic system, with capital and labour as production factors and a parameter representing the level of technological progress. With this production function and some assumptions on the savings rate (which can be endogenous), the depreciation rate, the growth rate of technology and of the population, and the assumption that markets are always in equilibrium, these models allow the analysis of the role of capital accumulation, population growth, and technological improvement on economic growth.

  Over time, these approaches have incorporated additional modelling possibilities; for example, the technological progress that was considered to be exogenous in the early models is mostly modelled as being endogenous. Moreover, in addition to the classical factors of production such as capital and labour, some economists working with these models have begun to be concerned with environmental issues and constraints and, therefore, have introduced another factor into the production function, namely natural resources. These models are oriented towards analysing the factors of economic growth, by focusing on the production activities in an economic system. Finally, and most importantly, from an energy and climate policy point of view, the possibility of connecting economic growth models to climate models has emerged in the economic literature in the form of integrated assessment models (IAMs).

- **IAMs**: IAMs are used to analyse the effects of the functioning of an economic system on the environment and to evaluate the effects of policy measures on the economic and environmental systems. These models tend to be interdisciplinary in nature and based on different models developed across scientific fields such as climatology, ecology, economics, and sociology. The main goal of IAMs is to link together different models that represent, for instance, the climate, the economic system, and the biosphere. Thus, these models provide a comprehensive representation of the interactions between these systems.

Related to energy and climate issues, IAMs combine a description of the economy along with a formulation of the climate system to help us understand the effects of climate change across economic sectors and agents and enable us to learn about the implications of energy and climate policies. Several IAMs are currently available, many of which combine a neoclassical growth framework with a climate model. However, some models may also use other economic models, such as a general equilibrium framework. An important example of an IAM is the DICE (Dynamic Integrated Model of Climate and Economy) model, which is based on neoclassical economic growth theory, and in which economic agents undertake investments in capital, education, and technology to increase consumption in the future. Other examples include RICE (the Regional Integrate Model of Climate and Economy, which assumes different regions of the world) and the MERGE (Model for Estimating the Regional and Global Effects of Greenhouse Gas Reductions) model, which includes a damage assessment module in addition to a general equilibrium economic module and a climate module.

- **Agent-based models (ABMs)**: When it comes to energy systems, computational models called ABMs can be quite useful. These models simulate the actions and interactions of economic agents in an energy system. Here, each agent is represented as an independent decision-maker who interacts with other agents according to a set of rules or heuristics. These rules can be simple or complex and are based on various factors that influence the agent's behaviour, such as economic incentives, social norms, and technological constraints. Unlike other approaches, ABMs are suited to modelling rational as well as boundedly rational agents and can also be used to model adaptive heterogeneous agents such as investors or consumers that change their behaviour depending, for instance, on the behaviour of other economic agents. Monte Carlo simulations can also be used to determine the probabilistic distribution of the outcomes in these models. ABMs can be used to simulate the behaviour of households and firms under different policy scenarios, such as the introduction of subsidies for renewable energy sources or energy-efficient technologies, or to assess the reliability and resilience of the energy system under different scenarios.

9.3.2   Modelling the Impact of Policies

Now, we will briefly review some of the methods that can be used to evaluate the impact of energy and climate policies on different economic outcome variables. As mentioned previously, one of the criteria to consider in the choice of a policy measure is its level of effectiveness, that is, if the policy measure has a significant impact on the economic variables of interest.

Identifying the impact of a policy measure on an economic variable is inherently difficult. One must isolate the policy's effect from all other factors that can potentially affect the economic variable considered in the evaluation analysis. For example, before it can be said that a subsidy for the purchase of electric cars led to an increase in sales of this type of car, it is necessary to understand what would presumably have happened to car sales in the absence of the subsidy. For instance, it may be that an observed increase in electric car sales can be attributed to other economic factors, for example, increased income, and not only to the subsidy. For this reason, from a methodological point of view, it is essential to base the evaluation on a counterfactual approach to identify the true impact of a policy measure. This implies that one must somehow reconstruct what would have happened without the intervention to determine the real effect of public policy. It is, therefore, a question of distinguishing a causal relationship (the occurrence of one event causing a second event) from a correlational relationship. A correlation (or association) between two variables does not imply a causal relationship.

Generally, to argue that a policy measure A causes a change in the outcome variable B, we must verify three conditions: (1) the introduction of the policy measure A must precede the effect observed on variable B; (2) cause and effect must be correlated; and (3) we need to exclude other factors/explanations that could account for the effect on variable B.

We can distinguish two main broad types of approaches for policy evaluation. The first set of approaches is experimental studies. In this case, researchers introduce an intervention or a policy using random assignment and study its effects using the methodology of randomised control trials. These effects could be analysed using a stated choice approach, or a revealed choice approach. In a stated choice approach, participants are asked to make a choice in a hypothetical situation, whereas in using the revealed approach, we look at the impact of the policy on actual choices.

Experimental studies are normally done *ex-ante*, that is, before the introduction of the policy measure. For this reason, this method is very attractive for undertaking policy evaluation. However, the implementation of experiments may not always be possible due to financial, ethical, or organisational reasons. The second set of approaches is quasi-experimental and does not involve random assignment of policies. Instead, by applying methods such as difference-in-differences or regression discontinuity, it is possible to derive causal estimates of a policy using observational data. This type of analysis is usually performed *ex-post*.

- **Randomised controlled trial (RCT)**: this methodology involves evaluating the impact of a policy measure by organising an experiment in which some observational units (individuals, households, firms, etc.) randomly chosen from a sample are 'treated', that is, they are subjected to the energy or environmental policy measure. In contrast, another group is not treated and is considered to be a

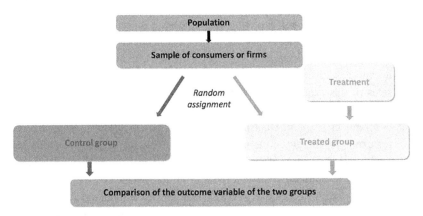

Figure 9.3 Randomised controlled trial

control group. This group approximates the counterfactual situation we need to perform the policy evaluation. After introducing the policy for the treated group (and, in some situations, allowing some time to pass), the researcher evaluates the impact of the policy by comparing the change in the outcome of interest between the treated and control groups. The random selection of the observations into each of the two groups participating in the experiment assures us that the two groups are similar to one another, in terms of both observable and unobservable characteristics. This type of experiment is called a **RCT** because it is based on the randomisation of the treatment or the intervention, and this process is controlled by the researcher, that is, the researcher has complete control over the introduction of the policy measure and the random selection of units into the treatment and control groups.

Figure 9.3 summarises the elements of conducting an RCT.

For instance, if policymakers are interested to know the impact of introducing a subsidy to promote the adoption of electric cars *ex-ante*, then they can collaborate with a research institution to organise an RCT. In this case, the researcher would start by selecting a sample of people interested in buying a car in the next six months (as an example). He or she would then conduct a baseline survey to obtain important information on this group (such as socioeconomic information) and then use randomisation to define the group of people that will have access to the subsidy (the treated group) and the control group that will not have access to it while ensuring that the two groups are similar to one another in terms of observable covariates. The next step would involve the researcher cooperating with the government on the practical aspects of the experiment, that is, in defining and implementing the procedure to obtain the subsidy from the government. The researcher could then organise another survey after six months and collect information on the cars that participants bought. The last step in the analysis would involve comparing the share of electric vehicles bought by the two groups. Suppose the percentage of electric cars purchased by the treated group is significantly higher (in a statistical sense) than the share of the control group. In that case, the researcher can provide evidence to the policymaker that the subsidy has been effective.

This RCT can also be organised in a stated choice framework, whereby participants are asked to choose a car hypothetically. However, it is important to keep in mind that this approach may result in participants not revealing their true preferences, also known as hypothetical bias. Therefore, from a methodological perspective, it is better to organise an RCT on revealed choices whenever possible.

Can information about energy costs affect consumers' choices? Evidence from a field experiment

In this paper, Boogen, et al. (2022) [123] investigated the impact of providing households living in Switzerland who were customers of two electric utilities with information on the potential monetary savings that could be achieved by replacing their current light bulbs or major appliances such as washing machines with new (and more energy-efficient) light bulbs and new appliances available on the market. A **RCT** was conducted in which the treated group of households received a letter with detailed information about potential monetary savings. After 1 year, the households were re-contacted. Both treated and control households, that is, those who didn't receive the letter, were asked to indicate which appliances and light bulbs had been replaced. The level of energy efficiency of the appliances and light bulbs purchased during the year by the two groups of households was then compared. The main result of this study was that providing information on monetary savings led households to purchase more energy-efficient light bulbs and appliances. Figures 9.4 and 9.5 illustrate the overall organisation of the study, as well as an example of the information that the households received about the efficiency of washing machines.

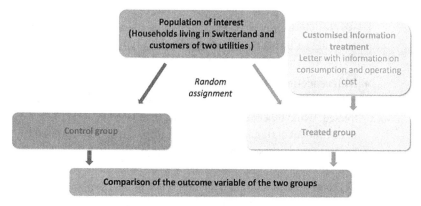

Figure 9.4 Elements of the RCT on monetary information

Washing machine

Characteristics of your appliance: Producer: Bosch, Width: 60cm, Height: 90cm, Year of Purchase: 2007

	Your appliance	Alternative appliance on the market (load capacity: 8kg)	
		A++	A+++
Consumption per cycle	1.050 kWh	1.170 kWh	0.470 kWh
Cost of one cycle	0.210 CHF	0.234 CHF	0.094 CHF
Annual operating cost[ii]	46 CHF	51 CHF	21 CHF
Approximate price range of new appliance		725-2309 CHF	440-4099 CHF
Estimate of potential annual savings on operating costs (compared to current appliance)		No savings	25 CHF

[ii] The annual operating costs for the washing machine are estimated using 220 cycles.

- You can save an estimated CHF 25.- per year in electricity costs by replacing your washing machine with a new A+++ appliance.

Figure 9.5 Information sheet on the efficiency of washing machines

---

Nudging adoption of electric vehicles: Evidence from an information-based intervention in Nepal

Filippini, Kumar and Srinivasan (2021) [124], in their study, shed light on some of the market failures, and especially behavioural anomalies, that hinder the adoption of electric motorcycles in Kathmandu, Nepal. Using survey data on about 2,000 potential motorcycle buyers and a stated-preference RCT, the authors showed that informational interventions related to the health and environmental benefits of electric motorcycles had an impact in determining the stated choice of respondents. Moreover, these effects varied across respondents, based on gender, education as well as health status. This study shows that information provision, a potentially less costly policy option, especially in developing countries, can influence vehicle choice (even if it is the stated preference) [124].

- **Difference-in-difference analysis (DiD)**: this method is quasi-experimental in nature. As with an RCT, this method also assumes that some economic agents are treated, while others aren't. However, compared to an RCT, in a quasi-experiment, the treatment assignment is not random, and it is not organised by a researcher. DiD analysis is based on collecting data on the treated group and the control group that are observed both before and after the treatment. In a simplistic version of the DiD analysis, we compute the difference in the economic variable of interest for the two groups before and after the treatment and then compare this difference across the two groups. In this methodology, treatment assignment is based on some

Table 9.1 Introduction of a subsidy for energy-efficient renovation of buildings in some regions

Region	Year 1	Year 2
A	No policy	Policy
B	No policy	Policy
C	No policy	Policy
D	No policy	No policy
E	No policy	No policy
F	No policy	No policy
G	No policy	No policy

other criteria, such as administrative or spatial rules, which result in some units receiving treatment, whereas others do not. For example, we can imagine a situation in which one city introduces a subsidy for purchasing solar panels, while other cities do not. In this case, we would have treated people in one city and untreated people in other cities, but the assignment to the respective groups was not randomised. For this reason, DiD analysis is considered to be a quasi-experimental method, since the treatment assignment is not organised and controlled by the researcher, but is observable in reality. In general, DiD analyses are conducted after the implementation of policies, and thus they are *ex-post* in nature.

A typical situation in which it is possible to apply a DiD approach is the one illustrated in Table 9.1. Let us assume that we have several regions in a country that, in year 1, have not implemented any energy and climate policy measures to promote energy-saving renovations of buildings. Then, some regions choose to implement a policy measure to promote energy-saving renovations in year 2. In this case, we have a quasi-experiment with treated economic agents (owners of buildings) in some regions and untreated economic agents in other regions. The owners of buildings in the treatment groups have the possibility to apply for the subsidy (but they are not obliged to do so), whereas owners in the non-treated regions do not have this possibility.

This type of situation allows the researcher to exploit the variation in the policy over time and between regions to analyse the impact of the policy, by comparing the number of energy-saving renovations in the treated and untreated regions. Because the data observed are over multiple time periods, we can calculate two types of differences in the outcome variable (the number of energy-saving renovations), and not only one as in the typical RCT. The first difference is obtained by subtracting the outcome variable in year 2 from the outcome variable in year 1 for each region, whereas the second difference is obtained by subtracting the first difference of the outcomes of the untreated from the first difference of the treated. Using a mathematical expression, we can say that the DiD estimate compares the variations over time of the treated group outcome $(Y_2^T - Y_1^T)$ with the variations over the same period of the control group outcome $(Y_2^{NT} - Y_1^{NT})$. The magnitude of this estimate is also shown in Equation 9.1.

$$DiD = (Y_2^T - Y_1^T) - (Y_2^{N^T} - Y_1^{N^T}) \tag{9.1}$$

It is possible to obtain more precise DiD estimates by using a regression-based approach that allows researchers to incorporate other variables that may influence the outcome variable. It is particularly interesting to use a regression model that includes fixed effects because this allows one to control for unobserved variables that are time-invariant. For example, a simple difference-in-difference regression model based on the use of panel data can take the following form:

$$\ln Y_{it} = \beta_0 + \beta_1 POLICY_i + \beta_2 POST_t + \beta_3 POLICY_i * POST_t + \lambda_t + \epsilon_{it} \tag{9.2}$$

where Y_{it} is the outcome variable, $POLICY_i$ is the treatment or policy variable, $POST_t$ denotes a post-treatment indicator, λ_t denotes dummy variables for time periods, and ϵ_{it} is the idiosyncratic error term.

For applying the DiD approach, it is very important that the regions that we are analysing are comparable to one another. Particularly, before the introduction of the policy, the evolution of the outcome variable of interest should be similar for treated and non-treated groups over time. This assumption is known as the 'parallel trends' or 'common trends' assumption. In Figure 9.6, we graphically present the mechanism of the introduction of a subsidy for energy-efficient renovation of buildings. In this graph, we plot time on the horizontal axis and the share of energy-efficient renovations on the vertical axis. We can observe two lines that describe the development of the share of energy-efficient renovations in two regions over time, and the vertical dotted line denotes the onset of the treatment. The line on top indicates the share of energy-efficient renovations in the untreated region, whereas the line on the bottom denotes the share in the treated region. From this figure, it is clear that before the introduction of the subsidy, the two lines were parallel, that is, the shares of energy-efficient renovations were growing at the same rate for both groups. This indicates that the parallel trends assumption was satisfied. After the introduction of the subsidy,

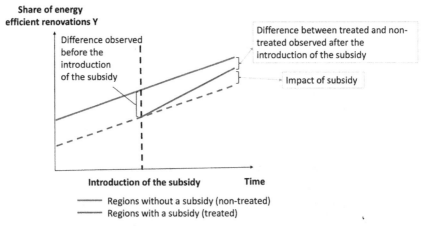

Figure 9.6 Introduction of subsidy for energy-efficient renovations

the dashed part of the line on the bottom indicates an increase in the rate of change of the share of energy-efficient renovations in the region that adopted the policy. This visual analysis indicates that the subsidy had an impact on increasing the number of renovations in the treated region.

If in a natural experiment setting, we observe that the treated and untreated groups are very different from one another in terms of socioeconomic variables, it is possible to use a method that focuses the analysis on comparable subgroups within the sample. This method is called matching, and the comparable subgroups can be obtained using different matching algorithms. The researcher usually selects some important socioe-conomic characteristics of the household, or economic characteristics of a firm, on the basis of which to find a suitable match for each observation in the data. This implies that observations in both treated and untreated groups that do not find a match are excluded from the analysis. Once this matching is complete, the researcher performs a DiD estimation on the matched sample. It is important to keep in mind that the matching approach can also be used by itself to analyse the impact of policy measures. In this case, the researcher simply compares the outcome variable after matching observations in the treated and untreated groups. However, this approach suffers from certain shortcomings; for instance, it is not possible to account in any way for unobserved variables that may influence the outcome variable.

Application of DiD for the evaluation of rebates for energy efficient appliances
In this paper, Datta and Filippini (2017) [125] estimated the impact of rebate policies on the quantity of ENERGY STAR household appliances sold using data from the United States. The authors of this study exploited a natural experiment, given that only some of the US states introduced subsidies to increase the adoption of energy-efficient appliances with an 'ENERGY STAR' label. Therefore, no state had introduced a rebate for ENERGY STAR appliances in the pre-treatment period, whereas in the post-treatment period, some states introduced a rebate for them. The empirical analysis, using a classical DiD regression model, was performed using socioeconomic and sales data for washing machines, dishwashers, refrigerators, and air conditioners at the state level for the period from 2001 to 2006. The empirical results showed that rebates have a positive impact on the share of ENERGY STAR electrical appliances. The authors estimated the following econometric model:

$$ES_{ait} = \alpha_0 + \beta RebatePolicy_{it} + \gamma X_{it} + \delta_i + \lambda_t + \epsilon_{it} \qquad (9.3)$$

where the subscripts 'a', 'i' and 't' denote appliance type, state, and year, respectively. In the model, the authors considered four types of appliances, that is, washing machines, dishwashers, refrigerators, and air conditioners. ES_{ait} is the share of each of the ENERGY STAR appliances sold, $RebatePolicy_{it}$ is a dummy variable for the presence of the rebate policy in a state in period 't', X_{it} is a matrix of all other explanatory variables, δ_i denote the individual fixed effects, λ_t are the time fixed effects, and ϵ_{it} captures the idiosyncratic error term.

Application of DiD for the evaluation of a demand side management strategy

In this paper, Boogen, Datta, and Filippini (2017) [126] estimated the impact of demand side management (DSM) measures introduced by some Swiss electricity companies on residential electricity consumption. The authors of this study exploited a natural experiment, given that only some of the Swiss electricity distribution companies introduced DSM measures to promote energy savings. Therefore, no company had introduced a DSM programme in the pre-treatment period, whereas in the post-treatment period, some of the companies decided to introduce a DSM programme. The empirical analysis is based on a classical DiD estimation, and it is performed using socioeconomic and residential electricity consumption data from thirty companies observed for the period from 2006 to 2012. The empirical results showed that DSM programmes had an impact on reducing the demand for residential electricity. A 10 per cent increase in DSM spending resulted in a 0.14 per cent decline in electricity consumption. This implies that the cost of saving 1 kWh of electricity was around 0.04 cents, while the price of 1 kWh for a household was around 20 cents. The authors estimated the following econometric model:

$$\ln EC_{it} = \beta_0 + \beta_1 DSM_{it} + \gamma X_{it} + \delta_i + \lambda_t + \epsilon_{it} \qquad (9.4)$$

where the subscripts i and t denote indices for electric utility and year, respectively. EC_{it} is the residential electricity consumption, DSM_{it} is the DSM policy variable, X_{it} is a matrix of all other explanatory variables that include the electricity price, the average taxable income per taxpayer, the household size, and the heating and cooling degree days. α_i are the utility fixed effects, λ_t are the time fixed effects, and ϵ_{it} is the idiosyncratic error term.

Regression discontinuity design (RDD): the RDD is an empirical method that can be used to analyse policy measures determined by thresholds, that is, instruments in which eligibility for treatment may be based on a cut-off condition related to some socioeconomic variables. For instance, the South African government has implemented the Indigent Programme to provide poor households (below an income threshold) with free electricity of up to 50 kWh per month. In this case, income (the variable on which assignment to treatment is based) is known as the 'running variable'. From a policy perspective, it may be interesting to verify if this measure has had an impact on households switching from using more polluting fuels (such as kerosene or firewood), to cleaner sources such as electricity, and thus to understand whether this policy reduced health costs from the indoor air pollution in developing countries.

The regression discontinuity approach, which is also quasi-experimental, evaluates the impact of a policy measure by comparing the outcome variables of interest for the treated and untreated units that are very close to the cut-off. For instance, in the example above, this approach compares the electricity consumption of households that have an income that may be 5–10 per cent higher than the cut-off (the untreated group), with the electricity usage of those 5–10 per cent below the cut-off (the treated group). If this difference is statistically significant, it implies that the policy has had an impact on electricity consumption, and thus indirectly on the health outcomes of households, within this bandwidth or interval.

In order to apply the RDD approach, we have two prerequisites: first, we need a continuous running (or eligibility) variable, and second, a clearly defined cut-off point. Moreover, this approach is based on the following two assumptions:

- No manipulation of the running variable, that is, no clumping of individuals just above or below the cut-off, and
- Similarity of households and firms around the cut-off.

The second assumption implies that we would then compare very similar groups in the econometric analysis.

regression discontinuity design (RDD) can be applied to both cross-sectional (as in the example above) and spatial contexts. In the latter case, the researcher exploits the spatial variation in a policy. For instance, one region can introduce a bonus to adopt energy-efficient cars, while another nearby region may not. In this case, the researcher can compare the shares of energy-efficient cars sold in the vicinity of the border between the two regions. Recently, in energy and environmental economics, researchers have begun to estimate RDD-based methods along the time dimension as well. For instance, one could consider the moment when an energy price shock occurs to be a threshold point. In this case, the researcher is comparing the outcome variable (let's say, energy consumption) just before and after the shock. However, RDD-based models with time as a running variable are not very easy to implement, and the results can be biased, because of the difficulty in controlling for unobserved factors varying over time that may also affect energy consumption.

In Figure 9.7, we present a typical situation in which the state decides to give a subsidy for energy-efficient electrical appliances only to low-income households. This policy is enacted with the objective of improving the level of consumption of energy services by low-income households. Therefore, its effectiveness can be measured using the RDD approach. The figure plots income on the horizontal axis, which

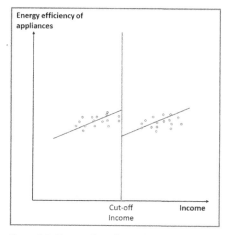

Figure 9.7 Regression discontinuity design (RDD)

is the running variable in this case, as well as the cut-off that determines eligibility for the programme. On the vertical axis, we plot the level of energy efficiency of the electrical appliances. In the same figure, we can also see scatter points that represent the combination of income and energy efficiency for both households that are eligible for the subsidy (left of the cut-off) and not eligible for it (right of the cut-off). We can observe that close to this threshold, the level of energy efficiency of the electrical appliances by households that are eligible for the subsidy is, on average, higher than the level of energy efficiency of similar households ineligible for the programme.

Application of RDD for evaluation of labels

In this paper, Filippini and Wekhof (2021) [127] employed the RDD approach to analyse the effect of culture, captured through language, on the average level of energy efficiency of cars. Switzerland is an interesting case study to evaluate the impact of culture on economic and environmental decisions, due to the presence of different cultures/language regions that share the most important institutions at the federal level, but that are also spatially separated. In fact, Switzerland has different cantons in which the primary language varies from Italian to French, to German. Furthermore, variations exist in language and culture even within some cantons, where some regions within the canton have French as the primary language, and others have German. Such situations provide a natural experiment to analyse the impact of culture on economic decisions, by exploiting the variation in languages across the borders of regions as a threshold in the spatial RDD approach and using the distance of each municipality to the language border as a running variable. The empirical results of this study indicated an important effect of French-speaking culture on the energy efficiency of cars, that is, French-speaking car owners tended to buy more efficient vehicles.

9.3.3   Review Questions and Problems

The online question bank contains review questions and problems for this chapter, including solutions (see https://wp-prd.let.ethz.ch/exercisesfortextbookeep/).

Special Terms

ATC average total cost. 129, 142, 151, 244

CAPM Capital Asset Pricing Model. 82, 244
CER Certified Emission Reduction. 200, 244
CIS Commonwealth of Independent States. 13, 244

DSM demand side management. 240, 244

EECs energy-efficient cars. 177, 183, 244
EE energy efficiency. 244
ETS Emissions Trading Scheme. 187, 244

FiT feed-in-tariff. 166, 184–186, 244
FLH Full Load Hours. 244

GDP gross domestic product. 4, 11, 12, 106, 107, 224, 244
GHG greenhouse gas. 1, 8, 10, 11, 17, 28, 40, 164, 165, 171, 187, 189, 200, 244
GHGs greenhouse gases. 28, 244
GHI Global Horizontal Irradiance. 244

IPCC Intergovernmental Panel on Climate Change. 11, 244
IRR internal rate of return. 76, 77, 244

LCoE levelised cost of energy. 73, 85–87, 89, 90, 244, 257, 258
LMICs low and middle-income countries. 46, 123, 244
LNG liquefied natural gas. 157, 158, 244
LPG liquefied petroleum gas. 200, 244
LTC lifetime cost. 244

MAC marginal abatement costs. 173, 188, 204, 205, 210, 217, 244
MC marginal cost. 244
MEB marginal external benefits. 177, 212, 244
MEC marginal external cost. 244
MERC marginal energy reduction cost. 177, 178, 183, 212, 213, 217, 244
MPB marginal private benefits. 26, 171, 177, 183, 209, 212, 244
MPC marginal private costs. 244

MR marginal revenue. 244
MRTS Marginal Rate of Technical Substitution. 53, 244
MSB marginal social benefit. 96, 177, 178, 183, 204, 205, 209, 210, 212, 217, 244
MSBs marginal social benefits. 244
MSC marginal social costs. 244

NOCs National Oil Companies. 244
NPV net present value. 76, 77, 79, 81, 85, 87, 97, 98, 244

OECD Organisation for Economic Co-operation and Development. 4, 13, 14, 64, 65, 68, 69, 154, 157, 158, 244
OLS Ordinary Least Squares. 61–63, 91, 92, 244
OPEC Organization of the Petroleum Exporting Countries. 32, 152, 154–157, 244
ORB OPEC Reference Basket. 157, 244

PDV present discounted value. 112, 244
PM10 Particulate Matter 10. 12, 244
PM2.5 Particulate Matter 2.5. 12, 13, 24, 244
PV photovoltaic. 18, 40, 90, 92, 244

R&D research and development. 25, 27, 33, 44, 100, 167, 171, 182, 188, 223, 244
RDD regression discontinuity design. 241, 242, 244
RRT resource rent tax. 136, 244

SDG Sustainable Development Goal. 244
SDGs Sustainable Development Goals. 43, 244

UN United Nations. 29, 42, 166, 167, 244
UNEP United Nations Environment Programme. 219, 244

WACC weighted average cost of capital. 78, 244
WNOCs Western National Oil Companies. 244
WSSD World Summit on Sustainable Development. 42, 244

References

[1] Hanna Ritchie, Max Roser, and Pablo Rosado. 'Energy'. In: *Our World in Data* (2022). https://ourworldindata.org/energy (cited on page 3).

[2] EIA. *Energy Intensity*. 2023. www.eia.gov/opendata/index.php#bulk-downloads (cited on page 3).

[3] Energy Institute. 'Energy intensity'. In: *Energy Institute Statistical Review of World Energy* (2023) (cited on page 3).

[4] IEA. 2023. *Energy Efficiency Indicators Data Explorer*. www.iea.org/data-and-statistics/data-tools/energy-efficiency-indicators-data-explorer (cited on page 4).

[5] IEA. 2021. *Data and Statistics*. www.iea.org/reports/key-world-energy-statistics-2021/final-consumption (cited on pages 4, 6, 7).

[6] Hannah Ritchie. 'Global comparison: How much energy do people consume?'. In: *Our World in Data* (2021). https://ourworldindata.org/per-capita-energy (cited on page 5).

[7] SFOE. 'Buildings'. In: *Startseite* (2023) (cited on page 6).

[8] Anjali Jaiswal and Prima Madan. 'Towering possibilities in India: Efficient buildings'. In: *NRDC* (2019). www.nrdc.org/experts/anjali-jaiswal/towering-possibilities-india-efficient-buildings (cited on page 7).

[9] Malini Goyal. 'How car ownership is changing rapidly and irreversibly in India'. In: *The Economic Times* (2018). https://economictimes.indiatimes.com/industry/auto/auto-news/how-car-ownership-is-changing-rapidly-and-irreversibly-in-india/articleshow/66296079.cms?from=mdr (cited on page 7).

[10] Megha Kumar. 'How car ownership is changing rapidly and irreversibly in India'. In: *International Council on Clean Transportation Blog* (2021). https://theicct.org/whats-the-business-as-usual-future-for-road-transport-in-india/ (cited on page 7).

[11] Hannah Ritchie and Max Roser. 'Per capita CO_2 emissions'. In: *Our World in Data* (2020). https://ourworldindata.org/greenhouse-gas-emissions (cited on page 8).

[12] Hannah Ritchie and Max Roser. 'Emissions by sector'. In: *Our World in Data* (2020). https://ourworldindata.org/emissions-by-sector (cited on pages 8, 10).

[13] IEA. 'Methane tracker 2021 – Analysis'. In: *CC BY 4.0* (2022) (cited on page 8).

[14] IEA. 'Methane tracker data explorer – Analysis'. In: *CC BY 4.0* (2023) (cited on page 8).

[15] Hannah Ritchie and Max Roser. 'CO_2 and greenhouse gas emissions'. In: *Our World in Data* (2020). https://ourworldindata.org/co2-and-other-greenhouse-gas-emissions (cited on page 9).

[16] World Bank. CO_2 *Emissions (metric tons per capita)*. 2020. https://data.worldbank.org/indicator/EN.ATM.CO2E.PC (cited on page 10).

[17] IPCC. 'IPCC summary for policymakers'. In: *Climate Change 2021: The Physical Science Basis. Contribution of Working Group I to the Sixth Assessment Report of the Intergovernmental Panel on Climate Change* (2021). https://doi.org/10.1017/9781009157896.001 (cited on page 11).

[18] Nicholas Herbert Stern. 'The economics of climate change'. In: *Stern Review* 30 (2006) (cited on page 11).

[19] Marshall Burke, Solomon M. Hsiang, and Edward Miguel. 'Global non-linear effect of temperature on economic production'. In: *Nature* 527.7577 (2015), pp. 235–239. https://doi.org/10.1038/nature15725 (cited on page 12).

[20] Matthias Kalkuhl and Leonie Wenz. 'The impact of climate conditions on economic production. Evidence from a global panel of regions'. In: *Journal of Environmental Economics and Management* 103 (2020), p. 102360. https://doi.org/10.1016/j.jeem.2020.102360 (cited on page 12).

[21] UN. 'Stressing air pollution kills 7 million people annually, secretary-general urges governments to build green economy, in message for World Environment Day'. In: *United Nations* SG/SM/19607-ENV/DEV/1957-OBV/1887 (2019) (cited on page 12).

[22] C40 Knowledge Hub. 'WHO air quality guidelines'. In: *WHO* (2021) (cited on page 12).

[23] Ian Tiseo. 'Most polluted capital cities 2020'. In: *Statista* (2021) (cited on page 13).

[24] IQAir. 'World Air Quality Report 2019'. (2020). www.iqair.com/world-most-polluted-cities/world-air-quality-report-2019-en.pdf (cited on page 13).

[25] IQAir. 'World Air Quality Report 2020'. (2021). www.iqair.com/world-most-polluted-cities/world-air-quality-report-2020-en.pdf (cited on page 13).

[26] Hannah Choi Granade et al. 'Unlocking energy efficiency in the US economy'. In: *McKinsey & Company* (2009) (cited on page 14).

[27] Anna Alberini and Massimo Filippini. 'Transient and persistent energy efficiency in the US residential sector: Evidence from household-level data'. In: *Energy Efficiency* 11.3 (2018), pp. 589–601. https://doi.org/10.1007/s12053-017-9599-z (cited on pages 14, 110).

[28] Massimo Filippini and Lester C. Hunt. 'Energy demand and energy efficiency in the OECD countries: A stochastic demand frontier approach'. In: *The Energy Journal* 32.2 (2011). https://doi.org/10.5547/ISSN0195-6574-EJ-Vol32-No2-3 (cited on pages 14, 108).

[29] ScienceFacts.Net. 'Types of Renewable Energy Sources: Sources, advantages & disadvantages'. In: *Science Facts* (Dec. 2020) (cited on page 18).

[30] Sendhil Mullainathan and Richard Thaler. 'Behavioral economics'. In: *National Bureau of Economic Research* Working Paper 7948 (Jan. 2000). https://doi.org/10.2139/ssrn.245828 (cited on page 22).

[31] Cheng-Yao Zhang et al. 'Impact factors of household energy-saving behavior: An empirical study of Shandong Province in China'. In: *Journal of Cleaner Production* 185 (2018), pp. 285–298. https://doi.org/10.1016/j.jclepro.2018.02.303 (cited on page 30).

[32] Graham Beattie, Iza Ding, and Andrea La Nauze. 'Is there an energy efficiency gap in China? Evidence from an information experiment'. In: *Journal of Environmental Economics and Management* 115 (2022), p. 102713. https://doi.org/10.1016/j.jeem.2022.102713 (cited on page 31).

[33] Mozhgan Alaeifar, Mehdi Farsi, and Massimo Filippini. 'Scale economies and optimal size in the Swiss gas distribution sector'. In: *Energy Policy* 65 (2014), pp. 86–93. https://doi.org/10.1016/j.enpol.2013.09.038 (cited on page 33).

[34] Christine Jolls, Cass R. Sunstein, and Richard Thaler. 'A behavioral approach to law and economics'. In: *Harvard Law School John M. Olin Center for Law, Economics and Business Discussion Paper Series* 50 (May 1998). https://doi.org/10.2307/1229304 (cited on page 34).

[35] Suchita Srinivasan and Stefano Carattini. 'Adding fuel to fire? Social spillovers in the adoption of LPG in India'. In: *Ecological Economics* 167 (2019), p. 106398. https://doi.org/10.1016/j.ecolecon.2019.106398 (cited on page 36).

[36] Harvey Leibenstein. 'Allocative efficiency vs. "X-efficiency"'. In: *American Economic Review* 56.3 (1966), pp. 392–415 (cited on pages 37, 38).

[37] Mehdi Farsi, Massimo Filippini, and Michael Kuenzle. 'Cost efficiency in the Swiss gas distribution sector'. In: *Energy Economics* 29.1 (2007), pp. 64–78. https://doi.org/10.1016/j.eneco.2006.04.006 (cited on page 38).

[38] Mehdi Farsi and Massimo Filippini. 'An analysis of cost efficiency in Swiss multi-utilities'. In: *Energy Economics* 31.2 (2009), pp. 306–315. https://doi.org/10.1016/j.eneco.2008.11.009 (cited on page 38).

[39] Massimo Filippini, Thomas Geissmann, and William H. Greene. 'Persistent and transient cost efficiency – an application to the Swiss hydropower sector'. In: *Journal of Productivity Analysis* 49 (2018), pp. 65–77. https://doi.org/10.1007/s11123-017-0522-6 (cited on page 38).

[40] Gro Harlem Brundtland. *Report of the World Commission on Environment and Development: 'Our Common Future'*. UN, 1987 (cited on pages 42, 43).

[41] Massimo Filippini and Shonali Pachauri. 'Elasticities of electricity demand in urban Indian households'. In: *Energy Policy* 32.3 (2004), pp. 429–436. https://doi.org/10.1016/S0301-4215(02)00314-2 (cited on pages 61, 64).

[42] William H. Greene. *Econometric Analysis*. Prentice Hall, 2018 (cited on page 63).

[43] Nina Boogen, Souvik Datta, and Massimo Filippini. 'Estimating residential electricity demand: New empirical evidence'. In: *Energy Policy* 158 (2021), p. 112561. https://doi.org/10.1016/j.enpol.2021.112561 (cited on pages 63, 64).

[44] John Dimitropoulos*, Lester C. Hunt, and Guy Judge. 'Estimating underlying energy demand trends using UK annual data'. In: *Applied Economics Letters* 12.4 (2005), pp. 239–244. https://doi.org/10.1080/1350485052000337789 (cited on pages 64, 69).

[45] Lester C. Hunt and Yasushi Ninomiya. 'Primary energy demand in Japan: An empirical analysis of long-term trends and future CO_2 emissions'. In: *Energy Policy* 33.11 (2005), pp. 1409–1424. https://doi.org/10.1016/j.enpol.2003.12.019 (cited on page 64).

[46] Paresh Kumar Narayan, Russell Smyth, and Arti Prasad. 'Electricity consumption in G7 countries: A panel cointegration analysis of residential demand elasticities'. In: *Energy Policy* 35.9 (2007), pp. 4485–4494. https://doi.org/10.1016/j.enpol.2007.03.018 (cited on page 64).

[47] Chandra Kiran B. Krishnamurthy and Bengt Kriström. 'A cross-country analysis of residential electricity demand in 11 OECD-countries'. In: *Resource and Energy Economics* 39 (2015), pp. 68–88. https://doi.org/10.1016/j.reseneeco.2014.12.002 (cited on page 64).

[48] Isabella Schulte and Peter Heindl. 'Price and income elasticities of residential energy demand in Germany'. In: *Energy Policy* 102 (2017), pp. 512–528. https://doi.org/10.1016/j.enpol.2016.12.055 (cited on page 64).

[49] Namrata Chindarkar and Nihit Goyal. 'One price doesn't fit all: An examination of heterogeneity in price elasticity of residential electricity in India'. In: *Energy Economics* 81 (2019), pp. 765–778. https://doi.org/10.1016/j.eneco.2019.05.021 (cited on page 64).

[50] Yumin Li, Yan Jiang, and Shiyuan Li. 'Price and income elasticities of electricity in China: Estimation and policy implications'. In: *Regional Science Policy & Practice* 46 (2022), pp. 76–91. https://doi.org/10.1111/rsp3.12309 (cited on page 64).

[51] Carol A. Dahl. 'Measuring global gasoline and diesel price and income elasticities'. In: *Energy Policy* 41 (2012), pp. 2–13. https://doi.org/10.1016/j.enpol.2010.11.055 (cited on page 64).

[52] Massimo Filippini and Fabian Heimsch. 'The regional impact of a CO_2 tax on gasoline demand: A spatial econometric approach'. In: *Resource and Energy Economics* 46 (2016), pp. 85–100. https://doi.org/10.1016/j.reseneeco.2016.07.00 (cited on pages 64, 227).

[53] Massimo Filippini and Nilkanth Kumar. 'Gas demand in the Swiss household sector'. In: *Applied Economics Letters* 28.5 (2021), pp. 359–364. https://doi.org/10.1080/13504851.2020.1753875 (cited on page 65).

[54] Paul J. Burke and Hewen Yang. 'The price and income elasticities of natural gas demand: International evidence'. In: *Energy Economics* 59 (2016), pp. 466–474. https://doi.org/10.1016/j.eneco.2016.08.025 (cited on page 65).

[55] David Coyle, Jason DeBacker, and Richard Prisinzano. 'Estimating the supply and demand of gasoline using tax data'. In: *Energy Economics* 34.1 (2012), pp. 195–200. https://doi.org/10.1016/j.eneco.2011.07.011 (cited on page 65).

[56] Brantley Liddle. 'The systemic, long-run relation among gasoline demand, gasoline price, income, and vehicle ownership in OECD countries: Evidence from panel cointegration and causality modeling'. In: *Transportation Research Part D: Transport and Environment* 17.4 (2012), pp. 327–331. https://doi.org/10.1016/j.trd.2012.01.007 (cited on page 65).

[57] Amado Crotte, Robert B. Noland, and Daniel J. Graham. 'An analysis of gasoline demand elasticities at the national and local levels in Mexico'. In: *Energy Policy* 38.8 (2010), pp. 4445–4456. https://doi.org/10.1016/j.enpol.2010.03.076 (cited on page 65).

[58] Jihyo Kim and Eunnyeong Heo. 'Asymmetric substitutability between energy and capital: Evidence from the manufacturing sectors in 10 OECD countries'. In: *Energy Economics* 40 (2013), pp. 81–89. https://doi.org/10.1016/j.eneco.2013.06.014 (cited on pages 68, 69).

[59] Nicholas Bloom et al. 'Modern management: Good for the environment or just hot air?'. In: *The Economic Journal* 120.544 (2010), pp. 551–572. https://doi.org/10.1111/j.1468-0297.2010.02351.x (cited on page 69).

[60] Ralf Martin et al. 'Anatomy of a paradox: Management practices, organizational structure and energy efficiency'. In: *Journal of Environmental Economics and Management* 63.2 (2012), pp. 208–223. https://doi.org/10.1016/j.jeem.2011.08.003 (cited on page 69).

[61] Arti Grover and Valerie J. Karplus. 'The energy-management nexus in firms: Which practices matter, how much and for whom?'. In: *World Bank Group, Washington, DC,* Policy Research Working Paper 9397 (2020) (cited on page 69).

[62] David Kamerschen and David Porter. 'The demand for residential, industrial and total electricity, 1973–1998'. In: *Energy Economics* 26 (2004), pp. 87–100. https://doi.org/10.1016/S0140-9883(03)00033-1 (cited on page 69).

[63] Olutomi I. Adeyemi and Lester C. Hunt. 'Modelling OECD industrial energy demand: Asymmetric price responses and energy-saving technical change'. In: *Energy Economics* 29.4 (2007), pp. 693–709. https://doi.org/10.1016/j.eneco.2007.01.007 (cited on page 69).

[64] Nobuhiro Hosoe and Shu-ichi Akiyama. 'Regional electric power demand elasticities of Japan's industrial and commercial sectors'. In: *Energy Policy* 37.11 (2009), pp. 4313–4319. https://doi.org/10.1016/j.enpol.2009.05.045 (cited on page 69).

[65] Boqiang Lin and Weisheng Liu. 'Estimation of energy substitution effect in China's machinery industry–based on the corrected formula for elasticity of substitution'. In: *Energy* 129 (2017), pp. 246–254. https://doi.org/10.1016/j.energy.2017.04.103 (cited on page 69).

[66] Stefanie A. Haller and Marie Hyland. 'Capital–energy substitution: Evidence from a panel of Irish manufacturing firms'. In: *Energy Economics* 45 (2014), pp. 501–510. https://doi.org/10.1016/j.eneco.2014.08.003 (cited on page 69).

[67] Rossella Bardazzi, Filippo Oropallo, and Maria Grazia Pazienza. 'Do manufacturing firms react to energy prices? Evidence from Italy'. In: *Energy Economics* 49 (2015), pp. 168–181. https://doi.org/10.1016/j.eneco.2015.01.014 (cited on page 69).

[68] M. Aklin et al. 'Economics of household technology adoption in developing countries: Evidence from solar technology adoption in rural India'. In: *Energy Economics* 72 (2018), pp. 35–46. https://doi.org/10.1016/j.eneco.2018.02.011 (cited on page 71).

[69] Paul J. Gertler et al. 'The demand for energy-using assets among the world's rising middle classes'. In: *American Economic Review* 106.6 (2016), pp. 1366–1401. https://doi.org/10.1257/aer.20131455 (cited on page 72).

[70] Miguel Poblete-Cazenave and Shonali Pachauri. 'A model of energy poverty and access: Estimating household electricity demand and appliance ownership'. In: *Energy Economics* 98 (2021), p. 105266. https://doi.org/10.1016/j.eneco.2021.105266 (cited on page 72).

[71] Bjarne Steffen. 'Estimating the cost of capital for renewable energy projects'. In: *Energy Economics* 88 (2020), p. 104783. https://doi.org/10.1016/j.eneco.2020.104783 (cited on page 79).

[72] European Environment Agency. *Estimated average EU external costs for electricity generation technologies in 2005*. 2012. European Environment Agency. www.eea.europa.eu/data-and-maps/figures/estimated-average-eu-external-costs (cited on page 88).

[73] IEA. *Projected costs of generating electricity 2020 – Analysis*. CC BY 4.0. 2020. https://iea.blob.core.windows.net/assets/ae17da3d-e8a5-4163-a3ec-2c6fb0b5677d/Projected-Costs-of-Generating-Electricity-2020.pdf (cited on page 88).

[74] IRENA. (2018). Renewable Power Generation Costs in 2017, International Renewable Energy Agency, Abu Dhabi. (cited on pages 90, 91).

[75] Edward S. Rubin et al. 'A review of learning rates for electricity supply technologies'. In: *Energy Policy* 86 (2015), pp. 198–218. https://doi.org/10.1016/j.enpol.2015.06.011 (cited on page 92).

[76] Felipe A. M. de Faria et al. 'The local socio-economic impacts of large hydropower plant development in a developing country'. In: *Energy Economics* 67 (2017), pp. 533–544. https://doi.org/10.1016/j.eneco.2017.08.025 (cited on page 96).

[77] Janosch Ondraczek, Nadejda Komendantova, and Anthony Patt. 'WACC the dog: The effect of financing costs on the levelized cost of solar PV power'. In: *Renewable*

Energy 75 (2015), pp. 888–898. https://doi.org/10.1016/j.renene.2014.10.053 (cited on page 101).

[78]   World Bank. *World development indicators*. 2023. https://databank.worldbank.org/source/world-development-indicators (cited on page 107).

[79]   "Data Page: Primary energy consumption", part of the following publication: Hannah Ritchie, Pablo Rosado and Max Roser (2023) – "Energy". Data adapted from U.S. Energy Information Administration, Energy Institute. Retrieved from https://ourworldindata.org/grapher/primary-energy-cons [online resource] on 21st April, 2021 (cited on page 107).

[80]   Massimo Filippini and Lester C. Hunt. 'Measuring persistent and transient energy efficiency in the US'. In: *Energy Efficiency* 9.3 (2016), pp. 663–675. https://doi.org/10.1007/s12053-015-9388-5 (cited on page 108).

[81]   Julia Blasch et al. 'Explaining electricity demand and the role of energy and investment literacy on end-use efficiency of Swiss households'. In: *Energy Economics* 68 (2017), pp. 89–102. https://doi.org/10.1016/j.eneco.2017.12.004 (cited on page 110).

[82]   Bruno Troja. 'A quantitative and qualitative analysis of the super-efficient equipment program subsidy in India'. In: *Energy Efficiency* 9.6 (2016), pp. 1385–1404. https://doi.org/10.1007/s12053-016-9429-8 (cited on page 111).

[83]   Julia Blasch et al. 'Empower the consumer! Energy-related financial literacy and its implications for economic decision making'. In: *Economics of Energy & Environmental Policy* 10.2 (Apr. 2021), pp. 149–181. https://doi.org/10.5547/2160-5890.10.2.jbla (cited on pages 119, 120).

[84]   Massimo Filippini, Nilkanth Kumar, and Suchita Srinivasan. 'Energy-related financial literacy and bounded rationality in appliance replacement attitudes: Evidence from Nepal'. In: *Environment and Development Economics* 25.4 (2020), pp. 399–422. https://doi.org/10.3929/ethz-b-000328611 (cited on pages 119, 120).

[85]   Susanna B. Berkouwer and Joshua T. Dean. 'Credit, attention, and externalities in the adoption of energy efficient technologies by low-income households'. In: *American Economic Review* 122 (10 2022), pp. 3291–3330. https://doi.org/10.1257/aer.20210766 (cited on page 123).

[86]   Franz Fuerst and Ramandeep Singh. 'How present bias forestalls energy efficiency upgrades: A study of household appliance purchases in India'. In: *Journal of Cleaner Production* 186 (2018), pp. 558–569. https://doi.org/10.1016/j.jclepro.2018.03.100 (cited on page 124).

[87]   Faisal Jamil and Eatzaz Ahmad. 'Policy considerations for limiting electricity theft in the developing countries'. In: *Energy Policy* 129 (2019), pp. 452–458. https://doi.org/10.1016/j.enpol.2019.02.035 (cited on page 125).

[88]   Eliana Carranza and Robyn Meeks. 'Energy efficiency and electricity reliability'. In: *The Review of Economics and Statistics* 103.3 (2021), pp. 461–475. https://doi.org/10.1162/rest_a_00912 (cited on page 125).

[89]   Lucas W. Davis, Alan Fuchs, and Paul Gertler. 'Cash for coolers: Evaluating a largescale appliance replacement program in Mexico'. In: *American Economic Journal: Economic Policy* 6.4 (2014), pp. 207–238. https://doi.org/10.1257/pol.6.4.207 (cited on page 126).

[90]   Mehdi Farsi, Aurelio Fetz, and Massimo Filippini. 'Economies of scale and scope in multi-utilities'. In: *The Energy Journal* 29.4 (2008), pp. 123–143 (cited on page 134).

[91] Aurelio Fetz and Massimo Filippini. 'Economies of vertical integration in the Swiss electricity sector'. In: *Energy Economics* 32.6 (2010), pp. 1325–1330. https://doi.org/10.1016/j.eneco.2010.06.011 (cited on page 134).

[92] David Ricardo. *On the principles of political economy and taxation.* John Murray, 1817 (cited on page 136).

[93] Weijian Du, Mengjie Li, and Faming Wang. 'Role of rent-seeking or technological progress in maintaining the monopoly power of energy enterprises: An empirical analysis based on micro-data from China'. In: *Energy* 202 (2020), p. 117763. https://doi.org/10.1016/j.energy.2020.117763 (cited on page 142).

[94] Sahel Al Rousan, Rashid Sbia, and Bedri Kamil Onur Tas. 'A dynamic network analysis of the world oil market: Analysis of OPEC and non-OPEC members'. In: *Energy Economics* 75 (2018), pp. 28–41. https://doi.org/10.1016/j.eneco.2018.07.032 (cited on page 155).

[95] Muntasir Murshed and Muntaha Masud Tanha. 'Oil price shocks and renewable energy transition: Empirical evidence from net oil-importing South Asian economies'. In: *Energy, Ecology and Environment* 6.3 (2021), pp. 183–203. https://doi.org/10.1007/s40974-020-00168-0 (cited on page 158).

[96] Ioannis N. Kessides. 'The impacts of electricity sector reforms in developing countries'. In: *Renewable Energy* 25.6 (2012), pp. 79–88. https://doi.org/10.1016/j.tej.2012.07.002 (cited on page 159).

[97] Akshaya Jha, Louis Preonas, and Fiona Burlig. 'Blackouts in the developing world: The role of wholesale electricity markets'. In: *Energy Policy Institute at the University of Chicago* Working Paper No. 2022-01 (2022) (cited on page 160).

[98] European Environment Agency. *Environmental tax reform: Increasing individual incomes and boosting innovation.* 2012. www.eea.europa.eu/highlights/environmental-tax-reform-increasing-individual#:~:text=Environmental%20tax%20reform%20is%20defined,types%20of%20effects%20of%20ETR (cited on page 179).

[99] Jaume Freire-González. 'Environmental taxation and the double dividend hypothesis in CGE modelling literature: A critical review'. In: *Journal of Policy Modeling* 40.1 (2018), pp. 194–223. https://doi.org/10.1016/j.jpolmod.2017.11.002 (cited on page 181).

[100] Arief A. Yusuf and Budy P. Resosudarmo. 'On the distributional impact of a carbon tax in developing countries: The case of Indonesia'. In: *Environmental Economics and Policy Studies* 17.1 (2015), pp. 131–156. https://doi.org/10.1007/s10018-014-0093-y (cited on page 181).

[101] Davide Cerruti, Claudio Daminato, and Massimo Filippini. 'The impact of policy awareness: Evidence from vehicle choices response to fiscal incentives'. In: *Journal of Public Economics* 226 (2023), 104973. https://doi.org/10.1016/j.jpubeco.2023.104973 (cited on page 184).

[102] Yucai Hu et al. 'Can carbon emission trading scheme achieve energy conservation and emission reduction? Evidence from the industrial sector in China'. In: *Energy Economics* 85 (2020), p. 104590. https://doi.org/10.1016/j.eneco.2019.104590 (cited on page 187).

[103] Shanjun Li, Joshua Linn, and Erich Muehlegger. 'Gasoline taxes and consumer behavior'. In: *American Economic Journal: Economic Policy* 6.4 (2014), pp. 302–342. https://doi.org/10.1257/pol.6.4.302 (cited on page 190).

[104] Raj Chetty, Adam Looney, and Kory Kroft. 'Salience and taxation: Theory and evidence'. In: *American Economic Review* 99.4 (2009), pp. 1145–1177. https://doi.org/10.1257/aer.99.4.1145 (cited on page 190).

[105] Martin L. Weitzman. 'Prices vs. quantities'. In: *The Review of Economic Studies* 41.4 (1974), pp. 477–491. https://doi.org/10.2307/2296698 (cited on page 191).

[106] Suchita Srinivasan. 'The light at the end of the tunnel: Impact of policy on the global diffusion of fluorescent lamps'. In: *Energy Policy* 128 (2019), pp. 907–918. https://doi.org/10.1016/j.enpol.2019.01.001 (cited on page 195).

[107] Richard H. Thaler and Cass R. Sunstein. 'Libertarian paternalism'. In: *American Economic Review* 93.2 (2003), pp. 175–179. https://doi.org/10.1257/000282803321947001 (cited on page 195).

[108] Anant Sudarshan. 'Nudges in the marketplace: The response of household electricity consumption to information and monetary incentives'. In: *Journal of Economic Behavior Organization* 134 (2017), pp. 320–335. https://doi.org/10.1016/j.jebo.2016.12.015 (cited on page 196).

[109] Anne Sofie Elberg Nielsen et al. *Nudging and pro-environmental behaviour.* https://norden.diva-portal.org/smash/get/diva2:1065958/FULLTEXT01.pdf. Nordic Council of Ministers, 2016 (cited on page 197).

[110] *European Commission. 'EU Ecolabel- Guiding your sustainable choice'. Retrieved on October 1st 2022.* https://environment.ec.europa.eu/topics/circular-economy/eu-ecolabel_en (cited on page 197).

[111] Magnus Bergquist et al. 'Field interventions for climate change mitigation behaviors: A second-order meta-analysis'. In: *Proceedings of the National Academy of Sciences* 120.13 (2023), e2214851120. https://doi.org/10.1073/pnas.2214851120 (cited on page 198).

[112] Julia Blasch, Massimo Filippini, and Nilkanth Kumar. 'Boundedly rational consumers, energy and investment literacy, and the display of information on household appliances'. In: *Resource and Energy Economics* 56 (2019), pp. 39–58. https://doi.org/10.1016/j.reseneeco.2017.06.001 (cited on page 198).

[113] Energie-Umwelt.ch. *Renovation und Heizung.* Energie. 2023. www.energie-umwelt.ch/haus/renovation-und-heizung/gebaeudeplanung/waermebedarf-und-geak (cited on page 206).

[114] Conrado Augustus de Melo and Gilberto de Martino Jannuzzi. 'Energy efficiency standards for refrigerators in Brazil: A methodology for impact evaluation'. In: *Energy Policy* 38.11 (2010). Energy Efficiency Policies and Strategies with regular papers, pp. 6545–6550. https://doi.org/10.1016/j.enpol.2010.07.032 (cited on page 214).

[115] Tabare Capitan et al. 'Time-varying pricing may increase total electricity consumption: Evidence from Costa Rica'. In: *Resource and Energy Economics* 66 (2021), p. 101264. https://doi.org/10.1016/j.reseneeco.2021.101264 (cited on page 215).

[116] United Nations Environment Programme. (2021). 'Regulating Air Quality: The First Global Assessment of Air Pollution Legislation'. www.unep.org/resources/report/regulating-air-quality-first-global-assessment-air-pollution-legislation (cited on page 219).

[117] Esther Duflo et al. 'Truth-telling by third-party auditors and the response of polluting firms: Experimental evidence from India'. In: *The Quarterly Journal of Economics* 128.4 (2013), pp. 1499–1545. https://doi.org/10.1093/qje/qjt024 (cited on page 219).

[118] Michael Greenstone and Rema Hanna. 'Environmental regulations, air and water pollution, and infant mortality in India'. In: *American Economic Review* 104.10 (2014), pp. 3038–3072. https://doi.org/10.1257/aer.104.10.3038 (cited on page 220).

[119] Paul E. Carrillo, Arun S. Malik, and Yiseon Yoo. 'Driving restrictions that work? Quito's Pico y Placa Program'. In: *Canadian Journal of Economics/Revue canadienne d'économique* 49.4 (2016), pp. 1536–1568. https://doi.org/10.1111/caje.12243 (cited on page 221).

[120] V. Brian Viard and Shihe Fu. 'The effect of Beijing's driving restrictions on pollution and economic activity'. In: *Journal of Public Economics* 125 (2015), pp. 98–115. https://doi.org/10.1016/j.jpubeco.2015.02.003 (cited on page 221).

[121] Angus Deaton and John Muellbauer. 'An almost ideal demand system'. In: *American Economic Review* 70.3 (1980), pp. 312–326 (cited on page 231).

[122] Steven Berry, James Levinsohn, and Ariel Pakes. 'Automobile prices in market equilibrium'. In: *Econometrica* 63.4 (1995), pp. 841–890. https://doi.org/10.2307/2171802 (cited on page 231).

[123] Nina Boogen et al. 'Can information about energy costs affect consumers' choices? Evidence from a field experiment'. In: *Journal of Economic Behavior Organization* 196 (2022), pp. 568–588. https://doi.org/10.1016/j.jebo.2022.02.014 (cited on page 235).

[124] Massimo Filippini, Nilkanth Kumar, and Suchita Srinivasan. 'Nudging adoption of electric vehicles: Evidence from an information-based intervention in Nepal'. In: *Transportation Research Part D: Transport and Environment* 97 (2021), p. 102951. https://doi.org/10.1016/j.trd.2021.102951 (cited on page 236).

[125] Souvik Datta and Massimo Filippini. 'Analysing the impact of ENERGY STAR rebate policies in the US'. In: *Energy Efficiency* 9.3 (2016), pp. 677–698. https://doi.org/10.1007/s12053-015-9386-7 (cited on page 239).

[126] Nina Boogen, Souvik Datta, and Massimo Filippini. 'Demand-side management by electric utilities in Switzerland: Analyzing its impact on residential electricity demand'. In: *Energy Economics* 64 (2017), pp. 402–414. https://doi.org/10.1016/j.eneco.2017.04.006 (cited on page 240).

[127] Massimo Filippini and TobiasWekhof. 'The effect of culture on energy efficient vehicle ownership'. In: *Journal of Environmental Economics and Management* 105 (2021), p. 102400. https://doi.org/10.1016/j.jeem.2020.102400 (cited on page 242).

Index

Printed in the United States
by Baker & Taylor Publisher Services